Vietnam

McNamara

McNamara

Henry L. Trewhitt

Harper & Row, Publishers

NEW YORK, EVANSTON, SAN FRANCISCO, LONDON

1817

The lines by T. S. Eliot on page 298 from "Little Gidding" from *Four Quartets* are reprinted with permission of Harcourt Brace Jovanovich, Inc.

For Barbara

Contents

Foreword

W E had crowded into a Paris hotel room, about thirty American correspondents who lived in Europe or who had come from Washington for the NATO meeting. After the chairs were taken, we sat on the floor, and we stepped over each other to reach the table laid out as a bar. In our talk as we waited, we all sounded a bit more sure than we really felt. The Cuba missile crisis was not long past. It was not clear whether the Russians really had subsided around Berlin. NATO was in "disarray"—one of our favorite words.

Suddenly Robert McNamara burst through the door, carrying the heavy briefcase that seemed never to leave his side. "Hello, fellows," he said, his wide grin sweeping us all in, and immediately he got down to business. For most of an hour we listened to one who seemed to know precisely where NATO had to go, whose conception of Western security bridged the uncertainties of the alliance. When it was over, the reaction of those who had never seen him in action before was fretful. They were in near awe of his brilliance, but there was an undercurrent of skepticism, even cynicism, just the same. To the doubting journalistic mind, no one could be *that* certain.

I have been interested in Robert McNamara ever since. For the

first half of the decade I remained in Europe, and I watched him
partly through the eyes of European politicians and military officers. When I returned to the United States at the end of 1965,
the view became much closer; for more than a year I was assigned
to the Department of Defense. In 1968 Harper & Row asked me
to help with the editing of some of McNamara's speeches and
other public statements. These were published in McNamara's
book, *The Essence of Security*, later that year. This present book,
in turn, grew out of my participation in that project.

The book has been neither authorized nor approved by its
subject. It is rather a book of journalism, an attempt to fit one
man into his time with representative evidence now available. I
plead guilty to the possible accusation that I am perpetrating
"instant history," which is what journalism is all about. That the
evidence will become fuller I have no doubt. I do not believe it
will change substantially the conclusions, firm and tentative, I
have reached.

I hope this is a book free of all prejudices but one. To me government is not peopled by good and bad men, with rare exceptions, but by men trying, each within the limitations of his abilities and his weaknesses, to perform the roles assigned them. Those
who undertake the missions on the outer reaches of human capability deserve our understanding even when we cannot approve.
They deserve, at least, dispassionate treatment from those they
serve. That has been my objective here.

Of all those who helped with the research on this book, I am
most grateful to Robert McNamara himself. He agreed to talk
with me without getting any assurance of favorable treatment.
He did not see the manuscript, nor had he any idea of its content
in advance of publication, beyond what he might deduce from my
questioning. For the most part, our talks were about details, to
check technical points in information I had acquired elsewhere.
Not once did he make classified information available to me, nor
did he utter a word of criticism toward the Presidents he served.
It will be clear that others did both.

Therefore I must warn that not all of the judgments and insights I have ascribed to McNamara were imparted by him. I have talked to dozens of his friends, admirers, critics, and associates, most of whom must remain anonymous, to supplement the public record, and I am indebted to them for their help.

Among my colleagues, I owe special thanks to Lloyd Norman, the military correspondent of *Newsweek,* one of the finest reporters I know. Lloyd shared without reserve his knowledge and experience, and his personal library is a wonder. Valuable comments on the manuscript were given freely by William M. Beecher, the military correspondent of the *New York Times,* Ernest B. Furgurson, Jr., my former associate on the Baltimore *Sun,* and Henry Hubbard, my colleague at *Newsweek.* Murrey Marder and George C. Wilson of the Washington *Post* generously advised me on points in their fields of special interest. To my editors at *Newsweek,* and especially Mel Elfin, chief of the Washington Bureau, I am grateful for their patience and for welcoming me back from many forays away from my assignment in diplomacy. I am grateful also to Thomas B. Congdon, Jr., of Harper & Row. However this book is judged, it is the better for his editing.

None of those who contributed, however, is responsible for the inevitable errors of fact and the possible misjudgments. Those are mine alone.

HENRY L. TREWHITT

1

Transition

ROBERT STRANGE MCNAMARA began the special day at the pace with which he began almost every day. A few seconds after 7:30 on the morning of January 3, 1961, the heavy glass doors of Washington's Shoreham Hotel parted abruptly and McNamara strode to a waiting ten-year-old Cadillac. McNamara hardly ever just walked anywhere. He strode, he hurried, and Rossie Lee Hamlin, the driver from the Pentagon, was hard put to return the brisk "Good morning" and get the door open before McNamara reached the car.

The big limousine followed Rock Creek Park through the cold half-light toward the Potomac. McNamara glanced through the Washington *Post* and the *New York Times* and some of the official documents that provided the background of the morning's headlines. By 7:50 he was in his modest temporary office in Suite 3E880 of the Pentagon, the suite of the outgoing Secretary of Defense, Thomas S. Gates, Jr. Almost three weeks before the inauguration McNamara had begun keeping the regular office hours and setting the pattern that would continue—actually he was a bit late that morning—for the next seven years.

Two days before, he had been president of the Ford Motor Company. Today he was Secretary of Defense-in-waiting. Care-

1

fully the generals, lieutenants, civilian careerists, and office secretaries of OSD—the Office of the Secretary of Defense—studied him to learn what manner of man the young President-elect had chosen. "The overall impression was of energy, controlled energy," a secretary recalled, and added: "I thought he was handsome."

By most standards he was. His 165-pound frame carried hardly an ounce of excess fat. His black hair, thinning only slightly, longer than that of most executives, was slicked back with a part just to the left of center. He seemed to worry little about fashion, for his lean body moved about with too much room to spare inside his dark blue suit. His glasses were old-fashioned, half-rimmed with metal in a style that would become popular with rebellious youth several years later. He seemed warm enough; his smile was friendly, though some people felt he regarded the amenities as a waste of time, and he left the impression that he wanted to get on to something more substantial. "If he wore horn-rims and unwound just a little, he'd be quite human," a staff member offered in tentative judgment. The impact McNamara set out to make, however, was based on quite different criteria.

From the beginning it was a startling performance. The eighth Secretary of Defense brought to his new job a brilliant mind, inquiring and trenchant, honed by the new theories of scientific management, and total dedication. Yet even for Robert McNamara, to whom failure was an unacceptable alternative, the challenge he had accepted was formidable.

Of his seven predecessors, one had been driven to suicide. Others had been made by history to look merely a bit foolish. One had left in thinly camouflaged disgrace. Still others, who understood what needed to be done, had been prevented by lack of time, or by counterforces at work in the White House, from becoming fully effective. McNamara never betrayed a moment's doubt as to where he was going or who was in charge.

In those first weeks of the year, even before he was sworn in, the strategists of the Defense Department's continuing internal struggles were uneasily aware that this was a new kind of civilian leader. Staff members, arriving at conventional office hours, found the Secretary-designate already hard at work. They became accustomed to his familiar posture—slightly hunched behind the desk, eyes boring into a document, feet hooked behind the front legs of the chair. Usually he was without a jacket.

Key phrases that later became doctrine drifted out of the inner sanctum to circulate about the Pentagon. What in the world, traditionalists wondered, did "cost effectiveness" mean? The new Secretary would stimulate argument and a full airing of views on controversial issues, but once he—*he*—decided, he expected support for the decision by the military and civilians alike. A manager could referee or judge the disputes of his subordinates, or he could lead: the new Secretary would lead. He was so impatient to get started that he had to be dissuaded from firing off memorandums even before he took office.

It was all vaguely unsettling. But some in high Pentagon positions claimed to be unimpressed: "We just keep the new ones busy with public relations and personnel." Not this one.

In those first weeks McNamara listened carefully to the established experts and asked questions endlessly. After two weeks of twelve- to fifteen-hour days, the questions disclosed that in many cases he knew more answers than they did.

The procedure, though not the tempo, changed after January 20. On that day John Fitzgerald Kennedy, forty-three, took the oath of President of the United States. The next day McNamara, forty-four, became Kennedy's Secretary of Defense. He abandoned the old Cadillac for a newer limousine, moved into the twenty-one-by-forty-nine-foot office of the Secretary in Suite 3E880, transferred his papers into the five-by-nine-foot walnut desk that General Black Jack Pershing had used for twenty-six years, and took charge.

Twelve days later he appeared before the press to expand upon the first national security decisions announced by the President. In careful detail he listed plans to increase airlift and to speed up the Polaris submarine program. By adding more transport planes, McNamara aimed to refine mobility for conventional warfare, reflecting a concern the Administration shared with a large body of military and civilian strategists. Adding to the Polaris fleet strengthened the nuclear arsenal. The Polaris submarines, each armed with sixteen missiles to be launched from beneath the sea, were the most sophisticated "weapons system," as the jargon had it, in operation.

McNamara also eliminated two positions for assistant secretaries "in order to streamline the organization and increase our administrative efficiency." That left thirteen senior officials reporting to him or to his deputy; "still far too many," he claimed, "but at least a step in the right direction." He formed an Office for Management Planning and Organizational Studies, noting that "the reason for this is obvious, I think." Yet it would remain one of his failures that although he could assert total control of policy, he never was able to reduce the executive staff to the quick-reacting nucleus he wanted: in fact it grew.

McNamara's announcements only confirmed the charted direction of the new Administration. Considered along with the new activity surging through the endless corridors of the Pentagon, however, they suggested a fresh situation in the defense establishment. Power was passing rapidly from the feuding military services—which for years had been at each other's throats in competition for vital and prestigious missions, and therefore money—to the Secretary of Defense.

It seems paradoxical to say that McNamara erupted out of obscurity into the excitement of the political transition in that miserable winter. How could the president of the Ford Motor Company, a pillar of American industry, be obscure? Still, he was little more than a name to most of the professional politicians, members of the Eastern Establishment, and ecstatic, newly franchised intellectuals waiting for power in Washington. Their ignorance was understandable. In his fifteen years at Ford McNamara had come up through an inside route. His strength lay in the gray areas of statistical analysis, finance, and scientific management rather than in the more public fields of engineering and marketing. There is little public interest in such a man, no matter how brilliant, especially when he avoids personal publicity. When, at forty-four, he became the first Ford president without the family name, McNamara moved for the first time into the spotlight. That was on November 9, 1960, the day after John Kennedy was elected President of the United States.

Although he was not generally known in the incoming Administration in Washington, he had some of its most cherished credentials. At the University of California he had been Phi Beta Kappa. After graduation from Harvard Business School in 1939, he had taught there. At Ford he had advanced through the organization at a spectacular pace and had earned a great deal of money. He read widely, and he eagerly tapped the intellectual reserves of the academic community to which he turned for respite from business. By the time he became president of Ford he had built a record that made him eminently desirable in the new Democratic Administration, even though he was a Republican.

He had no claim on the Kennedy Administration, however, and he might easily have been overlooked if the Kennedy team had not made the widest possible search for talent. The Defense Department appointment was a crucial one, for defense had been a prominent issue in the campaign. For almost a decade, as he built up to his drive for the Presidency, Kennedy had often criticized the defense policies of the Eisenhower Administration. In later years his particular target had been the reliance upon the nation's nuclear arsenal for massive retaliation as the beginning and end of formal strategy. As he saw it, the Republicans had failed to honor even the formal policy. That weakness became symbolized in the so-called missile gap, which implied the superiority of the Soviet Union in strategic weapons development.

The point lost some of its luster in the final months of the Republican Administration. Considerable confusion had developed on both sides. Republicans who also had feared a gap began to raise a sturdier defense. Some leading Democrats were beginning to suspect that the disparity might not be so great, after all. During the campaign a Navy intelligence captain flew to Hyannis Port, Massachusetts, to caution John Kennedy that the national intelligence estimates did not support the frightening calculations of Soviet strength. Kennedy would not accept the figures: he was, after all, a politician just short of the greatest prize the nation could offer. In any case, massive retaliation remained both politically and militarily vulnerable as a strategy. Many Republicans seemed to have lost their confidence in it, without ever being sure how to compensate. No one, in fact, was certain fifteen years after World War II how to plan nuclear warfare.

As Kennedy's own awareness of strategy matured, he insisted that the nation must do essentially two things in defense: it must build its nuclear forces as a deterrent and expand its nonnuclear forces for response to provocation short of nuclear war. He also wanted the fragmenting rivalries in the Pentagon brought under control. It promised to be a consuming challenge for his Secretary of Defense.

McNamara's name was introduced into the talent search for a Secretary of Defense during an exercise in political cross-fertilization. It was an ironic set of circumstances, as it turned out, for it involved the man who would succeed him seven years later. Clark Clifford, the former aide to Harry Truman who had become an immensely successful lawyer, first had sought the Presidential nomination for Senator Stuart Symington of Missouri. After he failed, he rallied immediately to Kennedy, to whom he was both friend and counselor. One of Clifford's first missions for Kennedy was an attempt to recruit for the Cabinet Robert A. Lovett, the witty, urbane New York investment banker who had made a decidedly positive record as Secretary of Defense a decade earlier. Lovett had been a naval hero in World War I and, after earning a fortune, had been in and out of government several times. This time he feared his health, much abused in Washington's internal wars, would not bear another tour at the Pentagon.

Whether or not Lovett was the first to mention McNamara is uncertain: several Kennedy talent scouts came across it. But Lovett had been in the background at more than one turning point in McNamara's life. He knew that McNamara had built a brilliant record with statistical control in the military during World War II, while Lovett was civilian head of the Army Air Force. He recommended McNamara without reservation, and a quick check impressed the Kennedy staff.

As a result, Robert F. Kennedy called McNamara a month after the election and asked him to talk with Sargent Shriver, the President-elect's brother-in-law and a principal recruiter of talent. What about? McNamara asked. Let Shriver explain, Kennedy suggested. When? Shriver would be in Detroit that afternoon, Kennedy said, and would like to see McNamara as quickly as possible. The meeting produced a tentative suggestion of Treasury or Defense—and a negative reaction from McNamara. After all, he had been president of Ford for only a month.

Memories falter and accounts differ. Shriver recalled later that at least one potential barrier was cast aside during that first interview—the lure of money. In his precise one-two-three, A-B-C manner, McNamara ticked off the central problems of both Treasury and Defense. He fretted over leaving Ford just at this point. Briefly, he noted that he would have to sacrifice several million dollars to enter the Cabinet, then he added: "You know, I've got more money now than anyone in my family ever dreamed of having. I've got more money than I'm ever going to need or use." That settled that point. Still, he was reluctant.

Shriver handled the situation deftly. At least McNamara ought to show Kennedy the courtesy of a response in person, he said. A meeting was arranged for the next day, December 8, at the Kennedy home on N Street in Washington's exclusive Georgetown section. It was an exploratory mission on both sides. McNamara rejected the Treasury, claiming lack of qualification—though, in fact, the idea bored him. On the other hand, he was fascinated by the challenge of the Pentagon, although he had been away from the military for more than fourteen years.

He suggested other possibilities, including the retention of Tom Gates. Although Gates had made his mark on the Defense Department in a short time as Secretary, the incoming Administration had already decided against asking him to stay. It would be too difficult to rationalize keeping a man who had administered policies the Democrats had criticized so strongly.

McNamara still hesitated, though the conversation had generated strong mutual interest. McNamara asked Kennedy directly about a rumor that had been circulated by the President-elect's critics. Had Kennedy really written *Profiles in Courage?* Kennedy said he had, with the explanation that of course others had done much of the research. It was not an idle question on McNamara's part, for the heart of the book was that conflict between principles and practicality which McNamara had faced so often in his own career.

Another meeting was scheduled. The scales of McNamara's final decision may have been tilted by the weather. A heavy snowstorm forced postponement of the second meeting. In the interim he wrote a thoughtful letter to Kennedy. Instead of mailing it, however, he carried it with him when the second conference in Georgetown took place.

As before, McNamara entered the back door of the N Street house to avoid the reporters in front. He handed Kennedy the letter and asked him to read it before they talked. McNamara had written, in effect, that he would want authority to choose his own men in the Department of Defense, and he wanted time to study the controversial recommendations of a Kennedy Task Force on defense and make his own judgment on them before acting.

The second was an important point, resulting from a long and bitter debate over the defenses required for the nation at a time of breathtaking change in technology. Congress had before it a complex range of solutions. Kennedy's Committee on the Defense Establishment, led by Senator Symington, had met the issues in a frontal attack.

Symington had been the first Secretary of the Air Force after it was separated from the Army, and now he was one of those most vocally disturbed by the continuing disarray in the defense establishment. His task force concluded that previous legislation had failed to give the Secretary of Defense the executive power essential at a time when there might be, at best, only fifteen minutes' warning of nuclear attack. Noting that the Secretary's authority still was challenged from time to time within the Department, Symington's report summed it up: "The doctrine of civilian control will be compromised as long as any doubts exist on this vital point."

As a solution, it proposed to eliminate the separate structures of the Army, Navy, and Air Force. The Secretary would have direct operational and administrative authority in an unbroken chain from the President down through the military commands. Some students argued that the Secretary already had the power the Symington report aimed to guarantee. In practice, it had not worked out that way.

All this was in the background as Kennedy glanced through the letter McNamara had asked him to read. When he had finished, Kennedy nodded and agreed. It was a turning point in the administration of national defense policy. Without compromising his own supreme command, Kennedy acknowledged that his Secretary of Defense would be a policy-maker as well as a manager, with broad authority for individual initiative.

There were still several bases to be touched. McNamara continued to express doubt as to his own competence. Kennedy responded dryly that he didn't know of any school for Cabinet officers, "or Presidents either." Off to the Pentagon, McNamara extended what was supposed to be a brief chat with Gates into a discussion of several hours. Finally, after a weekend of soul-searching, he called Kennedy again and announced crisply, "I have talked with Tom Gates and I am confident I can handle that job." To which Kennedy is alleged to have replied, "Well, I just talked with President Eisenhower and I am confident I can handle that job."

The President-elect introduced his Secretary of Defense at a press conference on December 13. "After much thought," McNamara told the press corps, "I came to the conclusion that personal considerations must be subordinated to the responsibility of the President of the United States and to serve the public when requested to do so."

The reporters were interested in those personal considerations. They recalled that Charles E. Wilson, former president of General Motors, had given up a salary and bonuses of $600,000 a year and had sacrificed millions more in stock in order to become Secretary of Defense under Eisenhower. McNamara estimated that his own losses in stock and options—he owned 24,500 shares of Ford stock, had options on 30,000 more—would be $3 million "during the next three or four years." He also was giving up a salary and other benefits that totaled $410,000 in 1960. It was McNamara himself who insisted on sacrificing his stock, rejecting suggestions that there might be some way to retain the potential for a great fortune without a conflict of interest.

By he time he left the Pentagon seven years later, of course, McNamara's direct loss was much greater. But money for its own sake was of secondary interest to him. There is an adage of the Southern mountains, "Money don't matter if you got enough." It applied to McNamara. He was a self-made millionaire whose fulfillment required challenging work, comfort for his family, books, intellectual stimulation, and vigorous outdoor vacations, preferably skiing and climbing. It was not an extravagant life. It called for large amounts of money, but McNamara had enough.

More important to McNamara in the circumstances was the challenge itself—the disorder in national security, as he saw it, to be put right, the underbrush to be cleared by the application of reason and unemotional analysis. There also was a compelling attraction in the prospect of raw power.

McNamara computed his personal sacrifice over the next "three or four years" with good reason. He had committed himself to remain in office as long as the President wanted him; or, in the practical sense, for the length of a Presidential term. As he turned to his own executive recruitment problem in mid-December, he looked for the same commitment in his civilian assistants. For three weeks he spent most of his time in the Ford suite at the Shoreham Hotel, without a secretary, moving from one telephone to the next. He called executives whose judgment he respected—including Lovett—as sources for candidates. Every contact with a prospect was recorded on a three-by-five-inch card in his atrocious left-handed squiggle.

The result was a balance between the free choice authorized for McNamara and political practicalities. Kennedy and his associates proposed for Deputy Secretary Roswell Gilpatric, a lawyer who had been Under Secretary of the Air Force under Thomas K. Finletter during the early fifties. There is no reason to believe McNamara was not pleased with the choice. Gilpatric, fifty-four, had worked on both the Symington Task Force for Kennedy and on an advisory commission headed by Nelson Rockefeller which had recommended defense reorganization in 1958. McNamara therefore had to make certain Gilpatric was not committed to any specific reorganization plan in the new Administration. They reached agreement with a hurriedly arranged conversation in McNamara's car at the Baltimore airport during a snowstorm.

One Kennedy suggestion was a bit more than McNamara could take. He rejected Franklin D. Roosevelt, Jr., for Secretary of the Navy. The name alone was enough to discourage putting it in a subordinate position. But it was a bit difficult to divorce from politics the choice of John B. Connally, Jr., which followed. Connally, forty-three, was a close political friend of Vice President Lyndon B. Johnson. Yet he also was an established attorney and businessman, and he had a distinguished Navy record from World War II.

Slowly the staff grew. McNamara chose Cyrus R. Vance, forty-three, a keen, imperturbable New York lawyer, former counsel to the Senate Preparedness Subcommittee, to be general counsel of the Department. As Assistant Secretary for International Security

Affairs, the office charged with bringing together military and foreign policy, he assigned Paul H. Nitze, fifty-four, a former State Department planner and Democratic Party adviser. Nitze was widely respected as a man unafraid to generate and examine new ideas in political-military relations. Harold Brown, at thirty-three director of the University of California's Livermore Laboratory, became Director of Defense Research and Engineering.

For comptroller, a highly critical assignment in McNamara's conception of rational management, he reached beyond conventional accountancy for Charles J. Hitch, fifty-one, of the RAND Corporation. Hitch, quiet and reserved, had been a Rhodes Scholar and was an economist who had produced revolutionary ideas on the formidable economics of defense. He was happy, however, at RAND (Research and Development), the freewheeling idea center associated with the Air Force, and he had just bought a new home. To get Hitch, McNamara borrowed the tactics the Kennedys had used on him. At least, he told Hitch by telephone, he ought to refuse in person. McNamara himself was on a skiing vacation at Aspen, Colorado. He arranged to meet Hitch, who was flying from the East Coast to the West, at the Brown Palace Hotel in Denver. The upshot was that Hitch agreed finally to talk it over with his wife, and later he accepted the appointment.

For Secretary of the Army, McNamara recruited Elvis J. Stahr, Jr., the president of West Virginia University—who, as it turned out, never fitted in—and for Secretary of the Air Force, Eugene Zuckert, a former associate at Harvard Business School.

At lower levels, McNamara sponsored a group of young intellectuals who ultimately caused more fuss than those at higher ranks. These were the "Whiz Kids," a term carried over from McNamara's own management group at Ford, so-called because of their self-assured disrespect for tradition as they ranged happily among the sacred cows of the Pentagon. The group included Alain C. Enthoven, thirty, dark and intense, towering in both physique and intellect, an economist who earlier, at RAND, had specialized in strategy and strategic weapons.

Enthoven did not lack self-confidence, and one often told Pentagon story concerns an occasion when he visited U.S. Air Force Headquarters in Germany. He was met by an assortment of generals, with decades of accumulated experience and yards of ribbons. Enthoven, fresh-faced and youthful, listened with growing impatience as the number one general outlined plans for briefing the visitor. Finally Enthoven interrupted. "General," he said, "I don't think you understand. I didn't come for a briefing. I came to tell you what we have decided." From RAND also came Henry Rowen, first as deputy to Nitze in International Security Affairs, like the other RAND graduates eager to put into practice the theories evolved during the fifties in the California think tank.

Soon after the transition Adam Yarmolinsky, thirty-eight, who had worked as a Kennedy talent scout, became an assistant to McNamara. Yarmolinsky was a product of both Harvard and Yale; he had practiced law and had been a consultant and teacher. He was, in short, something of a legal and intellectual free-lance, with impressive credentials. In his new assignment he was generally recognized as the inside liaison between the Pentagon and the White House.

Out of his own experience, McNamara asked a commitment from his aides for the first Kennedy term. He was well aware of the time required for an outsider, no matter how well qualified, first to learn and then to shape the routine of a huge, complex organization. As it worked out, the organization generally held up well, particularly the members of McNamara's personal team, though a few of the early appointments collapsed soon. Connally left for politics within the year. Stahr quit within a year and a half. Some remained to the end, and others stepped from the Pentagon into an even brighter spotlight. After holding a wide range of assignments, ending as Deputy Secretary, Vance left in mid-1967, partly because of a chronic back problem. President

Johnson promptly recruited him again as a diplomatic trouble-shooter. Hitch, after four and a half years as comptroller, moved to the University of California, and later became its president. Nitze also became a high-level utility man, eventually succeeding Vance as Deputy Secretary.

In some cases there were elements of disenchantment, as with Stahr, who never commanded McNamara's respect, and who left with the conviction that the centralization in the office of the Secretary of Defense ultimately would not work. With rare exceptions, however, the parting of the ways at high levels was carried out smoothly and without public rancor.

The McNamara team overall was a formidable array of finely tuned intellects, heavily weighted with Ivy Leaguers. So much intellectual assertiveness in the routine of the Defense Department, where even interservice conflict had overtones of tradition, was bound to cause a convulsive reaction. McNamara in fact counted on it. By the turn of the year members of the McNamara administration were already understudying their predecessors.

McNamara returned to Ann Arbor, the university town where he had lived while he was with Ford, only once after accepting his appointment. Most of the details of moving he left to his wife, Margaret. In a twelve-hour tour of Washington during her husband's orientation she arranged a year's lease on a home at 80 Kalorama Circle, in a fashionable, quiet section of Northwest Washington, and prepared to move the family. Their elder daughter, Margaret, nineteen, was a student at Stanford; their two younger children, Kathleen, sixteen, and Craig, ten, were enrolled at Sidwell Friends' School in Washington.

The staff of OSD, the Office of the Secretary of Defense, soon learned the routine of its new leader. He regularly appeared in a rush shortly after 7 A.M. Homework or the daily papers, or both, had been disposed of on the way in. When he left the private elevator from the Pentagon basement, he was ready for the documents arranged on his desk. From that point forward, the days were invariably too short.

He wanted an efficient office, yet he did not much like making heads roll. When it came time to choose a personal secretary, he summoned both Miss Margaret Stroud and another senior secretary to his office. "Well, we'll continue things just like they are," he said brightly. "You"—to Peg Stroud—"will continue to be number one, and you"—to the other secretary—"will be number two." Unfortunately, he had mixed them up. Miss Stroud was the junior secretary. For several minutes she and McNamara listened in astonishment as the other woman lectured the Secretary of Defense on bureaucratic proprieties.

When it was over, McNamara shooed them both out of the office. "You'll just have to work it out between you," he said. But a few minutes later he called Miss Stroud back in. "That woman," he said worriedly, "has got to go." Two days later an office director told the senior secretary she was no longer needed in OSD. Peg Stroud, efficient and personable, remained McNamara's secretary, both during his seven years in the Department and afterward.

He was a bit more subtle in disposing of a Navy aide who was more concerned with tables of organization and his place in them than in performance, and who thus was a general office irritant. McNamara decided this officer was far better suited for sea duty. Word came in from Navy headquarters that a ship command was available. The officer fretted at some length because Annapolis classmates had more choice commands—perhaps he shouldn't take it—until it was gently suggested that he had better move while he was still in good standing.

McNamara "was utterly merciless in criticism of error or in achieving a goal," remarked a former assistant. "But he seemed to see nothing personal in it. Personal friction made him nervous."

Only after he was firmly settled behind the big Pershing desk did he fully appreciate the enormity of the job he had taken on. "This place is a jungle, a jungle," he said with disbelief a few weeks after he took over. He would not remain checked for long, however. He set out to command the allegiance of the feuding factions with a determination that soon earned his administration an unwanted title, "The McNamara Monarchy."

The techniques were those that had always carried him to the top. This time, of course, he had entered at the top. But the challenges, as he saw them, in many respects were the same. Ford Motor Company was a fair-sized undertaking, he reminded questioners, and once you passed a certain level mere size became irrelevant.

He sought mastery first by being totally immersed in his job. Carl Vinson, who had something of a monarchy of his own in the House Armed Services Committee, was astonished when he telephoned at seven o'clock one morning to check with the duty officer about an appointment later in the day. The rasping voice that answered said crisply, "McNamara." Senior aides hurrying to work on Saturday morning sometimes felt the hood of his limousine and found it discouragingly cold. Such fragments melded into the reputation of the superman. He played as hard as he worked, according to the word in the Pentagon corridors. He would rush into the Pentagon's executive gymnasium, change to athletic shorts, thrash Agriculture Secretary Orville Freeman at squash, shower, and return to his office with breathtaking speed.

The new breed of defense intellectuals leaped enthusiastically to provide data in forms strange to the military. McNamara digested it at the massive Pershing desk. He had a walk-in vault installed at the south end of the cavernous office to hold the stack of black notebooks, stamped "Secret" and "Top Secret" in gold, which he piled on his desk and constantly updated. The telephones on the General Sherman table behind him—four in various colors (white to reach the President), plus a beige call director with twenty-nine buttons for assistants—were used often and with dispatch. Few in the Pentagon would have believed that he sometimes paused to look reflectively across the green mall reaching into the distance.

He had an extraordinary capacity to absorb facts and file them where he wanted them in his mind. "If you like," he told a committee of Congress, "I will consult my memory." Once he explained his own thirst for data: "I am sure that no significant military problem will ever be wholly susceptible to purely quantitative analysis. But every piece of the total problem that can be quantitatively analyzed removes one more piece of uncertainty from our process of making a choice. There are many factors which cannot be adequately quantified and which therefore must be supplemented with judgment seasoned by experience. Furthermore, experience is necessary to determine the relevant questions with which to proceed with any analysis."

Those remarks had been prepared for a speech. Yet McNamara was capable of speaking just as precisely without notes. Subordinates summoned to the Secretary's office soon learned to take "the walk"—that considerable distance from the door to the desk. Frequently McNamara's eyes remained focused on the document he was reading until the precise moment the visitor reached the desk. Then he looked up, conducted business in perfectly constructed sentences with no wasted words, and dismissed the caller by looking down at the document again. It was disconcerting, to say the least.

Predictably, the hierarchy of the Pentagon at first was stunned. McNamara listened to senior military officers, but he was not prepared to accept their opinions as gospel. He wanted to know how they reached their conclusions and why he should follow them. More than once an august military personage had to excuse himself with barely disguised humiliation as McNamara's questions revealed that he knew more than his teacher. To the extent that he accepted the judgments of his young aides over those of experience, military and civil service pride was sorely bruised.

General Thomas D. White, former Air Force Chief of Staff, put the dominant military reaction bluntly after his retirement that year: "I am profoundly apprehensive of the pipe-smoking, tree-full-of-owls type of so-called professional defense intellectuals who have been brought into this nation's capital. I don't believe a lot of these often overconfident, sometimes arrogant young profes-

sors, mathematicians, and other theorists have sufficient worldli-
ness or motivation to stand up to the kind of enemy we face." Yet
the early criticism was muted.

McNamara simply regarded this kind of reaction as inevitable,
one more factor to be integrated into the decision-making process.
"Obviously," he said, "a decision made in these circumstances
cannot satisfy every differing viewpoint, it cannot please every
protagonist, but it must be made. I am charged by law with the
decision-making responsibility, and I have no hesitancy in making
the required decisions, always, of course, subject to the approval
of the President."

As he established control, McNamara's uncompromising,
thrusting personality fascinated the press and Congress. For a
time the rush to assess what manner of man had appeared in the
Department of Defense overwhelmed in the public mind the issues
he had come so confidently to resolve.

The issues were not new; they were, in fact, chronic. Nor were
they to be defined as simply as they usually were in terms of party
politics or interservice rivalry. The Department of Defense at the
beginning of 1961 was neither quite the disoriented juggernaut
depicted by the incoming Administration nor a model of balanced
security, as some Republicans wistfully had it. As usual in such
debates, the truth lay somewhere between. Time and painful experience had demonstrated that the Eisenhower Administration
did not really intend to invoke massive nuclear retaliation against
lesser Communist provocations. It was equally clear, however,
that there was little flexibility in national strategy, nor the means
to enforce an assertive strategy when it was challenged. In his last
years even John Foster Dulles had seemed to concede the inade-
quacy of the massive retaliation doctrine he had stated.

As a management challenge alone the Department had never
been mastered. Yet it had direct jurisdiction over almost 2.5 million military personnel and more than one million civilians. It
claimed about half the national budget, 10 percent of the gross

national product. Apart from the United States and Soviet Governments as a whole, it was by far the biggest management operation in the world. The United States Secretary of Defense was surely among the most powerful half dozen men in the world. When McNamara took over, the outgoing Administration had asked for $41.8 billion to run the Department for a year.

Yet it seemed to Kennedy and McNamara that the defense budget since World War II had been determined with too much regard for immediate political and fiscal considerations, though these were important, and not enough for the kind of military balance it would support. Leadership was not always sure. One result was frequently savage, always unseemly rivalry among the services for what each regarded as its just share. More recently, conventional forces had been sacrificed to the rapid development of new strategic missiles. Thomas S. Gates, the outgoing Secretary, had been judged, across party lines, as one of the best. Yet he lacked the time, the essential White House support, and possibly the ruthlessness, to bring the military establishment to order.

The new Secretary had all these resources. Kennedy set the early pace for McNamara in his State of the Union message on January 29. In the past, the President said, "lack of a consistent, coherent military strategy, the absence of basic assumptions about our national requirements, and the faulty estimates and duplications arising from interservice rivalries have all made it difficult to assess accurately how adequate, or inadequate, our defenses really are.

"I have therefore instructed the Secretary of Defense to reappraise our entire defense strategy: our ability to fulfill our commitments; the effectiveness, vulnerability, and dispersal of our strategic bases, forces, and warning systems; the efficiency and economy of our operation and organization; the elimination of obsolete bases and installations; and the adequacy, modernization, and mobility of our present conventional and nuclear forces and weapons systems in the light of present and future dangers.

I have asked for preliminary conclusions by the end of February, and I then shall recommend whatever legislative, budgetary, or executive action is needed in the light of these conclusions."

That seemed clear enough. It required, as McNamara remarked, "compressing fifteen years of postwar history into four weeks." What followed in those weeks did much to establish both the reality and the mythology of McNamara's seven years in the Pentagon. He first carved that colossal assignment into four separate studies, covering strategic warfare and weapons, limited war, research and development, and bases and installations. Then he assigned responsibility for each to one of his principal civilian aides. It was a month of little sleep and grinding work. McNamara on February 2 announced the initial, interim steps mentioned earlier: faster delivery of the nineteen Polaris submarines already authorized; an emergency order of fifty-three new transport planes for men and cargo. Then as his staff cut a path through the paper jungle of the Pentagon, the Secretary got himself into trouble for the first time.

It came from one of those background conversations with reporters that are supposed to be beneficial to both sides. McNamara, still an innocent in the ways of Washington, wrote off the "missile gap" that had become so cherished in the Democratic lexicon. Years later the reporters still disagreed among themselves over his exact language. The obvious sense of the Secretary's remarks was that the gap did not exist. The unattributed news reports that followed said as much. Telephones began ringing in Kennedy's office early the next morning. McNamara, in turn, quickly heard from the President. It was easier for the Secretary of Defense to set the record straight in a background conversation than for the President to abandon publicly a central point in his critique of Republican defense policy.

The Secretary had to shed anonymity, of course. What he had told reporters, he explained to the Senate Armed Services Committee later, was that there was no "deterrent" or "destruction" gap, without dealing in numbers of missiles.

"There appeared . . . no signs of a Soviet crash effort to build intercontinental missiles, though the overall Russian military preparations continue at a rapid pace," he said. He still was being somewhat less than candid, presumably out of concern for the political sensitivities of the Administration. For it was in fact clear to him that the missile gap in the form under discussion never had developed.

In its then current state the gap was chiefly the product of Air Force intelligence. The Air Force was riding the crest of its own missile-building program, and a higher assessment of Soviet capability naturally reinforced its position. McNamara came to grips with moderating evidence by taking Gilpatric along with him one day to the Air Force intelligence shop.

His interrogation of officers there left him disturbed. The missile gap, it turned out, had been calculated largely by anticipating all the weapons Soviet technology could produce. There had been little allowance for physical evidence, anything short of total strategic commitment, or the economic burden for the Soviets. Gates had tried to make the same points the year before, but had failed to still the critics.

In fact, the United States at that point had deployed about seventy intercontinental missiles, the Soviets were just getting started, and the United States was widening the gap. From that moment, through the next five years, the missile gap was dead as a realistic immediate issue, though critics of the Administration belabored Kennedy and McNamara with the carcass for some time. Weeks later McNamara was heard fervently telling Gates during a visit by the former Secretary, "I hope I never hear of a missile gap again."

The embarrassment did not detract from work on the strategic weapons systems, however. There was a careful distinction in McNamara's language between the missile gap and a "deterrent" gap. Though the United States was not behind on either point, the Soviets were progressing rapidly in overall strategic capability, including the development of big rocket engines.

By mid-month in that convulsive February, McNamara was settling in. The basic studies were well under way. The Secretary also was at work on the first edition of a sweeping list of tasks that became known irreverently about the Pentagon as "McNamara's 92 Trombones," drawn, naturally, from the designation of the civilian team as "McNamara's Band." The list of 92 tasks, circulated the following month, "covered damn near everything," as a military officer described it.

Some were infinitely complex and sensitive: "Prepare a doctrine which if accepted would permit controlled response and negotiating pauses in event of a thermonuclear attack." The assignment suggested that even if nuclear war came, it might be cut short by limited retaliation and then negotiation. McNamara gave General Lyman L. Lemnitzer, Chairman of the Joint Chiefs of Staff, five weeks to answer that one. The list ranged widely over nuances of strategy, management, tactics, and hardware, and on down to such hoary problems as leaks to the press. In the years that followed, the list grew and shrank as McNamara raised new questions. Of the 131 tasks assigned in 1961, 112 were completed by the end of the year.

To carry them out, McNamara relied upon individuals rather than the endless chain of committees that filled the Department. "I want you to assume responsibility for . . ." he would say to an assistant. The aide either performed or found himself without further prestigious assignments.

McNamara quickly detected continuing probes of his authority within the Department. On February 17 he grasped an opportunity to explain his own conception of his role to both the public and his subordinates: he granted a request for a television interview.

"I think the role of the public manager is very similar to the role of the private manager," he said. "In each case he has the option of following one of two major alternative courses of action. He can either act as a judge or leader. . . . In the one case, it is a passive role; in the other case an active role. . . . I've always believed and endeavored to follow the active leadership role as opposed to the passive judicial role." Ten days later Arthur Sylvester, the Assistant Secretary for Public Affairs, formally circulated the text of the interview throughout the Pentagon in case anyone had missed the point.

The review of strategic defense meanwhile was completed almost on schedule and poured into the White House for translation into policy. Kennedy presented in his first special defense message on March 28 the "preliminary conclusions" he had promised.

The United States never would attack another nation first, he said. But its power must be "adequate to meet our commitments and insure our security, without being bound by arbitrary budget ceilings." He emphasized heavily the necessity for absolute civilian command and control of strategic forces at all times—even after an attack.

"Our defense posture must be both flexible and determined," the President continued. "Any potential aggressor contemplating an attack on any part of the free world with any kind of weapons, conventional or nuclear, must know that our response will be suitable, selective, swift, and effective."

The amendments to the Eisenhower budget that accompanied the message were quite plainly what the Pentagon called a quick fix. They provided a net increase of only $1.9 billion in spending authority, heavy on strategic weapons, but they did reinforce the course the new Administration intended to follow.

Ten more Polaris submarines would be added to the nineteen already authorized, McNamara announced. In addition, the Administration planned both to improve the land-based Minuteman long-range missile and to step up production within the total already authorized. Production capacity would be doubled against the possibility of an emergency. Minuteman was still in the test and development stage, but it promised to be successful as a basic strategic weapon, with a 5,000-mile range and a nuclear warhead equal to a million tons of conventional explosive.

With his program as it then stood, McNamara set in motion his

basic strategic conception: deterrence through the absolute ability
to destroy the aggressor, but including a wide range of lesser responses to lesser aggressions. It differed from massive retaliation
in the formal recognition that nuclear response was not the answer to all, or even most, forms of aggression. All else flowed
from those conclusions.

McNamara left without increase the existing plans for the
bomber forces, which he saw as hopelessly vulnerable to enemy
attack in the long run. The controversial and costly B-70 bomber
was held at the development stage with little prospect for production. Bomber advocates accurately read the decisions as gloomy
omens for their cause. The fifteen-year, billion-dollar effort to develop a nuclear-powered plane was a less lamented casualty:
McNamara sent it back to the scientists for more basic research.

It was no accident, of course, that some of these decisions saved
money—billions of dollars—apart from their strategic influence.
In fact, when McNamara found an opening through which he
could cut costs, he did so with little regard for internal or external politics. But the magnitude of some of the conclusions
often was lost in the matter-of-factness with which they were
presented.

McNamara vetoed for the time being production of the Nike-
Zeus antimissile system, which was supposed to intercept incoming enemy missiles and which the Army hoped would secure its
claim to a nuclear role. First, he said, there was grave doubt that
it would work. Second, it would have a paradoxical strategic
effect. It could be overwhelmed by sheer numbers of less expensive offensive missiles and thus contribute little or nothing to net
security. No one could foresee then the implications of that
argument for the antiballistic missile (ABM) debate of the future.

Another decision that would provide one of the bitterest tests of
McNamara's administration also was little noticed in the disposition of more controversial subjects. The Secretary asked for $45
million to begin development of a new tactical plane to serve both
the Air Force and the Navy. Progress in engines and aerody-

namics, including the concept of a "variable geometry"—movable —wing, made it possible to meet the requirements of all services with one plane, he said confidently. It was an early chapter in the drama of the TFX (for Tactical Fighter, Experimental), later to become the F-111 in all its variations.

Overall, the new Administration's first proposals for nonnuclear forces were less impressive than those for strategic weapons. This was particularly noticeable in the light of its proclaimed goal of flexible response. For one reason much of the nonnuclear effort was concentrated in planes and new arms for the forces already in being, and thus was less dramatic than nuclear hardware. The plan added only 13,000 men to all three services, 3,000 of them for the Army Special Forces whose antiguerrilla potential fascinated the President. McNamara was not yet ready to expand the Army substantially, though that service was pleading to break the bonds of the Eisenhower Administration. It seemed to some members of Congress that the new government was just putting a new gloss on the course of its predecessor. "In the time available," McNamara conceded, "we have not been able to give this program all the study it requires, and our present recommendations are not offered as a final solution."

They did, however, mark the end of a vigorous and eventful transition. If the first decisions of the new Secretary were not obviously revolutionary, they did underline important changes in execution. Strategic deterrence was being cast into a more diverse and, McNamara hoped, more believable perspective. Behind that shield he was committed to develop forces versatile enough to meet a wide range of threats below the nuclear threshold.

McNamara had demonstrated beyond doubt his readiness, even eagerness, to confront volatile issues without flinching. He dominated the Pentagon with unprecedented authority and self-confidence. Washington was as intrigued by the personality and character of the new Secretary of Defense as by the actions that flowed from them.

2

Before Washington

A distraught colonel once insisted that Robert McNamara was born "fully programmed when somebody flipped a switch in the Harvard Business School." The sarcasm betrayed a misunderstanding of the subject. The colonel had never heard McNamara's sudden shout of glee at a wry story well told when he was relaxed. Those moments occurred less often, however, than for most men, and McNamara deliberately avoided any display of emotion around most of his subordinates.

Yet the colonel had a point. The Harvard years marked one of the turns that directed McNamara ultimately to Washington. But there were several of these turns, and the path began in San Francisco.

He came from a family that could have modeled for the traditional American success story of the period. His father, Robert James McNamara, was the son of Irish immigrants. The senior McNamara had worked his way to San Francisco from Boston while he was still in his teens. Success grew from high personal standards and hard work. When he passed his mid-forties, he was still single, solidly established as sales manager of Buckingham &

Hecht, a wholesale shoe firm. Though he had little formal education, McNamara was known among his associates as a man of
keen intelligence and rather awesome dignity.

On June 30, 1914, he was married in St. Mary's Cathedral to
Claranel Strange, a native of Yuba City whose family had moved
to San Francisco. McNamara was a wobbly Catholic, she a Protes-
tant of Scottish-English ancestry. In some respects it was a marriage of opposites. He was forty-eight, she was only twenty-eight.
He was reserved and conservative, she was vivacious and outgoing, and, as an acqaintance noted, something of a scatterbrain
except where her children were concerned.

Robert Strange—bestowed with his father's first name and
his mother's maiden name—was delivered at Mount Zion Hospital at 5:45 A.M. on June 9, 1916. His sister Margaret Elizabeth
was born three years later. The family lived in a somewhat
crowded, rigidly lower-middle-class area in San Francisco's northern hills. But the senior McNamara was well paid, well enough
finally to raise his and his wife's gaze toward something better
for their children. Precisely why they chose Oakland, across the
bay, is not clear. Some factors, at least, were obvious. As their
family grew, the McNamaras needed more room, and the same
money bought a better house in a more attractive neighborhood
in Oakland than in San Francisco. Then, too, the parents must
have been thinking of schools, and their choice of locations in
Oakland indicates that they were.

Even before Bob started school, his parents were aware that
they had an unusual child on their hands. His sister made that
point years later to an interviewer as she scoffed at suggestions
that their father's age contributed to an abnormal childhood. She
and her brother, she said, "came from a very normal, middle-
class California home, and we both enjoyed a very normal youth.
Stories that there was a generation gap between us and our father,
that he didn't understand us, are nonsense. We had a very happy
home life. The only thing nontypical about it was Bob. Even as
a little boy my brother was terrific. He was something special.

All of us knew he'd grow up to be something special, and I believe he has."

Whatever the reasons for the move, the McNamaras bought a modest three-bedroom home at 1036 Annerly Road in Oakland in 1924. It was then and still is a pleasant neighborhood of manicured lawns on small lots, with hedges trimmed and flowers carefully planted to set off the alternating frame and California-Spanish houses. Annerly Road is one of the first streets in the transition from the rolling Oakland hills into the sharper ridges of the town of Piedmont. In fact, though the McNamaras lived in Oakland, the houses on the other side of Annerly Road were in Piedmont. To understand the significance of the move in the life of young Robert McNamara, it is necessary to understand Piedmont.

The town was an anomaly in 1924 and is even more of one today. Entirely surrounded by Oakland, it is a bastion of what one resident calls the "upper middle and lower upper class." Secure against the tax-hungry government of deteriorating Oakland, it is a hilly fortress of conservatism. Most important for the McNamaras, it had a splendid high school in which academic excellence was the supreme goal. In those days outsiders could get into Piedmont High, and as a resident of Annerly Road, McNamara was eligible.

He already had set his academic pattern at Westlake Junior High School in Oakland. Miss Marie Carriker, who taught him social studies at Westlake and lived a block away from the McNamaras, recalled him as "a student of perfection. When we did research on different countries, he would make beautiful books. He sat in the last seat in the back row, but you knew he was there. He was conspicuous for his scholarship, not his personality. What I mean is, he was not pushy, but when you called on him he was ready."

When Bob entered the rarefied atmosphere of Piedmont, he was more than ready. The atmosphere was closer to that of a prep school than that of the ordinary public high school. Girls wore middy blouses with ties, simple skirts, and white buck or saddle shoes. Tailored grounds surrounded the yellow California stucco building, perched on a hillside. Good paintings hung in the corridors. The teachers cared. In his three years at Piedmont, Bob McNamara achieved a record of twenty-six A's and seven B's. Four of the B's were in French—apparently more the result of a tin ear than a failure to understand the structure of the language —and two were in physical education. His other solid courses— English, mathematics, history, commercial law, chemistry—produced a string of A's broken only by one B in Junior English.

By his senior year he was one of the big men on campus, though a rather quiet one. He was a member of the Board of Control, in effect the student government organization; the Boys' Council, which arranged boys' activities; the Alpha Clan Council, an executive committee of the school's leading honor society; and editor of the 1933 *Clan-O-Log*, the yearbook, from which he peers solemnly with his hair slicked back in the style that became familiar to the nation years later. He also was a member of the Glee Club and the Opera, undertakings that still inspire giggles from former classmates, for his voice had a tendency to break. As president of Rigma—a secret fraternity pledged to service, which a faculty member recalls as "more of a nuisance than anything else"—his social standing was secure.

He developed lasting friendships at Piedmont. In most cases they were with students whose ability was even greater than McNamara's own. Even with his record, he was neither the smartest nor the most active student in the school. An IQ test in 1930 put him at one standard deviation above the norm—quite bright but not exceptional. He gravitated toward excellence and sought it in himself. Years later he would proclaim his good fortune at "having people around me who are smarter than I am," but he displayed early the quality of attracting bright people and reacting to their challenge.

"Bob always came to the surface through his abilities," remarked Stanley Johnson (President of the Student Body, Alpha

Clan, Masonic Oratorical Award), now a San Francisco attorney. "He didn't work his way deliberately into prominent positions. He arrived because of his natural qualities, but he refused to exploit them for personal advancement."

McNamara's friendship with Vernon Goodin (Alpha Clan, drama, football, opera), now also a San Francisco trial lawyer, remains his closest from the Piedmont days. A warm but never quite romantic relationship developed with Annalee Whitmore, whose five lines of achievements in the *Clan-O-Log* surpassed McNamara's three. She went on to become a Time-Life correspondent in the Pacific and wrote *Thunder out of China* with Theodore White. McNamara frequently went out with Hallie Booth, a close friend of Annalee, who also made an outstanding record at Piedmont and later at the University of California, but who died not long after graduation.

With all the Piedmont activity, McNamara retained a certain reserve. He met the challenges, but he was not extended. One classmate recalled him as being "not aloof, but self-contained." Still missing, apparently, was the awesome drive that would become famous later. Classmates and adults who knew McNamara during this period assumed that whatever special drive was necessary came from his mother. It was she who appeared at the school to clear up any questions about grades. A faculty member recalled with a grin that "it was a good idea to have answers."

Students who visited the McNamara home could immediately provide thirty-six years later vivid descriptions of Claranel McNamara but had difficulty remembering the father beyond the fact that he was quiet and friendly. One Piedmont teacher recalled the mother's saying years later that Bob felt she had pushed him too hard, and that Bob had told his mother so. Yet McNamara often would drop casual remarks indicating deep affection for both his parents and evidence of a firm fatherly hand at crucial times. "Bob never actually discussed his father and mother," Stanley Johnson once said. "I never saw signs of anything but a close, informal family relationship."

McNamara left Piedmont with recommendations to both Stanford and the University of California. He chose the latter and immediately began the process of what Stanley Johnson called "coming to the surface." He was pledged by Phi Gamma Delta social fraternity, and was a subchairman of the Mardi Gras dance, the first big social event of the year for the freshman class. All of this suggests that McNamara might have become a bit more socially conscious in college than he was in high school, but a fraternity brother discounted the evidence: "He never was much of a frat man; at least his heart wasn't in it." Still, the next year he was listed as a member of a "Vigilante Committee," of all things, to restore hazing traditions to the campus.

Other, more important things were happening to McNamara during his sophomore year. He had gotten off to what was, for him, an indifferent start as a freshman. Against A's in math and philosophy, he recorded a C in advanced French and a C and a B in English. But in his second year he built a spectacular record of eleven A's and one B, and he fell only slightly below that level as he worked his way through economics and philosophy courses —with astronomy as an elective—to a degree in economics with honors in 1937. He was voted into Phi Beta Kappa for his performance as a sophomore.

For McNamara that sophomore year was crucial, grades aside. It brought his own intellectual awakening in a university that was a peculiar mixture of traditional campus exuberance, with beer and football on Saturday, and uninhibited political exchange. It was a time of intellectual ferment, with old idols teetering and substitutes being proposed from across the political spectrum. Malcolm M. Davisson, a professor of economics who worked closely with McNamara, recalled him recently as being "very broadly based. He read widely outside his courses. Frankly, he didn't have to work too hard for his grades, so he had resources to spend elsewhere. I regarded him as a genuine intellectual, and I fully expected him to become a teacher."

McNamara watched with fascination as Robert Gordon Sproul,

the president from 1930 to 1958, built a great university, even during the nadir of the Depression, coaxing money from a rural-dominated legislature that regarded much of the liberal campus activity as near treason. As he grew older, McNamara would put Sproul and Monroe E. Deutsch, the University provost, as much as his teachers, in the forefront of those who shaped his thinking as an undergraduate.

By every standard the years at Berkeley were varied and stimulating. McNamara was chairman of the Men's Judicial Committee, which dealt with such problems as cheating, a role in which Charles T. Post, editor of the *Daily Cal*, found him a bit naïve. McNamara, Post felt, had too much faith in his fellow man. In his junior and senior years, McNamara was a member of the leading honor societies, the Winged Helmet and the Order of the Golden Bear. As Malcolm Davisson had said, he could maintain classroom excellence with time to spare. McNamara and Vernon Goodin several times drove down to Stanford on weekends to visit Annalee Whitmore, who would scratch up a date for Vern. "They were always broke," she told an interviewer. "They used to come by some circuitous route through Alviso to avoid the twenty-five-cent toll bridge. I must say we had fun." On a blind date he met Marion Sproul, the daughter of the University president. She later married Vern Goodin, and the Goodins and McNamaras remained close friends after college.

At Cal McNamara developed a liberal social outlook tempered by a hardheadedness that kept him from flying emotionally into causes. Leonard W. Charvet, who knew him as a co-worker in senior organizations rather than as a close personal friend, explained that "I was more liberal, more likely to fly off the handle. He was more thoughtful, working his way through issues. But he was not a stuffed shirt. He had time for those who were less quick than he. None of us was as quick as he was, that was obvious."

He tried out for crew and managed to become stroke of the second freshman boat in 1933. Carroll (Ky) Ebright, crew coach emeritus, recently recalled him instantly: "He was a good kid, tenacious. But he wasn't big enough. He weighed less than 160, and was only five feet eleven. He couldn't beat out the bigger fellows." McNamara became one of the crew managers during his sophomore and junior years, but finally lost out to a classmate in his senior year.

Outside the University as well, he began during the four years to demonstrate the pattern of self-testing that would become so prominent later.

Stanley Johnson accompanied him on the first of the searches for adventure that filled his summers from Piedmont forward. In the summer of 1933, with the price of gold up, the two set out to prospect at Spanish Creek, in the Feather River area of the Sierras. An old-timer taught them to make a sluice box and use a pan. The undertaking had netted about seventy-five cents' worth of gold when word arrived of a strike in the Siskiyou Mountains. Johnson and McNamara picked up their sluice box and set out for the new terrain. Along the way the sluice box fell apart, the bottle of gold was lost, and the expedition turned into a fishing trip—or at least Johnson fished while McNamara climbed.

McNamara fell in love with the mountains, for both the physical and mental challenge. From that time forward he always returned to them, to remote places with a few close friends, whenever his internal resources flagged. Joseph Cooper, a classmate at Cal, used to take McNamara home with him to the family ranch in northern California and had visions of making a fisherman of him. The effort was doomed from the start. Never much at formal athletics, McNamara nevertheless preferred vigorous sports and attacked them with fury.

Stanley Johnson also was along the first time McNamara skied, during his sophomore year at Cal. "Bob was bound and determined to be a good skier," Johnson said. "And he kept practicing on whatever was weakest."

Not all of his summers were spent in the mountains, however. Still looking for excitement, he wanted to ship out on a freighter in the summer of 1934. It was the year of a savage standoff be-

tween shipowners and seamen demanding relief from shameful
wages and working conditions. McNamara, blissfully ignorant of
the issues, proudly signed on as a seaman and was planning to
sail despite the strike that ultimately brought the National Guard
onto the docks. Those plans were abruptly canceled, however,
when his father learned what was happening. "He gave me hell,"
McNamara recalled. "It was the first time I had ever addressed a
labor question, and I didn't go." The elder McNamara was conservative, but he held no brief for strikebreaking. The son got a
job the next summer at thirty-three dollars a month—through the
union hiring hall created as a result of the strike.

His most memorable experience at sea occurred in the summer
of 1937 after graduation from Berkeley, when he shipped out on
the *President Hoover* for the Far East. The Japanese had attacked Shanghai on August 18, and the *Hoover* lay off in the
Yangtze to evacuate Americans. In the confusion the Chinese air
force, identifying the *Hoover* as Japanese, attacked with bombs,
killing two men and wounding several others. McNamara was so
busy wielding a camera that he had to be told to go below.

In the fall of 1937 McNamara went off to Harvard Business
School. Plan, set goals, consider the alternatives and consequences, adjust as necessary, but above all plan: this was the
message of the Graduate School of Business Administration.
McNamara's principal mentor was Ross G. Walker, who recognized the brilliance of the student immediately and who, with
Professor Thomas H. Sanders, steeped him in the principles of
accounting control. These two men, as well as Edmund P.
Learned, who taught merchandising, had the greatest impact on
McNamara as a graduate student. "These professors opened my
eyes to American business," he once told a friend. "A whole new
world of management techniques became clear to me."

It was of no small significance to McNamara that many of these
techniques were imparted, with General Motors cited as a case
history. With the Du Ponts in control and Alfred P. Sloan, Jr., in

charge, GM had risen from near collapse in 1920 to supremacy
in the automobile industry. McNamara was fascinated by the
process that enabled the GM high command to segregate trouble
anywhere in one of its divisions, and by the cost controls that
were a critical tool in the process. Moreover, he was impressed
by the fact that experts in finance and organization, not in manufacturing or sales, had rescued GM.

By all accounts, McNamara's first year at Harvard was a spectacular success. The school uses a case system, in which a group
of students is assigned to work on a specific business problem.
Walter Haas, Jr., a classmate who now is president of Levi Strauss
& Co., reported that "it was terribly tempting to the rest of us to
let Bob do all the work."

A cloud fell over the second year, however, with the death of
McNamara's father in November, 1938. Bob, of course, returned
to California. Unfortunately, his oral examinations for his
master's degree were scheduled shortly after his arrival back in
Cambridge, and apparently his performance was less than outstanding. At any rate, it prevented him from receiving his degree
with honors. "Some of us were terribly upset," Edmund Learned
recalled thirty years later. "I have felt badly about it ever since.
But one professor failed to make allowance for the death of his
father. His work generally was splendid."

McNamara remained uncertain about a career. After leaving
Harvard, he returned home to work for Price, Waterhouse & Co.,
the accounting firm, in its San Francisco office. For a while he
went out with several girls in the old crowd from the Piedmont
and Berkeley days. Then in April, 1940, he bumped into Margaret Craig, whom he had known casually at Cal. This time
sparks flew.

Margaret Craig, small, brown-haired, vivacious, was born in
Seattle, but her family moved to Alameda, across the bay from
San Francisco, when she was two. She had dated Vernon Goodin
several times during their college years and thus met McNamara.
When he returned to the Bay area from Cambridge, she was

teaching biology and physical education in a San Rafael high school, and their romance flourished that summer. McNamara's prospects took a sudden turn at this time when Ross Walker asked him to return to Harvard to teach. By August McNamara had made a conditional decision: he would accept the Harvard offer if Margaret would go along. They were married on August 13 in Christ's Church of Alameda.

At Cambridge they moved first into a rooming house converted from a dormitory, as McNamara, with the rank of instructor, began teaching accounting. Later they settled into a faculty apartment, but "things still were rather lean," as Margaret McNamara saw it in retrospect.

McNamara very quickly became what Edmund Learned described as "a very good teacher. He organized his work well." Donald David, who became dean of the school the following year, called him "rather inspiring, really. He was able to give students confidence." With the approach of war, however, McNamara became more and more concerned at his isolation from the mainstream. He tried to enlist in the Navy and was rejected because of his poor vision. Then "Tex" Thornton entered his life.

Charles Bates Thornton was a young officer who had propelled himself from odd jobs in a small Texas town into a government job in Washington and the favor of Robert Lovett, then Assistant Secretary of War for Air. The Air Corps was growing to proportions never dreamed of, and the potential for waste was horrendous. With Lovett's backing, Thornton approached the business school with a plan to train likely young officers in statistical control. In the summer of 1941 Dean David called in several of his most promising young faculty members to sound them out on participation.

For McNamara the choice was relatively simple, and he abandoned his thoughts of volunteering for the Army. Edmund Learned, placed in charge of the program by Donald David, put it to the faculty in terms of a straight challenge: They had been chosen, he said, because they "were able, promising young men who might be able to take a project that vague and make something real out of it." Thornton could offer them their choice of commissions or positions as civilian consultants; for the time being McNamara remained a civilian.

As the program got under way, McNamara's responsibilities grew quickly. Often he was sent to Washington for talks with the military, and each time, as David reported, "he did it well. He came back with the situation all tied up in a neat package: there were no loose ends."

After more than a year of teaching Thornton's Air Corps candidates on his home ground, McNamara was sent to England to work out problems in the B-17 bomber program. For a poor civilian, the premium on $10,000 life insurance covering an Atlantic flight in those days was high. It was a measure of McNamara's standing that Dean David insisted on paying the premium and keeping the young teacher's place—he had become an assistant professor with the formation of the "Stat School"—in the University's pension program. David anticipated McNamara's return to teaching after the war, and McNamara himself had no other career in mind. But it quickly became apparent in England that military officers did not react kindly or quickly to civilian consultants. On March 12, 1943, McNamara, needing the force of rank and able to obtain a higher commission in the field than he could Stateside, became a temporary captain in the United States Army.

Those were the days when Colonel, soon to become General, Curtis E. LeMay was introducing brilliant new ideas on tactics and leadership into aerial bombardment with the B-17s. Edmund Learned today treasures a letter from Captain McNamara full of praise for Colonel LeMay—with whom his differences over high policy would become almost total twenty years later.

McNamara's task, in the simplest terms, was to make things work the way they were supposed to work, especially in the movement of men and materials—getting the proper number of men to mesh with the right amount of equipment at the appointed

hour. Thornton's entire operation, in fact, was directed at achieving this ideal state. In September, after he had been in England
about nine months, consistently impressing his superiors, McNamara returned to the United States to apply his talents to the
B-29s at Salina, Kansas.

Arriving in New York, McNamara was met by his wife and
little Margaret, who had been born on Halloween Day, 1941, and
was then almost two. They set out for the Midwest in a 1940 con-
vertible so overloaded that the baby rode sitting on her potty-chair
for the first stage of the journey. History may have little use for
the footnote that Captain Robert S. McNamara finally yielded to
exasperation and stealthily abandoned his daughter's potty-chair
on a curb in Allentown, Pennsylvania.

After six months in Kansas, McNamara flew off to Calcutta with
the B-29s in April, 1944, leaving Margaret to bear their second
daughter, Kathleen, on July 22. His promotion to major became
effective on April 10, the day after his formal transfer to the
China-Burma-India theater. The assignment in India, which included planning the flow of matériel across the hump into China,
also lasted six months. Even before his return to the United States
in October, McNamara was promoted to lieutenant colonel, having
served only four months as a major.

Learned later judged McNamara's work for the Twentieth Air
Force to be "spectacular." His techniques for damage assessment
on the B-29s were "entirely new." "The best logistics report the
Air Force ever received was originated by him in China," Learned
said flatly.

Back in Washington, McNamara was assigned to Pentagon
Room 4D1053, in the Office of Management Control, Statistical
Control Division, of Army Air Force Headquarters. It was only a
short walk from Suite 3E880, which later would become the office
of the Secretary of Defense. Of course, there was no Secretary of
Defense then, and the thought of high position in the Pentagon
never crossed the mind of Lieutenant Colonel Robert S. McNamara, twenty-eight, who expected to return to teaching at Har-

vard. The McNamaras moved into an apartment in Arlington, a short distance from the Pentagon.

The following spring McNamara was transferred for the last time in his military career, to headquarters of the Air Technical Service Command at Wright Field, Dayton, Ohio. With his service nearing an end, he judged it to have been far more than an obligatory exercise. He had been able to apply the management techniques of the Harvard Business School in a practical environment. There were military honors as well. Apart from the standard geographic service ribbons, he wore a Legion of Merit, awarded in December. His service record contained three letters of commendation. A notation in the Department of Records says tersely: "Effectiveness reports on file indicate overall evaluation of not less than superior."

Shortly after the McNamaras reached Wright Field, however, official applause faded to unimportance. There had been a wave of polio in Washington as they left, and McNamara came down with a mild case. At first it was thought to be malaria, a memento of his service in Asia. Then his wife was stricken with a more serious attack, and there was no longer any doubt about the diagnosis. After the immediate danger was past, the McNamaras still faced difficulties. The children had to be farmed out while their mother received extended hospital care. She was to spend four months in a military hospital, and then five months at Children's Hospital in Baltimore, and then to wear a brace for a year. Meanwhile the bills mounted, and McNamara, who had looked forward to a comfortable career as a teacher, faced the prospect of having his wife cared for by the polio foundation. He was deeply in debt.

Rescue came in an unusual form—one of those short-term decisions of necessity that take on historical significance. Tex Thornton had become one of the younger colonels in the U.S. Army, and he was a man with more than conventional ambition. His wartime team, which at one point included as many as 2,800 officers, had saved millions, and perhaps billions, of dollars for the government while yielding a profit in faster, more efficient operations. Why not sell the services of a small statistical control and management team on the open market? McNamara automatically fell into the group of brightest candidates Thornton set out to collect. A package of ten was chosen simply for convenience.

McNamara reacted with skepticism when Thornton called. The scheme at first appeared harebrained, and McNamara's sense of commitment to Donald David and Harvard was strong. Thornton drew him along with the device by which Kennedy recruited McNamara later, and which McNamara then employed to collect his own defense team: at least, Thornton said, McNamara owed him the courtesy of discussing it in person.

By early fall of 1945 Thornton had begun prospecting among a long list of companies, most of them believed to be in varying stages of financial trouble. His first encouragement came from Robert R. Young, whose massive Allegheny Corporation needed help. But the youngest member of Thornton's group, Lieutenant George Moore, twenty-six, heard of an even more fertile challenge. Henry Ford II, who had just gained control of the shaky Ford empire from his aged and deteriorating grandfather, was reported to be in sore need of bright young men. After talking it over with others of his group, Thornton decided on a direct approach with a wire to Henry II.

"I wasn't too impressed," Ford remembered later. "Colonels were like pebbles on the beach at that time." He was interested enough, however, to have a Washington representative get in touch with Thornton the next day. Thornton and Moore made one hurried visit to Dearborn, and then in early November eight of the young officers arrived to talk with Ford and men close to him in the resurgent management. Besides Thornton, thirty-two, and Moore, the group in the Rotunda dining room included Charles E. Bosworth, twenty-nine, J. E. Lundy, thirty-one, McNamara, twenty-nine, Arjay R. Miller, twenty-nine, Francis C. (Jack) Reith, thirty-one, and James O. Wright, thirty-four. Despite their youth, the officers represented considerable business and professional experience apart from their Air Force service. Three had taught business or economics: McNamara at Harvard, Miller at U.C.L.A., and Lundy at Princeton. The other members of the Thornton team, missing from that first conference, were Ben Davis Mills and Wilbur R. Andreson, both thirty.

By the end of the day most had made up their minds tentatively in favor of working for Ford. They had been drilled thoroughly by John S. Bugas, the former FBI agent who became one of young Henry's most trusted and effective managers. "They'll do," Bugas told Ford. Almost to a man, the young officers scented courage and resolve in Ford, who was only twenty-eight himself, and thus opportunity for themselves as he set out to bring the reeling giant under control. When Thornton returned to Washington, he sent Ford a salary schedule for the group: the Indians would receive $9,000 to $12,000—McNamara was down for $12,000, a comfortable level at the time—and the chief, Thornton, a premium rate, about $16,000.

Actually the decision was not final that day; far from it. McNamara still had questions. He talked with Donald David, who was reluctant to let him go but thought two or three years in private business might be good for him. A full professorship in the prestigious business policy course would be waiting when he returned to Harvard to teach. Thornton knew McNamara was broke and that his wife was recovering from polio. "You owe it to her," he said—and McNamara dropped his reservations. On January 29, 1946, still on terminal leave from the Army, he arrived in Dearborn ready to report to work.

There were moments in the early weeks when the new team wondered what sort of madhouse it had entered. It had been given full authority to search and question at will throughout the Ford system, for none of its members knew much about the automobile industry. The Ford Motor Company was a model of inefficiency: it had nothing even remotely approaching the system with which Thornton's crowd had kept fingers on the Air Force pulse. A great measure of hostility—or fear—greeted the young executives as they probed supervisor after supervisor in the Ford plants. Rumors were out that the team was really an execution squad, gathering material with which to fire those out of favor. It was a notion consistent with the way Harry Bennett, old Henry's powerful confidential aide, had run things in the recent past.

Slowly the new recruits learned, and at the end of four months the "Whiz Kids" or "Quiz Kids," as they quickly became known, had a better general knowledge of company operations than anyone else. One thing was clear: Henry Ford II had accepted an awesome challenge when he set out to turn the company around. Formal organization was haphazard at best, and where it existed it was as likely as not to duplicate efforts elsewhere. Planners and producers found themselves crossing each other's paths. Ford had to unravel the administrative mess as he struggled to make the transition from wartime to peacetime production. There had been no new cars at all in 1943–44, and only a few thousand in 1945.

Young Henry had several important assets, however. Despite the current losses, he had money, and the company was free of debt. Cash reserves in mid-1945 were $685 million, so he was able to spend in order to create corporate vitality for the long pull.

Ford had no hope that the neophyte managerial team could remake the company for him—though some of its members might have thought they could. He had to have quickly the sort of experienced, decisive general executive who would serve as his right arm, a man who would reach out for the special talent Ford needed in almost every area of company operations. Apparently Ford had hoped to have new management muscle in place by the beginning of the year, but as it worked out he was still negotiating to obtain it even as McNamara and his colleagues fanned out through the company.

The key to new health for Ford's vast enterprises was decentralization, beneath a strong top management, in contrast to the former autocracy that merged all undertakings into an amorphous

whole and prevented sharp definition of responsibility. Henry
Ford II recognized this fully, and he recognized also that General
Motors was the best example of what he had to do. Old Henry's
legacy of disdain for paper work and for financial experts had to
be discarded.

The choice to become his all-important first lieutenant was
Ernest R. Breech, forty-nine, the president of Bendix Aviation
Corporation, who had been in General Motors management for
twenty-one years. Strongest in finance, Breech also was an exceedingly competent generalist. He was first appalled, then intrigued,
and finally challenged by the chaos at Ford. The company was
losing almost $9 million a month, yet had awesome resources
rattling around. In May, 1946, he agreed to join Ford as executive vice president.

With him he brought Lewis D. Crusoe, who had retired from
the high executive level at General Motors at fifty, but had returned to become Breech's assistant at Bendix, and Harold T.
Youngren, who had been engineer for the Oldsmobile division
and later chief engineer for the Borg-Warner Corporation. For
purchasing, Ford recruited Albert J. Browning, former director
of War Department purchasing, from the Department of Commerce. Delmar S. Harder, former chief of production for General
Motors, was quite content as President of the E. W. Bliss Company, and it was not until October that he agreed to become
Ford's vice president for operations.

Even before the new executives arrived, Thornton's crew,
working directly under Ford himself, began putting together ideas
for reorganization. When Crusoe arrived, he was placed in charge
of the group. It had been decided early on that each of the ten
would go his own way within the company. Sifting out into the
structure was necessarily a slow process, however, and for a time
Crusoe kept them busy on organization in a special planning
office. McNamara, Lundy, and Miller worked directly under
Crusoe on finance, and two of these three—McNamara and Miller
—went on to become presidents of Ford.

McNamara hardly could have drafted a situation more suited to his particular capabilities. Here was a company with massive resources, waiting to be harnessed under a bright new leader who was eager for change. Change meant decentralization, breaking out the various company operations into individual profit-and-loss centers under executives who would rise or fall on their performances. It was a conscious swing toward the staff-and-line officer system of General Motors in the 1920s and 1930s, of which Breech as broad-based executive, Crusoe with special talent in finance, Youngren as engineer, and Harder as production expert, had been part.

Then here was McNamara, trained by Ross Walker at Harvard, as familiar with the system as any man could be without coming from GM. There was an additional quality in the Ford transition which McNamara was especially suited to exploit: a receptiveness to professional management, to imagination rather than the traditional automaker's instinct. Planning and finance, rather than production and sales, would become the ways to advancement in the new Ford system.

McNamara almost immediately began once again the process Stanley Johnson had identified during his high school years: "coming to the surface." There never had been any question that Thornton was the leader of the Air Force Whiz Kids. McNamara had not even been a member of the smaller circle that planned the combined assault on industry. Yet he shortly began to emerge as the most promising of the young executives. Thornton, dissatisfied with progress he considered too slow, quit in the spring of 1948 for grander things at Hughes Aircraft and later at Litton Industries. McNamara managed Ford's Planning Office and Financial Analysis Office until 1949, when he was promoted to comptroller. From there he moved steadily: August, 1953—assistant general manager of the Ford Division, the heart of the company; January, 1955—general manager of the Ford Division and vice president of the company; May, 1957—vice president and group executive, all car and truck divisions; August, 1957—director of

the company, member of the executive and administration committees; November, 1960—president of the company.

It was a remarkable record, and it was achieved for the most
obvious reasons: McNamara made the right moves in the automobile jungle when they counted most. The course was not always
smooth. Reports filtered out that Breech at times took McNamara
aside, counseled patience with the density of other executives,
and urged him to sell himself. McNamara relied instead on performance. As the company surged in one of the spectacular
recoveries of U.S. industrial history, McNamara's career moved
with it. When the Ford Division was created in 1949 as the meat
and potatoes branch of the company, Lew Crusoe was put in
charge. With McNamara's transfer to that division in 1953, he
again moved under a demanding teacher. And when Crusoe
moved up to become executive vice president, he left McNamara
in position to make or break his own reputation outside the comptroller's office, the area in which he was most comfortable.

Ford men are reluctant to pinpoint blame publicly for failures,
though the system usually points to individuals. Yet a comparison
of the planning that culminated in the Edsel with that which led
to the small Falcon and its larger offspring reveals why McNamara succeeded in the automobile industry.

When the Edsel was conceived in 1955, Ford was searching for
products to broaden its share of the market. The company offered
nothing between the Mercury and the Lincoln, a gap in which
General Motors had three cars and Chrysler two. Ford planners
looked carefully at sales statistics and buying behavior, which
indicated buyers wanted to move up in automobile status. To a
great extent, however, the Edsel was shaped ahead of the consumer research, which was concentrated, when finally ordered,
more on the presumed prestige of Edsel ownership than the details of the car. No one really knew what the buyer wanted.

When Edsel finally reached the market in the fall of 1957, the
economy was in recession, and medium-priced automobiles were
selling poorly. The car had more defects than normally are ex-

pected in a new line. Its styling features and the public reaction became staples for comedians. Whether the Edsel could have been saved with better planning is subject to debate, but there was no question that there were flaws in its development. Only 110,000 cars were sold before McNamara—who had been promoted in the meantime—had it withdrawn in 1959.

The cost of the Edsel experience has never been fully disclosed. Outsiders have put it between $200 million and $350 million. And there were other costs as well. Francis C. (Jack) Reith, of the original Thornton group, had risen rapidly to become managing director at Ford of France in 1952. When Ford sold out to Simca, Reith returned to Dearborn, just in time to direct for Crusoe the studies that produced a plan for future products— including the Edsel. With acceptance of his proposals in 1955, Reith was promoted to vice president in charge of the Mercury Division. But the market turned sour, and the division, as a former executive recalled, was "in a mess." Ford again folded Mercury and Lincoln, with the Edsel, into a single division, and Reith was bypassed. McNamara, by then one step away from the presidency, called for his resignation. Reith left to become president of the Crosley Division of Avco Manufacturing Corporation. Three years later, at forty-five, he shot himself to death.

Many people, in fact, were to blame for the Edsel, but some paid a higher price than others. Records of the time indicate McNamara raised a few doubts about the planning. His role, however, was negligible: the car was outside his responsibility when it was conceived and developed.

When Ford assaulted the compact car field, however, the story was quite different. With McNamara in charge, a team of specialists in every aspect of automobile development, from finance and style through production and sales, set out to learn all that could be learned in advance. Consumer surveys ranged across the spectrum from owners of foreign and U.S. economy cars through the higher brackets. Designers put on paper various combinations of engines and body styles, and these too were exposed to the criticism of potential customers. Whenever cost or design problems forced a change, the alternatives then were tested on consumers as well.

What resulted was a new lightweight engine with fewer moving parts than that of the standard Ford, and a body structure that also was lighter and offered replacement features that resulted in lower insurance premiums for owners. When the car went on the market in 1959, McNamara could price the basic Falcon at less than General Motors' Corvair. By the end of 1961 more than a million Falcons had been sold.

Under Detroit standards it was a car both simple and economical, characteristics that did not endear McNamara to traditional automakers. He was shooting for function and quality first, not simply for the sale of the most cars for the most money. Despite the reservations on the part of some executives, Ford had learned several important lessons about broadening its base of products to cover the market. Soon after the compact made its appearance, McNamara detected a gap between the Falcon and the Ford. Within eighteen months a new Fairlane had been produced to sell for $200 less than the standard Ford. "Never in this world could such a record have been made without the Falcon experience as precedent," a writer in *Fortune* remarked.

From the Falcon also came the Mercury Comet as a higher-level counterpart. From the new Fairlane, Mercury devised the Meteor. In addition, along the way, McNamara had successfully converted the Thunderbird from a two-seater to a four-seater for repressed swingers who also had a couple of children.

The success of the new models had an unhappy side effect in the decline of the standard Fords, providing fuel for McNamara's detractors. The company did not seem worried at the overall results within the Ford Division, however. As Lee Iacocca, who had mixed emotions about McNamara and who was one of his successors in the division, noted later, "Our stockholders are interested in profits per share, not profits per car." Iacocca was something of a phrasemaker. Observing the eagerness with which buyers accepted extras on the basic Falcon, he quipped, "The American public wants economy, and they don't care what they pay for it." Ford had learned the whimsicality of the auto owner, and had provided optional features—automatic transmission, whitewall tires, fancy interiors, a souped-up engine—for those who wanted to start low and build up. Most buyers wanted at least some of the options.

At work here in part was a financial practice raised almost to the level of a new concept by McNamara. Ford had speeded its postwar recovery with the management methods applied by General Motors in the twenties and thirties. These meant diligent reduction of the costs required to achieve a given quality, and thus greater profits. Later Ford added asset control—carefully integrated cultivation of all company resources, an area long neglected—and revenue control. That last term was McNamara's application of the idea that close cultivation of income from a varied product base could have as much to do with profits as cost control. Give the buyer a broad choice of basic products and accessories, McNamara said in effect, at prices acceptable to both him and the company. Most students of the Ford recovery have cited car radios as a readily identifiable instrument of revenue control: many buyers discovered they needed a radio, a high-profit item, after only minimum investment in sales effort.

There was another aspect to the offering of options. Soon after McNamara took over the Ford Division, the company opened a campaign for safety belts as an extra-cost accessory. It was Ford's response to rising pressure outside the industry for safer automobiles—and to the prospect of a shellacking by GM that year. For a time its seat belts and other built-in safety features were well received. But automakers were horrified at acknowledging that somehow automobiles might be dangerous, and counter-pressures within the industry, and within Ford, caused the campaign to subside in 1957. It was the only time McNamara was in trouble at Ford, and it demonstrated that he was not above compromise.

Thus there were limits, though they were imprecise, to competition within the industry. One of the most remarkable examples developed in the pricing of the 1957 models. Ford's prices were already out to dealers when the word came that GM would be charging more for corresponding models. With a series of steps, including readjustment of dealers' discounts, McNamara brought Ford prices up nearer the General Motors levels.

As it had provided the inspiration for the Ford recovery, General Motors became the measurement of success. The result had a great deal to do with McNamara's status at Ford. In both 1957 and 1959, while he was in the line of direct responsibility, Ford fulfilled the rallying cry, "Beat Chevrolet." Quite properly others within the company shared the applause. It was not hard to understand, however, why McNamara was named when Ford reached outside the family for the first time to choose its president.

Along the way, he cultivated the work habits and the self-discipline that intrigued friends and infuriated the enemies he inevitably made as he moved purposefully through the corporate maze. He regularly worked from 7:30 A.M. to 6:30 P.M., what he called a "good, normal" working day, though it began at an hour that horrified most automobile executives. From the beginning he sought an objectivity on the job that reduced human considerations, including those applying to himself, to the status of one component among many with which he dealt on a given issue. "He's mature to the point that he eliminates his own feelings, and thereby automatically eliminates the feelings of others," another Ford executive once remarked. "If there are humans involved in a problem, he would have his equation as to the impact on them, but that's all it would be."

With this approach, McNamara could snap, "That's irrelevant," to a good friend. He had little tolerance for imprecise thought, and since most people, including high industrial executives, often think imprecisely, some subordinates reacted to McNamara with sick fear or suppressed fury. "He commands respect because of

his braininess, his mental ability," a former Ford official remarked
as McNamara was leaving the company in 1960. "But he's completely deficient in human qualities. He runs Ford through fear."

Stanley Johnson, of Piedmont and Berkeley, argued from
knowledge of the earlier years that such critics were mostly poor
performers. "He was neither a social snob nor an intellectual
snob. He might get impatient with laziness, not with lack of brain-
power." His personal relations—and he could make the distinction between business and personal relations with the same
individual—were often warm. Reserved with strangers, he could
be totally at ease with friends. "He could relax," a friend at Ford
said. "But his relaxation wasn't the same as that of others. The
idea of just sitting back and doing nothing . . . I can't conceive
of him not doing something."

McNamara had disciplined himself to nervelessness under
conditions that caused other men to tremble. One Ford executive
recalled a flight aboard a small plane from a Florida sales meeting back to Detroit in foul weather: "Our pilot had me looking
out the window to see how fast ice was peeling off the wings. It
was too turbulent for work, so McNamara had something to eat
from a box lunch and went to sleep."

Tex Thornton once summarized McNamara as a "very balanced, practical intellectual, highly respected by those who have
ability and show a willingness to work and shoulder responsibility. . . . He doesn't buy bags of wind." Another associate
recalled that McNamara was "very difficult to advise" because
"normally he was way ahead of the individual trying to advise
him." It could be an intimidating experience for the adviser.
James Wright, of the original Thornton group, once noted that
McNamara was hard to move once he had reached a conclusion.
It was a characteristic with which Congress and assorted military
leaders would become familiar later.

If McNamara had set out specifically to seek high office in the
company, no one ever learned it. He was ambitious, but his
approach was rather one of dedication to the success of the com-

pany first: the rest would follow. This concept of responsibility was another that Washington would learn about later. The Ford official who thought he finally had identified the driving force behind his colleague may have been closest to the truth: "Challenge. He must have that constant problem to solve, or another mountain to climb." Despite his sense of loyalty, McNamara was not prepared to yield his soul to Ford. In 1955 he insisted on including in a commencement address at the University of Alabama a paragraph which some superiors insisted had to come out. They thought it suggested something wrong with young people going into business for personal gain: "Today progressive taxation places limits on the earning power of the businessman, and hence upon his purely monetary motivation. More and more he draws his incentive from a sense of public responsibility. More and more, I believe, idealistic and progressive young people will seek and find in industry not just a road to personal enrichment, but a most direct and effective means of public service." All concerned might wonder today what the fuss was about, but McNamara went ahead with his speech.

There was still another, private side to McNamara, so different from his business life and so isolated from it that those who shared one sometimes had difficulty recognizing the other.

Even after he could afford to move there, McNamara shunned the fashionable Bloomfield Hills and Grosse Pointe areas, where great numbers of auto industry executives gravitated. "If you belong to the Bloomfield Hills Country Club," one of the clan remarked, "sooner or later you're going to meet almost every executive of General Motors, for example." The McNamaras chose another course.

When they arrived in Dearborn they were broke, and they lived in an apartment rented from the company, part of a block the residents called the Ford Foundation. In 1950, the year Robert Craig, their third child and only son, was born, they moved into a small house they had built near Ann Arbor, the university center. Two years later, as the father's success moved his assets from the red to the very black column, they moved into a more fashionable section of Ann Arbor, thirty-eight miles from Ford headquarters in Dearborn.

Margaret McNamara later would call the period that followed "wonderful years." The shaded fieldstone house, with two chimneys, dormer windows, and leaded panes, was a comfortable, well-lived-in haven. It cost about $50,000, but as McNamara rose in Ford it became less and less what was expected of an auto magnate. This worried the McNamaras not a whit. They led their private lives in the community at large, not in the tightly focused world of the auto industry. McNamara regarded the daily forty-five-minute drive to Dearborn, during which he sometimes road-tested a competitive car, as a cheap price to pay for that choice. Yet, given the individual competition within the industry, only a "very secure person," as Annalee Whitmore once described him, could have shucked off Dearborn without wondering how the other bright young men were spending their evenings and weekends.

"It wasn't a negative thing," an industry executive commented. "Bob makes up his own mind what he wants his life to be, and he doesn't let the judgments of others determine his course."

Ann Arbor had special attractions for McNamara, of course. He soon knew many of the teachers at the University of Michigan, and he himself gave an occasional lecture to graduate students. For a long period he met once a month with a dinner circle of a dozen university figures and local leaders to discuss regional, national, and international issues. Among those in the group were Harlan Hatcher, the university president, Neil Staebler, State Democratic party leader, and Warren Huff, a prominent cattleman and farmer. There were formal agendas, so each participant could come well prepared.

Associate Professor Leland Stowe found in McNamara "some of the qualities of Harry Hopkins—the same quickness of mind, the same alertness, a trigger-fast perceptivity. He's really a triple-

threat man: a highly skilled industrial executive, he has an intel-
lectually questing mind, and he is a person naturally extremely
able in dealing with people." That last, of course, was a quality
about which business associates were divided.

As a member of George Romney's Citizens for Michigan Committee—Romney was still head of American Motors—McNamara
was an eager gleaner of facts. He insisted, typically, in a study of
taxes, on beginning with the objectives of a sound tax program
and proceeding through the alternatives. "No matter how well he
prepares something," remarked Edward L. Cushman, a vice president of American Motors, "he has to be sure it's perfect. If there
is some weakness, or something that can't be quickly documented,
that thing seems to leap at Bob."

The McNamaras climbed and skied whenever possible and
brought up their children to love the highly personal challenge of
these sports. They went on expeditions with the old crowd from
California, and Vern Goodin noted that McNamara always refused to accept courtesy cars from Ford dealers: he rented and
paid. He thrived on chopping wood and sleeping in a frost-
encrusted sleeping bag, and he carefully studied topographic
maps of the High Sierras or the Grand Tetons to chart the course
of the party.

He never became much of a fisherman. Nor did he become a
golfer, though Ben Mills tried to help him. McNamara studied a
book recommended by Mills and, in the words of an associate,
"still had the worst hook I've ever seen. He couldn't hit a bull in
the ass with a spade."

If the picture of McNamara at play, however intensely, seemed
inconsistent with his work image in Dearborn, there was a simple
explanation: he recognized that men function better after recrea-
tion, and he knew that if he sacrificed his vacations to the job he
would be forcing subordinates in effect to do the same thing. So
he played—but in the same way as he worked: with all stops out.

In politics he concentrated on issues and individuals more than
party, though he was nominally a Republican. Locally his was a

lively and liberal voice in Ann Arbor's civic affairs. At one point he joined a movement to eliminate submarginal housing, and offered to invest some of his own money in the replacement project. At the First Presbyterian Church, where McNamara became an elder, he and his wife were among the first to sign a covenant of open occupancy, a church plan intended to end racial discrimination in the sale of real estate. Though the formal practice of religion was not a primary consideration, its philosophies fascinated him.

McNamara supported the campaigns of both Democratic Senator Philip Hart and Paul Bagwell, the unsuccessful Republican candidate for governor. He let friends know he had voted for John F. Kennedy for President, though the Democrats failed through an organizational mixup to enlist his public endorsement in advance of the election. Both the National Association for the Advancement of Colored People and the American Civil Liberties Union received his contributions.

Little of this attracted public attention as McNamara came to the surface at Ford. From the beginning of his career, he had held newspapermen at a distance. Above all, both he and his wife insisted on keeping private their personal lives. A reporter for the Ann Arbor *News*, thumbing through files as McNamara's name entered speculation about Cabinet appointments, was surprised to find that Mrs. McNamara's name had gone without mention in the society pages for six months. When he encountered her at the door of her home later that day, he noted that almost nothing of their private lives had been published. "That's the way we've tried to keep it over the years," she replied graciously. She added one further contribution to the interview: "We love it here. We'd hate to leave it."

Actually her husband granted few interviews in his business life either. To a man as precise as McNamara, the imprecision of much journalism seemed grossly irresponsible. In any case a man who was determined to protect his personal privacy and who relied for professional advancement upon performance divorced from internal politics was unlikely to encourage the curiosity of the press. Then, too, McNamara had a firm sense of loyalty to his organization, and the newspapermen around Detroit, though hardly hypercritical of the automobile industry, did not view Ford in quite the same light.

Lack of general public knowledge of McNamara's rise was understandable. What was more surprising was the extent to which he remained a mystery within the industry. Even when he moved into higher executive levels, McNamara's name was hardly an everyday word at General Motors and Chrysler. Executives there had to worry first, of course, about Henry Ford II and such people as Breech, Crusoe, and Harder. They knew about McNamara as a comer, but not, in fact, very much else about him.

Some outside the company had followed his progress, however. Most important, Robert Lovett, whose influence had so much to do with his career, directly and indirectly, knew a great deal about him. As a permanent fixture in the Eastern Establishment ("Hell, he *is* the Eastern Establishment," one member remarked), Lovett caught immediate interest when he mentioned McNamara's name as a potential member of the Kennedy Cabinet.

At that time McNamara had been president of Ford less than a month, so he had no substantive record in the position. Kennedy's election as President and McNamara's as head of Ford were only a day apart. Kennedy would have found it difficult, probably impossible, to take McNamara had he been only a vice president of the company. In any event the Robert McNamara who took over the Department of Defense the following January had come to maturity at Ford.

He cut across the molds of previous Secretaries of Defense. If Louis Johnson and George C. Marshall are set aside as a cause-and-effect aberration—Department prestige sank under Johnson; Marshall restored it—then there had been two sources for the office: big investment banking houses and big industry. Coming from the latter, McNamara brought the financial and statistical orientation more often associated with the former. He had enough money—his assets not long after leaving Ford were about $1.2 million—to qualify for the ex-Secretaries' club.

The immediate temptation in Washington was to place him in the Charles E. Wilson school, since Wilson, after all, had directed General Motors before the Pentagon. But Wilson was a rough-hewn engineer: GM had evolved in later years away from the model that inspired the Ford recovery. McNamara, on the other hand, had a curiosity that had given him wide knowledge, if not sophistication, in art, music, literature, and public affairs. He possibly was not an intellectual, as some would define the term, but the McNamara who went to Washington at the end of 1960 was a very broad person indeed.

McNamara had come to the surface. He had just reached the peak of career success, but he had not had time to make it his own. He had a great deal of money by usual standards, but he had not had time to earn great wealth as it was measured by his peers. The reasons tell much about the man. His friend Ben Davis Mills had identified them. "Challenge, not money," said Mills, made McNamara run. The United States Department of Defense offered McNamara's particular talents the greatest challenge in the world. It involved public service, a goal McNamara had revealed early to friends at Cal. And it offered power.

"Bob may think he was reluctant," a colleague at Ford said of the Kennedy overture. "None of us here had any doubt that he would go." Henry Ford once told an interviewer with a grin, "I don't think Bob's answer really took too much soul-searching."

The challenge in the end was irresistible. After clearing it with his family, he agreed to trade security of reputation and the prospect of great wealth for $25,000 a year and unrelieved risk and tension, the only rewards truly guaranteed.

3

The Legacy

WHEN McNamara arrived for his second Pentagon tour—in the first, he'd been an obscure lieutenant colonel—the Department of Defense still was searching for its place in the hierarchy of government. Its brief existence had been stormy. As a relatively new creation, crossing historic lines of power and responsibility, its administration had varied more than is normally the case with changes in leadership and policy. Its special institutions, still lacking the authority of history, reflected in great measure the men who preceded McNamara. Of the seven, none was more complex as an individual than the first, James Vincent Forrestal. Nor was any ever more acutely sensitive than Forrestal, in his final months in office and before his fatal illness, to the continuing identity crisis that lay ahead.

Forrestal was many things—a successful broker, zealous public servant, unabashed patriot, shrewd pathfinder in the political jungle of Washington. He was a warm and loyal friend to a chosen few. But his driven nature did not include much of a sense of humor. There is no reason to believe he was other than deeply serious with his often quoted remark after he was appointed Secretary of Defense in 1947: "This office will probably be the greatest cemetery for dead cats in history."

He must have grasped the irony in his own position, later if not then. Earlier, as Secretary of the Navy, he had been instrumental in weakening the National Security Act of 1947, which created the office of Secretary of Defense, so that it stopped short of unifying the services. The weaknesses of that first confederation of national defense forces at times have obscured its landmark importance.

The Act resulted from a long accumulation of pressures, not a very seemly progression. American military leaders had proved to be heroic and sometimes brilliant tacticians and strategists in times of war; they also could be petty and self-serving in times of peace. The need for more coherent civilian management of the armed services had finally begun to point toward unification.

But oddly, the building that became the symbol of the Department of Defense to the world, the Pentagon, was created ahead of the Department itself, born with appropriate controversy as lightning flashed in Europe for the second time in the century. Critics thought the idea of a central headquarters for the Army represented a boondoggle, even though the Army's offices were scattered inefficiently around Washington. At first no one planned on the Navy as a joint tenant. By January, 1943, when construction was complete, War Secretary Henry L. Stimson and General George C. Marshall, the Chief of Staff, were housed in the biggest office building in the world. It was designed for a population of about 25,000. Today there are close to 30,000 in its offices at peak hours, and there never has been enough space.*

The growth of the Pentagon coincided with a new role of power for the United States. At the same time the war forced a working form of unification on the armed services. Joint opera-

---

* Yet getting around is simple. Each floor and each corridor is numbered. The five concentric rings are designated by letters. Therefore 3E880, the office of the Secretary of Defense, is on the third floor, the E or outside ring, between the eighth and ninth corridors. More than one student of bureaucracy has been enchanted to learn that the Pentagon complex, first estimated to cost $31 million, finally was completed for $81 million—thus making it a rich illustration of military cost overruns.

tions demanded it, both among the American military services and for coordination between American and British commands. When the fighting ended, there was a nervous consensus in the White House, in the Army and its restless offspring, the Air Force, in Congress, and even, for a while, in the Navy, that somehow there must be new central direction of the military services short of the Presidency.

The war had produced several approaches to unification. Congressional hearings in 1944 showed everyone who mattered—except some Navy leaders—generally in favor of it. When discussion turned to specifics, however, the atmosphere changed. Views on integration ranged across service boundaries, but as positions began to sort themselves out, the contest developed broadly as one of the Navy versus everybody else. Naval officers who had supported reorganization as a result of military experience found parochial factors more compelling when they returned to Washington. Many of them reversed engines rapidly.

The Navy now believed it might be picked to the bone. It had the best of all military worlds: its fleet, which no one could take away; its own air arm, which the Air Force was eying hungrily; its own ground forces, the Marines, which the Army would have been delighted to absorb. With the Air Force and its nuclear bombers taking over the Navy role as the first line of defense, the Navy could see little but grief in unification.

For the Army the considerations were quite different. Generals wanted to avoid the decline their service had suffered historically after war. They were certain their chances were better in a unified structure, and they were fairly sure the top military man in such an organization would be Army.

The Army Air Force was wallowing in popular acclaim. It wanted to become a separate service, and the momentum it had created was great enough to overcome opposition hopes of preventing it completely. Yet the air generals would have to move carefully to meet the mood of the nation and civilian leaders. In order to get the distinct status it sought, the Air Force must support the concept of a unifying civilian authority at the top of the framework.

Forrestal was reading the signs correctly early in the debate. He had been Secretary of the Navy since the death of Frank Knox in 1944, and now he warned his admirals that total opposition to unification would get them nowhere. His course was to pursue the Navy's "constructive alternative." It was a plan that wove all the elements of national security into a single structure beneath the President. But it would force only a mild form of coordination on the services.

For more than a year the struggle fascinated Washington. Postwar cuts in the budget sharpened the feud between the services. Military forces that had totaled more than 12.1 million plunged through the 2 million level in 1946 and reached 1.582 million by mid-1947. Spending dropped from $80.5 billion in fiscal 1945 to $14.8 billion in 1947. The services fought desperately for individual recognition.

But finally a compromise began to evolve, weighted in favor of the Navy. On July 26, 1947, President Truman, who first had favored an Army integration plan, signed into law the National Security Act. It was a monument, for better or worse, to the tenacity and dynamism of James V. Forrestal.

What emerged from the years of controversy was unlike anything else in government. The Act created a "National Military Establishment," not a department, over separately administered departments of the Army, Navy, and Air Force. A Secretary of Defense would exercise "general direction, authority, and control" and "establish general policies and programs." With one of his few concrete powers, he could "formulate and determine the budget estimates for submittal to the Bureau of the Budget." The Joint Chiefs of Staff were assigned as "principal military advisers" to the President and the Secretary.

Outside the military structure itself, Forrestal got the National Security Council he wanted and, beneath it, a Central Intelligence Agency. The Council would "advise the President with respect to the integration of domestic, foreign, and military policies, relating to the national security." The CIA was to "correlate and evaluate intelligence relating to the national security." With the National Security Council, Forrestal hoped to assure a voice for the military that would keep power in phase with political commitments.

Elements that were obviously missing were as important as those included. The Secretary of Defense lacked clear authority to run his department, and the goodwill Forrestal anticipated simply never developed. The services were free to leapfrog the Secretary in appeals to the White House, Congress, and the public. Perhaps most important for the early history of the Act was that it did little to define service roles and missions.

Now that the deed was done, someone had to try to make it work. Harry Truman first tried Army Secretary Robert Patterson, who refused and went ahead with plans to retire. Then the President, possibly with appreciation for the irony, took a logical step: he handed the task to James Forrestal.

At the time he met this greatest challenge, Forrestal already had given the nation more than it ever demands except from those very few with total commitment. They march to a different beat, but often are unaware of it themselves. In Forrestal's case, the drummer set a murderous tempo.

He came to Washington from Wall Street, where he had become president of the investment firm of Dillon, Read and Company in 1938 at forty-six. Son of an Irish immigrant father, Forrestal had worked his way into Dartmouth, then Princeton, but dropped out shortly before graduation. He soon joined the investment house and rose swiftly.

Looking for organizing talent as the nation began its prewar mobilization of industry, President Roosevelt brought him to Washington in June, 1940, as a White House aide. But Frank Knox, the Secretary of the Navy, grabbed him quickly and within two months made him Under Secretary. Driving himself relentlessly, Forrestal ran Navy procurement and production through

the early war years. When authority was lacking in those days of
crisis, he created it. Though he was a tough master, his own dedication inspired subordinates. When Knox died in 1944, Forrestal
was in direct line to succeed him.

He was a complex man, and his very complexity helped neutralize whatever chance he might have had to make the National
Security Act work in its original form. Well before such a view
was generally acceptable, Forrestal perceived the threat of the
Soviet Union to an orderly postwar world. More clearly than most
in Washington, he recognized the need to balance military power,
and foreign and domestic priorities, in a long-term national security policy. Against such keen insight, his stubborn negotiation
of the Navy's case for confederation rather than integration is a
paradox. Forrestal felt he simply was pursuing the course of
reasonable compromise.

As Secretary of Defense, of course, he faced many of the same
old problems he'd encountered as Secretary of the Navy. Though
the Truman Administration accepted the developing Soviet challenge in Europe, the domestic mood dictated that it do so as
cheaply as possible. Truman asked for only $9.5 billion in new
military spending authority in 1947 and imposed a ceiling of $15
billion in 1948. As Air Force Secretary Stuart Symington told an
interviewer, "It was like throwing a piece of meat into an arena
and letting three hundred hungry tigers go in after it."

Working sixteen hours a day, six and seven days a week, the
Secretary tried to get the services to share the shortages and at
the same time to break through the President's budget ceilings.
But Truman did not intend to be pushed by Forrestal or anyone
else into a costly unrestrained overhaul of the armed forces. The
evidence that he judged the national mood correctly was hardly
disputable: he was re-elected in November against awesome odds.

Time was running out for Forrestal. He had tried to raise the
defense budget at a time when Truman was cutting it. He had
strong reservations about the United Nations, in which Truman
had a heavy political investment. He wanted military control over

nuclear weapons, and he saw the National Security Council as an instrument for the exercise of real power, neither of which Truman would concede. Instead of actively supporting the Truman political cause, he had briefed Thomas E. Dewey, the Republican candidate, on U.S. power. Near the end of the year Truman quietly signaled the abrasive Secretary of Defense that his days in office were numbered.

Despite the obstacles, Forrestal had accomplished more than one might assume from watching the visible brawling of the services. His ideas on political-military balance were winning greater acceptance. Though military integration was unacceptable, he planted seeds of consolidation in relatively uncontroversial areas—supply and communications, for example—which would flower years later. Meanwhile he urged the President to strengthen and broaden the power of the Secretary.

Finally, on March 1, 1949, Truman called Forrestal to the White House and asked him to resign. For a man with Forrestal's drive and temperament, it was a crushing confirmation of failure. On March 31, the day of his ceremonial departure, he received from the President the Distinguished Service Medal, the highest national award for a civilian; on Capitol Hill he was bathed in praise from members of the military committees in Congress. But that night his mind snapped. Friends rushed him to the Florida home of Robert Lovett, the fellow Wall Street broker whose Washington service had paralleled his own. The hope that Forrestal would recover with rest faded quickly. Three days later he was returned to the Naval Medical Center at Bethesda, Maryland, and there, in the early morning hours of May 22, he dropped from a sixteenth-floor window to his death. As surely as any trooper, Forrestal was a casualty of war. It was a war in which newly recognized elements, economic and political, blended with weapons, the old and the ominously new, as America tried to find its place in the postwar world.

It would be hard to imagine two men less alike than Forrestal and his successor, Louis A. Johnson. Forrestal was slight and wiry; Johnson at 250 pounds looked like an aging professional football tackle. Forrestal was a self-made Wall Street millionaire, with an almost compulsive respect for intellect, who had turned to public service with achievement there as an end in itself. Johnson was a politically oriented West Virginia lawyer with unlimited personal ambition.

He had survived one severe setback on his way up. A graduate of the West Virginia House of Representatives, he was appointed Assistant Secretary of War under Harry H. Woodring in 1937. It was Johnson who stumped the country urging rearmament—carrying the banner for Roosevelt—and he expected to be rewarded with the Cabinet assignment. Instead, Roosevelt appointed Henry L. Stimson, a Republican, and Johnson quit in frustration. He returned to favor during the war, however, and in 1948 he gathered the money that paid for Harry Truman's successful campaign.

The place of the United States in world affairs had changed fundamentally since Johnson's earlier War Department days. There was some doubt that he fully understood the changes. There was no doubt, however, that he intended to run the Defense Department with an iron hand.

Johnson was sworn in as Secretary on March 28. One month later he canceled the Navy's planned supercarrier. It was a severe blow to the Navy, and it focused attention on a development already under way at the time: the Navy's counterattack to the expert Air Force propaganda campaign for roles and missions. The feud included grossly self-serving leaks to the press. Backbiting between the Air Force and Navy became almost an art. The two services competed with showboating demonstrations of hardware that often proved very little but won space in newspapers.

Finally the wrangling evolved into the "revolt of the admirals." High Navy brass became tarnished by the excesses of their propaganda. In the end the Navy lost. General Omar N. Bradley, who by fall had become the first Chairman of the Joint Chiefs, testified in October that the Navy's "open rebellion," stemming partly from its historic opposition to unification, had done "great harm to the nation." Truman fired Admiral Louis Denfeld from the Joint Chiefs of Staff, and other officers who had led the revolt retired quietly.

The Air Force now was unquestionably more than first among equals. With its nuclear bombs, it represented hope for cheap salvation to a nation fretfully seeking balance between the commitments it felt compelled to make and the means to fulfill them. Most officials in Washington would not, in fact, concede the extent to which they were relying upon the atomic deterrent.

The President wanted economy; Johnson was prepared to provide it. In the later stages he was operating with new authority. During the brawling of 1949, Congress had approved substantial amendments to the National Security Act. The word "general" was dropped from the Secretary's "general authority, direction, and control" over the services, a gesture to secure his power. The National Military Establishment became the Department of Defense, losing some of the ambiguity of its earlier status. The overburdened Secretary of Defense received a deputy, and a chairman was added to the Joint Chiefs.

But pressures on the Administration's tight defense budget meanwhile were growing. The loss of the atomic monopoly, the interservice controversies, the Maoist victory in China, growing Soviet bellicosity, all deepened uneasiness concerning the nation's basic security position. The Soviet atomic bomb, tested earlier than American scientists had predicted, was forcing the President to an early decision whether or not to develop the vastly more powerful thermonuclear weapon. A review was decidedly in order.

Truman ordered it on January 31, 1950, in a letter accompanying the announcement of his decision to proceed with the hydrogen bomb. The reassessment fell to a joint State-Defense task force which in six weeks turned out one of those rare official documents that looks even better with time. Accepted by the National Security Council as NSC 68, the analysis rejected the policy extremes open to the United States—either preventive war or withdrawal to "fortress America." It said, however, that the United States needed to rearm, including a vigorous expansion of conventional forces as Soviet nuclear weapons offset the early American strategic advantage.

President Truman approved NSC 68, but how he ultimately might have executed it on its own merits remains uncertain. Though he accepted its broad principles, he did not endorse its specific recommendations in the early months of 1950, and time was running out for a free decision. All the while, Johnson felt he had the defense structure well in hand. Disillusionment came swiftly.

On June 24 North Korean forces suddenly attacked across the 38th parallel with the obvious support of Peking and Moscow. South Korea was a tempting target. U.S. forces had been withdrawn the year before, and America was showing every sign of abandoning continental East Asia. General Douglas MacArthur and Secretary of State Dean Acheson seemingly had put Korea outside the American defense perimeter. In any case, the United States hardly appeared capable of nonnuclear intervention, and the risk that Washington would use atomic weapons must have seemed slight to the invaders.

In the aftermath of the attack and the U.S. decision to step back in, the Administration's budget restrictions had to go. And so, inevitably, did Louis Johnson. As the military position worsened in those first months, Harry Truman needed both a sacrificial offering and a new figure in the Defense Department.

Johnson was shaken when the President asked for his resignation in early September. But he knew the rules of the game. He had enforced the Administration's defense economies with ruthless zeal and, as he said, had made "more enemies than friends." Presidents do not sacrifice themselves in such circumstances; Cabinet members do. Johnson took his public disgrace with what in the circumstances could only be described as good form.

To replace him, Truman called in George Catlett Marshall, a

man so towering in national stature that the conservative resistance to his appointment seemed a petty discord. Chief of Staff during World War II, special envoy to China in 1945–46, Secretary of State, 1947–49, Marshall was being summoned in the interest of stability at a time of emotional and military crisis. "General Marshall is . . . eager to play the role of a front man for traitors . . . a living lie," cried Senator William E. Jenner, the conservative from Indiana. But Congress agreed by heavy majorities in both houses to set aside the National Security Act's barrier to a former military man's becoming Secretary of Defense within ten years of his active duty.

Approaching seventy at the time, Marshall faced problems quite different from those that had confronted Forrestal and Johnson. Arbitrary ceilings on manpower and money vanished. In the year after June 30, 1950, military personnel soared from 1.46 million to 3.249 million. Defense Department spending surged from $12 billion in fiscal 1950 to $41.3 billion two years later. Overt interservice rivalry faded with the availability of funds and the pressures of war. Marshall meanwhile exerted a calming influence in such trying episodes as Truman's firing of General Douglas MacArthur, with whom Marshall had feuded for years, for insubordination. The President, said Marshall, who had urged caution on Truman during the early stages of MacArthur's rebellion against Administration policy, ultimately had "no other recourse but to relieve him."

The assault in Korea had repercussions elsewhere which Moscow may not have anticipated. Though the North Atlantic Treaty had been signed in 1949, little progress had been made toward a NATO defense structure until the shock wave from the Korean peninsula reached European capitals and Washington. But by December, 1950, the North Atlantic Council had worked out a basic defense plan. Many on both sides of the Atlantic feared the invasion of South Korea was a feint in a master plan directed ultimately at Europe.

These American decisions were traumatic breaks with the past.

Here was the world's most powerful nation, psychologically isolationist, now recommitting forces to a still peaceful Europe—four more divisions would go—while it fought a major, if limited, war in Asia. The decisions set off a great debate in Congress over fundamental principles of foreign policy.

Conservatives like Senators Robert Taft of Ohio and Kenneth Wherry of Indiana opposed the assignment of forces to either Europe or Asia. They argued, moreover, that the President lacked power to make such commitments without Congressional approval. It was not a unanimous Republican position. Some, like Governor Thomas E. Dewey of New York, who were trying to build General Dwight D. Eisenhower for the Presidency, called the Taft position "Operation Suicide." In any case the conservatives failed, partly because Eisenhower returned from an inspection trip in Europe to urge commitment of arms, equipment, and men. With growing substance, the United States began to assume the hazardous role of the world's greatest power, and, wisely or not, its policeman.

Marshall retired for the last time on September 17, just a few days short of his first anniversary as Secretary of Defense. He had achieved, in his unspectacular way, the primary purposes for which Truman had appointed him: to re-establish respect for the office and to hold the nation's hand in a time of trial. Choice of the man to succeed him followed naturally. Robert A. Lovett and Marshall had built deep mutual respect and affection during World War II, while Lovett was Assistant Secretary of War for Air and Marshall was Chief of Staff. Marshall summoned Lovett as his Under Secretary shortly after he became Secretary of State in 1947, then recalled him as Deputy when he returned to the Pentagon in 1950.

By most standards, Lovett had already lived a full professional life. After serving as a pioneering Navy pilot for France, Britain, and the United States during World War I, he was graduated from Yale and studied further at Harvard before getting a minor job in

the National Bank of Commerce in New York. His rise was spectacular, to a partnership in the Wall Street firm of Brown
Brothers, Harriman and Company and directorates in a number
of major corporations. The transition from Deputy under George
Marshall to Secretary of Defense was one of the easiest he made.
It meant to a large extent that Lovett simply would change offices
and accept undiluted responsibility for work he already was doing.

With only sixteen months of Truman's term remaining, Lovett's
administration of the Pentagon had something of an interim atmosphere. Yet he was remarkably effective under the circumstances. For one reason, he was operating in a budget climate
that inflicted pain but not agony on the services. He had the
essential support of the President. He also understood and liked
military men, and he was able through personal diplomacy to
effect changes that another might have failed to make.

Lovett was the first Secretary of Defense to look consciously
upon the budget as a tool for orderly development. The new
weapons, he warned, were costly and approaching obsolescence
even before they could be deployed. To strike the balance between short- and long-term defense needs, he said, was "a difficult
and expensive undertaking, but there is still no easy, quick, cheap,
or magic way to fight or win a war—or to prevent one."

Lovett also found that the new defense organization still
needed work, and he passed his thoughts on to the President in
late 1952 to be handed on to the next Administration. There still
was too much nit-picking over the authority of the Secretary of
Defense, he said, and the role of the Joint Chiefs needed to be
clarified. Some of his ideas were to turn up in the planning of the
incoming Eisenhower Administration.

Eisenhower inherited two basic strategic concepts: deterrence,
for which the Strategic Air Command had been provided a growing armada with nuclear weapons, and containment, honored most
dramatically on the ground in Korea. Obviously the new Administration would try to sustain the first. How it would treat the

second was unclear before the inauguration and for some time afterward. The lessons from the Korean experience had to be digested.

One immediate lesson, obviously, was that he had to end quickly an unpopular war. Public frustration demanded resolution, though it was only a gentle foretaste of the disenchantment to be released against another limited war in Asia fifteen years later. Eisenhower made the transition from bloody stalemate to troubled cease-fire in part by hinting that enemy sanctuaries in Manchuria would be attacked.

For Secretary of Defense, Eisenhower chose a man who symbolized his campaign theme of security with solvency. Then sixty-two, Charles E. Wilson had been at GM since 1919, and president of the company since 1940.

Very quickly the power alignment in the new Administration became apparent. The President himself, a renowned general, obviously would keep to himself the primary judgment on military decisions. John Foster Dulles was quite decisive, and would become even more so, on the foreign policy which the military was in existence to support. The influence of George M. Humphrey on money matters would reach far beyond the Department of the Treasury—into the entire spectrum of national policy. This disposition of power left Wilson to operate the defense system and make it work. It was a difficult enough job in itself, of course, but it also was one in which policy-making had visible boundaries.

Wilson himself was quite different from his predecessors. He was short, chunky, and white-haired, with a solid reputation as one of the nation's able industrial executives. He also was publicly amiable, irreverent, and outspoken—characteristics that made him a delight to jaded newspapermen and at times kept the rest of the government nervously waiting for what he might say next.

His famous remark, "For years, I thought what was good for the country was good for General Motors and vice versa," was grossly misrepresented. There was no denying, however, that he informed members of the august Senate Armed Services Committee, "The trouble with you men is you just don't understand the problem." The slip occurred during hearings on his confirmation, and it, among others, may have hardened the committee's resolve to bring him to heel. At any rate, it pounded at Wilson until he agreed to sell a fortune in stocks in order to get the thankless job.

In the office, Wilson was less a policy-maker than an administrator, at times a ruthless one, and he sharpened the organization of the Department considerably in the early months of the Eisenhower Administration. In April a commission headed by Nelson Rockefeller came up with a plan for further reorganization. What finally evolved was the President's own adaptation, which Congress, after brisk debate, allowed to stand. Its most important provisions dealt with the Joint Chiefs of Staff. The President directed members of the JCS for the first time toward national security as a whole and the policies of the Administration in power, and away from their parent services.

At the same time, Eisenhower began to unveil the outlines of his "New Look" in defense policy. He had adopted the principles of his predecessor's foreign policy and military programs, but he also included specifically the national economy as a fundamental element in defense planning.

Defense must be packaged in a program that "we can bear for a long and indefinite period of time," he said. He rejected the notion that the United States was approaching a "year of maximum peril," a premise on which the Pentagon had been basing its plans. He relied heavily, once again, on the strategic power of the Air Force for deterrence, though the atomic monopoly was long past. To strengthen the West's nonnuclear defenses, local forces would be built up with American aid in the nations where danger was greatest—though there was no intention to withdraw the U.S. divisions committed in Germany. Battlefield nuclear weapons, rapidly becoming more compact and sophisticated, would be utilized as part of the forces for limited war, to be used as military

circumstances indicated. With this plan the Administration hoped
to reduce personnel and thus the overall defense budget.

The strategic rationale for the "New Look" was stated most
clearly by Dulles in his landmark address before the Council on
Foreign Relations on January 12, 1954. Soon identified as a
strategy of "massive retaliation," the Dulles approach indeed
raised the threat of just that, though it also contained a calculated
element of ambiguity.

"Local defense will always be important," Dulles said. "But
there is no local defense which alone will contain the mighty land
power of the Communist world. Local defense must be reinforced
by the further deterrent of massive retaliatory power. A potential
aggressor must know that he cannot always prescribe battle conditions that suit him. . . . The basic decision was to depend primarily upon a great capacity to retaliate, instantly, by means and
at times of our own choosing."

Several weeks later Dulles cautioned reporters: "In no place
did I say we would retaliate instantly, though we might indeed
retaliate instantly under conditions that call for that." He thus
hedged his policy. The exercise of choice requires capability,
however, and he had left no doubt at all that the principal American effort would be in nuclear weapons.

The implication was that the United States would, or might,
punish with nuclear power the source of aggression, however it
appeared. Many critics were aghast. To men like Paul Nitze, the
former State Department planner who had helped nurse NSC 68
into life, a strategy of massive retaliation increased rather than
reduced the danger of war.

The strategic pattern was designed, in great measure, to save
money. On military spending overall, however, Eisenhower had
to yield, for his Presidency was marked by one of the truly historic, and most costly, revolutions in weaponry: the development
of long-range rockets and the refinement of the weapons they
could carry.

America had started slowly in what became the missile race.
But slowly a sense of urgency began to develop in the 1950s.

There were several reasons for the delay, among them, of course, the costs of the Korean War. The price of missile research and development was high, and for years no one was quite certain where the trail was leading. Early atomic warheads were far too heavy for the rocket engines then in sight. In 1954, however, an evaluation committee headed by Dr. John von Neumann came up with the clear prospect of both refinements in long-range rockets and dramatic shrinkage in the size of warheads.

By the end of 1955 all the services had major missile programs under way. From the Navy came one of those rare developments in which just about everything went right. Its entry was the Polaris, a smaller rocket that would use solid fuel, rather than volatile liquids, and be launched from beneath the sea: sixteen missiles to a submarine.

Progress in longer-range missiles was only a bit less dramatic. Much of the momentum flowed in a sort of gigantic reflex action, but it slowly became clear the United States was engaged in nothing less than a critical strategic race with the Soviet Union. All those German scientists who had gone to Russia after the war had been busy, there were more of them than of their colleagues who had elected to go to the United States, and they had jumped to an earlier start in missilry. American military leaders once more were competing among themselves as well: if the new weapons proved to be as effective as seemed likely, he who hesitated in securing his strategic role appeared doomed to inferior status.

The significance of much of the early competition was lost on the public and even many members of Congress. When Senator Stuart Symington of Missouri, true to his Air Force background, led an investigation in 1956 of what he charged was strategic deficiency, most of the emphasis was on air power. To be sure, General Curtis E. LeMay, commander of the Strategic Air Command, estimated that the Soviets would be able to destroy the United States with missiles by 1959. But the agitation for more B-52 long-range bombers was more strident and easier to comprehend.

It was a chaotic period in many respects. The Administration was trying to develop credible power while keeping spending to the minimum. Twice in 1957 Secretary Wilson announced plans for reductions of 100,000 men in military manpower. At the same time Administration leaders began to speak of "sufficient deterrence" instead of absolute superiority in numbers as the required strategic stance. It was a deterrent concept to be refined more precisely later. For the time being the nation was in no mood to accept such abstractions, and talk of a "bomber gap" and a "missile gap" developed rapidly.

The Soviet Union resolved much of the immediate American debate. On October 4, 1957, the first artificial earth satellite, Sputnik, told the listening Americans more just by being there than they learned from the bleat of its radios. The Soviets had proved their superiority in big rockets and created, as never before, the specter of a hail of missiles against the United States. For the first time the American public seemed to recognize fully the implications of the missile race. New money poured into the missile programs.

The excitement also spurred legislation which amended the National Security Act into the form it has retained to the present. What was still lacking, the critics felt, was a decision-making and command process fast enough for the times and firm enough to reduce waste and duplication. The Secretary, in short, still needed more power.

From the Reorganization Act of 1958 he received authority to assign development and operation of new weapons to individual services as he saw fit. On his own authority he could consolidate many formerly separate functions. The Act specifically authorized the President to create multiservice commands under a single commander, who would report to the Secretary of Defense rather than the services.

Eleven years after its creation, the Defense Department finally was exercising some of the functions envisioned by the early integrationists. The military departments had become essentially administrative, training, and supply operations. At both the operational and housekeeping levels, power flowed cleanly through the Secretary of Defense. The gaps in the authority of the office had been plugged—to await a Secretary prepared to use that power to its fullest.

Charles E. Wilson, meanwhile, had bowed out. When he submitted his resignation in August, 1957, he had remained more than twice as long as any predecessor. The years and the workload had exacted their inevitable price. One writer recorded Wilson as saying: "I'm leaving because I found myself making decisions from fatigue."

Wilson had remained more a manager, and a conservative one, than a policy-maker. He never truly mastered the military issues. He had encouraged competition among the services at first, applying his successful techniques from General Motors. But they had been excessively enthusiastic in their response. When he then tried to weld them into a coherent system, they frequently balked.

"Charlie's record would have been better if he had had a hot war," a senior Pentagon official remarked. "Then he would have had enough money to prevent friction."

Leaving just as Sputnik was launched, Wilson carried with him much of the public criticism for the assumed Soviet strategic advantage. Yet he had filled the role set out for him by the Administration. Most important, he had marshaled the forces for fundamental changes in weaponry, the transition to the true military symbol of the nuclear age: the intercontinental missile.

To succeed him, Eisenhower once again looked to the front ranks of business, this time to a man who had even less experience with defense. Neil H. McElroy, president of Procter & Gamble for nine years, had become the world's greatest soap salesman, thanks to his unquenchable gregariousness and his skill at marketing, finance, and promotion. The new Secretary was a big man, six feet four, and radiated assurance. It was well that he did, for he took his oath on October 9, 1957, five days after the Soviets launched Sputnik I. It was a time when the public and the Congress badly needed soothing. McElroy did it well in the early period of his two years in the Pentagon. Yet he, too, was unable to take the defense establishment fully in hand, although the final reorganization gave him greater power. He relied heavily on the advice of military and civilian subordinates, of course, and as the services competed for their individual programs, he found it difficult to get objective guidance.

This problem contributed to one of his most unfortunate remarks. Questioned in Congress about a choice between Army and Air Force missiles, he grumbled, "This is one area where we have not done very well in making a decision. It would not bother me if you held our feet to the fire and forced us in connection with this budget." It was hardly the language of deft leadership, and the question whether anyone really could run the Defense Department seemed to take on ever greater justification.

McElroy remained for two years, as he had promised. In late 1959, Eisenhower, little more than a year before he would leave office, had to appoint his third Secretary of Defense. McElroy had created a record in the Wilson tradition, that of a businessman executing policy faithfully. With his choice of McElroy's successor, however, Eisenhower broke his own pattern.

Thomas S. Gates, Jr., marked a return to the Forrestal-Lovett school of defense administration. Gates was a Philadelphia Main Liner who had become a successful investment banker. Navy Secretary Robert B. Anderson recruited him as Under Secretary in 1953, and Gates then succeeded Anderson in 1957.

He was preparing to return to private business again when Donald A. Quarles, Deputy Secretary of Defense and an anchor man in the Pentagon throughout the Eisenhower Administration, died on May 8, 1959. Eisenhower immediately asked Gates to replace Quarles. In effect, he went into training for McElroy's job, and he took the oath as seventh Secretary of Defense on December 2, 1959.

Tall—six feet two inches—and lean, Gates looked a decade younger than his fifty-three years. He had only fourteen months in office ahead of him. Yet a man like Gates could do a great deal in fourteen months. His long experience in the Pentagon helped, of course. He had the extensive background of Forrestal and Lovett on the job, and a great deal had been learned about running the system in the intervening years. Gates made maximum use of that experience.

When the Joint Chiefs disagreed among themselves, as they frequently did, Gates leaped into the arena with them and made decisions. He quickly established weekly meetings with the Chiefs, and the backlog of so-called split papers shrank rapidly.

Gates was a perceptive manager of men, and he paid close attention to morale, from generals down to seamen. Part of his technique was to give the services their innings on every issue. When he set out to create a joint planning group for targeting Air Force and Navy strategic weapons, Admiral Arleigh A. Burke, the Chief of Naval Operations, disagreed vigorously. Gates saw the folly of independent targeting. Burke feared the heavy hand of the Air Force. The Secretary finally won the support, if not the agreement, of the Admiral by sending him to talk it out with the President.

More than his predecessors under Eisenhower, Gates tried to integrate military planning with foreign policy by cultivating a close relationship with the State Department. He formed a central Defense Communications Agency and laid the groundwork for McNamara's later organization of the Defense Supply Agency and the Defense Intelligence Agency.

In his final months, as Democrats perfected their own targeting on the Eisenhower Administration, he was one of the most articulate defenders of the nation's military stance. He could cite the spectacular developments of the eight Eisenhower years: from the introduction of supersonic jet aircraft to ICBMs and tactical nuclear weapons, along with man's probing of space. The nation, he said, was well defended. As for the missile gap, he argued that the power to retaliate, numbers aside, was intact. He did not make a big thing of conventional forces, though he did assert that they were ready to fulfill their missions.

On the other side, a firm conception of what was wrong with the nation's defenses was voiced by Senator John F. Kennedy of Massachusetts. Kennedy belonged to a school of Democrats convinced that the nation would indeed confront a missile gap during the early sixties—years in which he aimed to be President.

In the public mind the argument over a missile gap had become mostly a matter of numbers. Gates had tried to dispel the nervousness that arose from the numbers game. It was based, he pointed out, on the assumption that the Soviets were producing missiles at maximum capability. His more moderate estimates made little impression in the heat of the election year, however. Though some Democrats began to have doubts about the missile gap, they were reluctant to let go of a good thing.

Politics aside, it was not only partisan Democrats and self-serving Army-Navy brass who feared the Eisenhower policies were leaving the nation without much of a strategy or the means to fulfill one. Many independent analysts also had rejected the notion that nuclear weapons were a strategic cure-all.

The strategic debate had been under way on a rising curve since World War II. Rational men could not agree how nuclear war would be fought. Must nations with these weapons prepare for a cataclysmic spasm in which civilization would disappear? Or would the threat of losses at some lower level deter aggression? Mankind could be thankful there was no body of experience for guidance. But in its absence, the responsibility for determining how resources should be divided between strategic and tactical forces, nuclear and nonnuclear, was especially trying.

Massive retaliation was advanced formally during the Eisenhower years to cover the spectrum, with uncertainty over the extent of U.S. tolerance to be part of the deterrent effect. Unfortunately the bare fact that the Soviets also had nuclear weapons reduced its value. Obviously Moscow might miscalculate and trigger nuclear war with the United States. But just as obviously there was vast room for Communist maneuvering within the boundaries of acceptable risk.

When Secretary of Defense Wilson set out to get "more bang
for a buck," unofficial strategists zeroed in on weaknesses of the
New Look policy. Bernard Brodie, B. H. Liddell Hart, and George
Kennan, among others, warned that massive retaliation as a
strategy was out of focus. Limited wars, Kennan argued, were
more likely in the future. In the Army, General Matthew B. Ridg-
way resisted so tenaciously the ceilings on limited-war capability
that he lasted only two years as Chief of Staff. His succcessor,
General Maxwell D. Taylor, struggled in frustration for four years
before he stepped out to become the most famous military symbol
of the demand for a modern army and a broader strategy.

In near despair, Lieutenant General James M. Gavin quoted
Secretary of Defense Wilson as saying, "We can't afford to fight
limited wars. We can only afford to fight a big war, and if there
is one, that is the kind it will be."

During Eisenhower's second term, the argument over limited
war at times approached the virulence of the "Revolt of the
Admirals" a decade earlier. The Navy, its strategic role secured
with the Polaris program, swung its support to the Army in the
argument for limited-war capability. To the Air Force, of course,
the complaints amounted to beating a dead horse. Limited war
would be covered more or less automatically, its leaders insisted,
by proper preparation for general war.

There were strong elements of parochialism, as the President
charged, in the competing arguments of the services, including
the Army's. Some of it appeared in General Taylor's book *The
Uncertain Trumpet,* published after his first retirement in 1959.
Still, the book was one of the most closely reasoned and ultimately influential criticisms of the Administration's defense doctrines.

The nuclear forces of the great powers, Taylor said, would
create a state of mutual deterrence once the United States got its
own house in order. The idea that the United States would use
nuclear weapons except to preserve itself or Western Europe
had limited credibility. Thus the United States could exercise its

power only with a balance of forces that enabled it to be truly selective. It would require strong, protected strategic forces, of course, but it also would require a modern Army so it could have a choice of conventional or nuclear weapons as circumstances demanded. There was a name for what Taylor was advocating, and later, substantially refined, it would become the military policy of the United States: the doctrine of flexible, or graduated, response.

The related, parallel discussion of how to fight strategic war if it came dealt in greater subtleties. The first answers were primitive: the United States simply would devastate the Soviet Union, its cities and its military capability. But with the development of long-range missiles, it became chillingly clear that the planning for nuclear war must be more intricate than imagined earlier if civilization was to survive. In 1957 Henry A. Kissinger, then a young instructor in Government at Harvard, produced one of the influential books of the period. In *Nuclear Weapons and Foreign Policy* he upheld the need for strategic deterrence but concluded that tactical nuclear weapons were the key to future wars.

By October of that year even Secretary of State Dulles was ready to moderate his dedication to massive retaliation. Returning to the Council on Foreign Relations, where he had first stated the policy, he noted that it might be "feasible to place less reliance upon deterrence of vast retaliatory power. It may be possible to defend countries by nuclear weapons so mobile, or so placed, as to make military invasion with conventional forces a hazardous attempt." What Dulles had in mind was a tactical nuclear barrier against conventional aggression. He still would force the aggressor to reckon with nuclear war, though initially, at least, a form of nuclear war somewhat short of total conflict with big bombers and missiles. This approach too would be used to justify fewer troops and de-emphasis of conventional weapons.

Still the armchair and slide-rule strategists continued to poke at the possibilities. At the RAND Corporation Albert Wohlstetter foresaw a time when the Soviet Union might strike first, coldly calculating and accepting its losses from retaliation, unless the United States carefully nourished its deterrent. After all, he noted, the Soviets were familiar with hideous losses: their dead numbered more than twenty million in World War II. The critical element in deterrence, he emphasized, was the certain capability to "strike second," to destroy the aggressor after absorbing an attack.

Most of the new ideas on nuclear warfare were presented cautiously and in restrained tones. But in late 1960 Herman Kahn, then of RAND, a physicist by training and a strategic generalist by choice, ripped the subject apart and analyzed its parts. In his *On Thermonuclear War* Kahn tried to project what that sort of conflict really might be like. He dealt with possibilities ranging from shades of crisis to horrifying variations on nuclear exchange. Kahn's matter-of-fact equations, in which variables might include tens of millions of deaths, were revolting to many. His findings that nations could survive nuclear war, that man in fact could adjust, and that economies could be revived seemed to some almost to rationalize nuclear war.

In the changing mood of the times Henry Kissinger took another hard look at his own ideas on war below total nuclear exchange and concluded he had been wrong. In a second book in 1961 he shifted his emphasis on tactical nuclear weapons and argued that massive effort must be made to keep conflict below the nuclear threshold.

The strategic argument boiled through to the end of the Eisenhower Administration. Massive retaliation, whatever it meant by that time, still was the official doctrine. But the Administration had modified it to even greater ambiguity with its emphasis on tactical weapons. In 1959 Christian Herter, who succeeded Dulles, told Congress, "I cannot conceive of any President involving us in an all-out nuclear war unless the facts showed clearly we are in danger of all-out devastation ourselves, or that actual moves have been made toward devastating ourselves."

As a deterrent to lesser challenges, nuclear weapons had been less than satisfactory in several areas. If the United States aimed to counter Soviet thrusts without using its nuclear power, it needed a coherent strategy covering both nuclear and conventional forces. Of the Army's fourteen divisions, five were committed in Germany and two in Korea. Three of those at home were training divisions. Much of their equipment was outmoded, and levels of supplies varied wildly. The Army, planning for long wars, was vastly overstocked with some equipment but short in many essentials. The Air Force was prepared only for a short, savage nuclear exchange.

By Election Day of 1960 there seemed no end to critics of the system, and the critics won. Whether or not the Democratic attack on Eisenhower defense policies may have won the election for John F. Kennedy is impossible to say. The margin was so close that any of several issues might have contributed the difference. There was no doubt at all, in any case, that the victors were pledged to overhaul the system: to build both strategic and conventional forces, to provide a real choice between, in Kennedy's words, "world devastation or submission," and to put the whole into a rational policy. On January 21 the following year Eisenhower and Gates handed the vast machinery over to Kennedy and McNamara, two young men confident they could make it work.

4

First Crises

Even Robert F. Kennedy, who admired the Secretary of Defense immensely, was moved to remark, "Bob McNamara is the most dangerous man in the Cabinet because he is so persuasive and articulate." Several times he made certain his brother heard arguments counter to McNamara's on critical issues just for the sake of balance.

McNamara needed all the persuasiveness and articulateness he could muster, and all of his enormous reservoir of energy, as he forced change upon the Department of Defense in 1961. He had resolved to accomplish his goals without another overhaul of the National Security Act. The first crash program that followed the transition revealed his conclusion that the reorganization proposed by the Symington Task Force of 1960 was unnecessary for one prepared to use fully the power already available. Without question he was prepared.

Soon after he took over, for example, McNamara decided to designate the Air Force as the primary agency for military space projects, in order to stop interservice duplication. He put Cyrus Vance, who worked out the plan in consultation with military specialists, in charge. McNamara sent a draft to General Lyman L. Lemnitzer, the Chairman of the Joint Chiefs, who criticized some of its terms and fretted over the Secretary's demand for a quick response. McNamara took some of Lemnitzer's points into account in his final directive.

Several days after it was issued, newspaper reports appeared detailing Lemnitzer's criticism. The leak, apparently inspired by the Navy, did not acknowledge that the General had argued with the early draft rather than the final version. One result was a House subcommittee hearing which offered a forum for the Army and Navy to unload some of their resentment at the move, and an occasion for some reporters to get in a few licks at McNamara's effort to limit their access to Pentagon sources.

In the end Lemnitzer himself disposed of the episode. "I am constantly consulted," he said. "I see [civilian superiors] on a daily basis and many times a day on some occasions." Asked whether he supported the directive, he replied simply, "Yes." McNamara was the boss, but such incidents were reminders that critical eyes were focused constantly on anyone who dared to assert control as McNamara had.

Despite his mandate to his Secretary of Defense, Kennedy himself unintentionally contributed to the continuing challenge to McNamara's authority in the early months. Always the activist, the young President was quick to grab the telephone and go to the most direct source when he wanted answers. One member of the Joint Chiefs of Staff basked happily in self-appreciation as he received repeated direct calls from the President. Slowly it dawned on him that no one else knew of them. The potential for an embarrassing misunderstanding, with the right hand proceeding independently of the left, outside normal command channels, was remote but disturbing. As a precaution, the officer began circulating memos of each such call to his counterparts in the other services. Finally, the calls decreased as Kennedy's confidence in McNamara grew.

As his grip became surer, McNamara moved steadily to ever more substantive changes. Some of them flowed naturally if not easily from patterns already established. Operational military control for the most part had been placed under unified commands, in which an officer of one service would direct the efforts of all the multiservice units charged with the same mission. The Commander in Chief, Europe, for example, was in command of the U.S. Army, Europe, at Heidelberg; U.S. Navy, Europe, in London; and U.S. Air Force, Europe, at Wiesbaden. McNamara soon was ready to complete this process, short of merger. He decreed unification of the 115,000-man Strategic Army Corps and the 50,000-man Tactical Air Force into the Strike Command, a force designed for putting out fires wherever they might appear. The order linked combat-ready troops to their means of transport. With that change, all combat forces were assigned within the unified command structure.

Important orders came on the housekeeping side. Remembering the unhappy missile-gap experience, he created the Defense Intelligence Agency on August 1, leaving the individual services only the intelligence role uniquely required by their forces. Three months later the Defense Supply Agency was established for central control over the tens of thousands of purchases required by all the services.

The most important management change developed out of the special talents of the new Secretary and the civilian team he brought to the Pentagon. Its key element was the budget, an awesome document which postwar administrations had controlled by imposing arbitrary ceilings, in total and for each service. The result had been a collection of individual, frequently contradictory and overlapping undertakings.

The Joint Chiefs of Staff had tried to come to grips with the problem in the mid-fifties when they began putting together what was called the Joint Strategic Objectives Plan (Jaysop). But it still was essentially a collection of individual Army–Navy–Air Force plans. It was an obvious weakness in the entire structure.

With the change of administration in the Pentagon, outside innovators and critics of the fifties were in a position to put new theories into practice. The result was the Planning–Programming–Budgeting System (PPBS), which brought together in the budget for the first time all those activities that are supposed to be basically related. Comptroller Charles Hitch outlined the proposed programming system to McNamara in the spring of 1961 and recommended that it be developed and applied within eighteen months. McNamara approved the system—but shortened the timetable to six months.

Despite the complexity of PPBS—which united resources into "program packages"—some of its implications were obvious even to the uninitiated. By considering together the Polaris submarines, which are the Navy's strategic system, and the bombers and missiles of the Strategic Air Command, for example, civilian leaders could shape more easily the overall strategic forces. There was no longer any excuse for random overlapping between the two services.

The system also tried to anticipate the long-range future, including costs, for each big undertaking. A primary purpose, of course, was to keep the nation's overall needs in clear perspective in contrast to the sometimes haphazard development by individual services in the past. The hope was to prevent advocates from starting small—in Pentagonese this was called inserting "the thin edge of the wedge"—and letting costs multiply later.

PPBS had essential points of simplicity. It remained possible to present to Congress the basic terms members were familiar with: soldiers and sailors and airmen, their pay and their weapons. One of the most critical consequences was simplest of all: PPBS further consolidated power in the office of the Secretary of Defense. The growing use of computers contributed to the same end. Civilian leaders often were getting more information, faster, than the services. McNamara did not really believe, as some critics had it, that all issues could be quantified; just most. He did believe that careful study of all available information contributed to more rational decisions, and he made a considerable point of getting data.

There was a fundamental management principle behind all this, wrapped up in the much-maligned phrase "cost effectiveness."

What the term implies in its broadest application is a determination—by "systems analysis"—whether a specific job must be done, and if so, how best to do it. More specifically, it means getting the most for the least money, or fulfilling a mission at an acceptable cost. Detractors, of course, hastened to suggest that it meant sacrifice of national security to cost factors.

Cost effectiveness was applied to such problems as determining whether to build ships with conventional or nuclear power or whether a new bomber was needed to complement a growing missile force. It is the sort of reasoning applied by a housewife when she decides which vacuum cleaner will do the job of getting the carpet acceptably clean within the shortest time at lowest cost.

These factors have been applied, whatever they were called, in producing weapons throughout history. Hitch pointed out in his book, *Decision-Making for Defense,* that the pendulum of cost effectiveness frequently swung from quantity to quality and back again. The armored knight was a splendid but costly weapons system; he finally fell to the inexpensive longbow. Here was cost effectiveness with a vengeance.

If the principles were old, McNamara gave them new point with intense personal concentration and institutional emphasis. He made the military think cost effectiveness from the start, and thus the technique was scorned by frustrated sponsors of projects that failed to pass his tests. McNamara forced the reasoning of the services on basic issues into the open for analysis and debate, but kept the high cards for himself. As in other areas, his commitment was total. He elevated systems analysis to bureau status in the Pentagon, assigned some of his best staff members to run it, and otherwise irritated traditionalists.

Obviously if anyone wanted to challenge a McNamara argument, he had to be faster with his facts and his handling of them. Unfortunately for the challenger, that seldom was possible. As a result, although he drilled mercilessly into programs beloved in Congress, McNamara fared better on Capitol Hill during his first year than might have been expected.

From the beginning he impressed Carl Vinson of Georgia, the

venerable chairman of the House Armed Services Committee. Vinson sometimes wavered, and sometimes he fought McNamara vigorously, but in general he was a McNamara supporter until his retirement in 1964. Usually McNamara and his team were simply so far ahead of their critics, Congressional and military, in that first year that they were rounding the next turn before the criticism landed.

When McNamara lost a significant skirmish, as he did when he opposed faster procurement of bombers in 1961, he still managed to win the battle. Harking to General Curtis E. LeMay, who succeeded General Thomas D. White as Air Force Chief of Staff, Congress provided more than $700 million beyond the Administration request for bombers. With Presidential support, McNamara refused, as had his predecessors in similar circumstances, to spend the money.

Some of the early irritations represented intensely human reactions to McNamara's civilian aides. For all their brilliance, some of them lacked the tempering of practical experience. They had been fretting for years over strategic weapons. Here they were ready with quick theoretical answers. They were less sure with their analyses of conventional forces, guns and men and airplanes. One infantry officer in the Pentagon reported mournfully that a young civilian high in the Secretary's office had asked him for a primer course in how a division was organized.

Some of the brightest of McNamara's civilians were the most abrasive, and, in harmony with their leader, the most assertive. These characteristics did nothing to soothe the instinctive military resentment at taking orders from a growing legion of civilians. One of the nation's most prominent strategic analysts, comfortable in both camps, has told of a young civilian who deliberately took over a three-star general's chair when he went to the officer's office for a talk. Understandably angry, the general filed what was described as an "almost formal complaint" with McNamara. The Secretary told him to forget it. "The military attitude was not anti-intellectual, it was more anti-civilian below the familiar command level," said the man who reported the byplay.

The military resentment at such bumptiousness—and boorish-ness, in the above case—was predictable. As seen by the young civilians, however, the new mood in the Pentagon was electric and inspiring. Ideas were the hard currency of power. Joseph A. Califano, Jr., who arrived in the spring, described the atmosphere as "almost unbelievably challenging."

Califano, bright, personable, was a young lawyer who applied to Cyrus Vance out of a simple but deeply felt desire to be where the action was. Their first conversation went about like this:

VANCE: "Have you read the National Security Act?"

CALIFANO: "No."

VANCE: "Have you had any intelligence experience?"

CALIFANO: "No."

VANCE, with twinkling eye, tossing over a copy of the Act: "Well, we're going to unite the intelligence services, and Mr. McNamara wants to know if it's okay."

"I got the feeling," Califano recalled, "that this must have been what the New Deal was like in the thirties." The next day he was hard at work on preparations to establish the Defense Intelligence Agency.

The events that did most to shape the new military-civilian relationship evolved, however, in less direct fashion. They arose, at first, out of the tendency of some senior military officers to outdo each other in the presentation of the Communist threat and denunciation of its perpetrators. As the rhetoric soared, the cumu-lative effect was to build an image of an increasingly bellicose United States at a sensitive time, much as the Soviet Union itself was doing through its official propaganda. As McNamara studied speech texts and the transcripts of military "Cold War seminars," he decided the Pentagon was poisoning American minds into an unreasoned fear.

McNamara began to apply the brakes for the more obvious reasons. Uninhibited remarks by military leaders sounded like foreign policy, and the Administration intended to control its own foreign policy. The issue was drawn, within a month of the inauguration, when Pentagon censors, or "reviewers," mutilated a speech planned by Admiral Arleigh A. Burke, the Chief of Naval Operations. It was a step never to be dared by even a senior officer without the approval of the Secretary of Defense. Cries that McNamara was "muzzling" the military began to waft from Capitol Hill.

Semantics aside, he was doing precisely that. Then the matter became further complicated and more acutely sensitive when the case of Major General Edwin A. Walker erupted.

General Walker was commander of the 24th Infantry Division in Germany, unquestioned as a leader of men, a hero of World War II and Korea. But the General had become more and more fearful of Communist influence, to the point that the liberal left in the United States, and even most in the great middle range of the political spectrum, appeared to him to be dupes, at best, of the Communist conspiracy. "The hour is late," he proclaimed, and he set out to inspire his troops with a fundamental goal: "the defeat of Communism." His men, he felt, had to be on guard against Communist influence in every aspect of their lives. The upshot was an indoctrination program, which he designated "pro-blue," and which followed closely the guiding principles of the right-wing John Birch Society.

In his lectures he warned of the leftist affiliation or influence of such citizens as former President Harry Truman, former Secretary of State Dean Acheson, Mrs. Eleanor Roosevelt, and leading figures in American journalism (he later would question the patriotism of Dean Rusk and Walt Rostow).

The manner in which his excesses were exposed had a great deal to do with subsequent events. The vehicle was the *Overseas Weekly*, a privately published paper distributed to American troops in Europe, which dealt heavily in scandal and sex. It was hardly the favorite publication of most military commanders, whether or not they sympathized with General Walker's political beliefs.

On April 16, 1961, the *Overseas Weekly* unloaded on General Walker with a carefully documented series of articles detailing his political activities. The Pentagon ordered a full investigation immediately. The outcome was an official "admonishment" for General Walker, basically on the ground that he had tried to influence the voting of his troops. It was the beginning of the decline that led to his resignation and a role as a raucous voice on the fringe of the political right.

But that would come later. For the time being, the events were too much for some conservatives in Congress to bear. This was especially true of Senator Strom Thurmond, of South Carolina, who at the time had yet to change his affiliation from Democrat to Republican. At his insistence, a special investigative subcommittee was formed under Senator John Stennis, the Mississippi Democrat, to look into the entire area of troop information and speech censorship.

McNamara refused to take a stand for or against hearings. That was up to Congress, he said, but he managed to suggest that such an undertaking was unnecessary and a waste of everyone's time. His own suspicion of Communist methods and intentions was as deep as that of any subcommittee member, however, and he refused to be outgunned by Thurmond on that issue when the hearings began.

"The threat is clear, and it is immediate," he said. "Our fighting men should know the positive values of the freedoms which the nation is calling them to defend, and they should know the nature of Soviet Communism which seeks to take them away." He promised a fresh appraisal of the troop information programs to make certain that military men had the best training possible without infringement on their rights to political choice.

There seemed to be little opening for political attack there. But Thurmond knew his constituency. Frequently it consisted of a

bevy of zealously patriotic, mostly middle-aged ladies who vocif-
erously endorsed every suggestion that the nation was sinking
into a political and moral abyss. In the background, General
Walker—after his retirement in the fall—kept the fires burning
with charges that he was the victim of a "no win" policy inspired
by international Communism. "Those women actually spat at me,"
McNamara said in wonderment after the hearings got under way.

Thurmond spent considerable time and concern on the character of the *Overseas Weekly*. Methodically, he dealt out copies
of the newspaper and asked for McNamara's opinion on those
"pictures of women who are almost naked." Wearily McNamara
responded that he found them "disgusting." But he doubted
whether personal revulsion outweighed the issue of press freedom
to be raised if the paper was removed from Army newsstands in
Germany.

Finally, however, the hearings crystallized on the issue of censorship of military speeches. On this point McNamara was
adamant from the beginning. He did not care much for the word
"censorship," but he was unswerving on the principle of "review."
It protected both the military officers and the civilian establishment, he said. Otherwise there was a "risk of violating civilian
control" and the possibility of presenting an "appearance of confusion" to the world.

"This is a particularly grave danger in the field of foreign
affairs," he remarked, "where foreign governments weigh with
great care every word spoken by our officials."

The conflict turned on the censorship treatment of more than
1,500 speeches given by military men. At one point, when the
subcommittee wanted to see them all, the Pentagon dredged them
out and delivered them, in all their mutations, within two days.
The rush was so great that Norman Paul, McNamara's legislative
assistant, was cruising the Pentagon corridors on a bicycle over-
seeing the project.

There were areas of vulnerability in the review system, of
course. For one thing, much of the process was arbitrary, with

deletions and changes to shift the tone, more than the substance, of a speech. How does one determine when a speech, taken as a whole, crosses the line between firmness of purpose and chauvinism? For every deletion, a phrase equally provocative might be left in. Some changes were patently silly. Thurmond, pursuing a good thing, insisted on learning the names of the individual reviewers who had made specific alterations in specific speeches. McNamara, from the beginning of the inquiry until February, 1962, firmly refused. He turned over the names of the fourteen men on the review staff, but he refused to associate individual reviewers with individual speeches. The overall responsibility, he said, was his, and no one else's.

The drama was played out in a carefully planned ritual on February 8, 1962. A day before, the Stennis subcommittee had voted to bring the issue to a test. On the morning of February 8 President Kennedy handed McNamara a letter instructing him to claim executive privilege. In effect, it held that the individuals who made specific changes in the speeches were answerable only within the executive branch, which bore the final responsibility. When Stennis convened his subcommittee that day, the question was put formally to a McNamara subordinate: Who had censored the statement to be delivered by Lieutenant General Arthur G. Trudeau before a committee of the House of Representatives in February, 1961? McNamara intervened, read the Kennedy letter, and instructed his subordinates not to answer.

Stennis then turned to a prepared statement which he had written on a yellow legal pad. With the precision drawn from his earlier years as a judge, he traced briefly the separation of governmental powers since George Washington. Finally he concluded: "The chair sustains the plea."

From that point forward the issue lost much of its sting. There had been moments reminiscent of the witch-hunting during the McCarthy period a decade earlier, but they never sparked a general reaction. Surely the American public had learned something from the earlier experience. But in the immediate case, much of the credit was due the American military. Few of its officers lost perspective on the background issue of civilian authority. Moreover, Senator Stennis had conducted the hearings and had ruled finally with impeccable judiciousness. From these events McNamara developed a respect for the conservative Mississippian which survived their many differences then and later.

Well he might. For the end result of the hearing was the implanting of his control, in both the general sense of civilian supremacy and in the personal sense, to an extent he might not have managed otherwise. McNamara himself regarded it as a fundamental point in the shaping of military-civilian relations.

Apart from the jousts with Congress, he had other image problems, especially in his relationship with the press. Newspapermen who covered Defense regularly were accustomed to feeding upon interservice rivalries—at least until Gates came along—and the calculated leak was a priceless resource. With McNamara, the individual service offices increasingly became administrative extensions of the Secretary's office. As overt interservice rivalries declined, so did opportunities for inside stories.

Given McNamara's own regard for secrecy, the press corps began to feed upon ever thinner fare. At the beginning the Secretary told aides he planned few press conferences, despite their warnings that he was asking for trouble. His reluctance stemmed from his belief that much of the reporting on defense affairs was superficial, and at worst irresponsible. In many cases he unquestionably was correct, but the fault was not all with the press.

McNamara's news values had been shaped in part by the relatively closed environment of big industry. He had a tendency to judge the rightness and wrongness of public information in the light of the Administration's—or Ford Motor Company's—views. He mistrusted reporters. Moreover, he added fuel for critics in testimony before the Senate Armed Services Committee about public reports he regarded as unwise.

"Why should we tell Russia that the Zeus developments may not be satisfactory?" he complained. "What we ought to be saying is that we have the most perfect anti-ICBM system that the human mind will ever devise. Instead the public domain is already full of statements that the Zeus may not be satisfactory, that it has deficiencies. I think it is absurd to release that kind of information for the public." In view of McNamara's own reservations about missile defenses, the likelihood that there was little mystery about this to the Soviets anyhow, and subsequent developments in the ABM debate, this was a vulnerable position indeed.

The Pentagon press office had to move quickly to keep that one from becoming a major flap. Under no circumstances, a spokesman said, did the Secretary feel "that the American public should be misled about a military program. But at the same time he does not think we should gratuitously provide any potential enemy with valuable information about any difficulties which may be encountered in the development of new weapons systems."

Few could argue with the basic security premise. But no journalist worthy of the name was prepared to accept without question the Pentagon judgment on releasable information. It was a dispute that always boiled down to a healthy antagonism between government and the press, one that McNamara, like his predecessors, was unable to erase. It was Hanson Baldwin of the *New York Times* who first perceived "The McNamara Monarchy." McNamara was concerned about his public image. The concern showed in the spectacular growth of the Pentagon public relations machinery in size and sophistication during his administration. But he refused to make deliberate personal gestures to improve his image. Performance, he seemed to believe, would establish the record. Thus he rejected the advice of aides who tried to get him to visit and personally console the unhappy Reservists called to duty later in 1961. Such an approach, he felt, would be insincere flackery on his part and an insult to men doing their duty. The attitude reflected perhaps as much the man as the circumstances. As a press aide remarked sourly, "He is sometimes a tough product to push."

Under those conditions it frequently appeared impossible that

McNamara analysts in Washington, a growing legion, were talking about the same man. The most powerful columnists with national exposure, interested primarily in high policy, were captivated. The reporters who covered the Pentagon on a day-to-day basis admired his awesome ability, but they also detected the warts and inspected them in print.

Within the Pentagon hierarchy associates found him determined to exclude emotion from his official responsibilities—a characteristic which he freely acknowledged. He was most comfortable with very bright, questioning, but loyal subordinates; with others he was usually courteous and businesslike, at worst cold and abrupt. In this he seemed to be consistent. He once authorized for direct attribution a remark by his wife in a private conversation, "Bob suffers fools badly." Presumably he had resolved for himself the point that one man's fool is not every man's fool.

Soon after the inauguration Admiral Burke, nearing the end of his third two-year term as Chief of Naval Operations when McNamara arrived, set out to unveil the human side of the Secretary. Burke was a World War II hero, a crusty saltwater fundamentalist who was intensely interested in human relations within the military, rules and traditions aside. He talked McNamara into attending a stag party of senior Department officials, military and civilian, just so they would know each other better.

It was a minor disaster. McNamara obviously made a genuine effort, as participants recalled later, but he was incapable of instant camaraderie. He had little talent and less liking for pointless conversation. He had one drink and stood around uncomfortably for an hour or so in the Officers' Club at Fort Myer, near the Pentagon, and everyone else carefully remained sober. Burke left the Department convinced that McNamara lacked the human qualities necessary for outstanding leadership.

But none of the internal adjustments, the adaptation of the old establishment to the new, the management revolution, the first gestures toward a new strategy, were half as important as the outside challenges. With his administrative takeover McNamara was on familiar ground. But 1961 also brought to a head a handful of inherited crises to educate the new Secretary in the application of power as well.

The first two, over Cuba and Laos, matured together in the early weeks after the inauguration. Arthur Schlesinger, Jr., has written that the President worried more about the Communist threat to Laos than any other issue during his first two months in office. The pending invasion of Cuba by a band of 1,500 exiles, trained and supported by the Central Intelligence Agency, ran a close second. Gnawing doubts on the part of some in the new Administration leaped to dismal certainty when the Bay of Pigs operation collapsed shortly after it began on April 17 in a shambles of Cuban lives, individual American reputations, and national prestige.

McNamara's role in the Bay of Pigs debacle is notable, in retrospect, for his lack of penetration into the issues. Certainly he bore no special individual responsibility. It was primarily a CIA operation, articulately and optimistically presented as the solution to Fidel Castro. McNamara was engrossed in harnessing the Pentagon. So he supported the operation firmly in White House councils, despite the hedged position of the Joint Chiefs of Staff.

In the aftermath Kennedy accepted full responsibility. McNamara himself was asked about the role of the Chiefs at a press conference on May 26.

"First," he said, "the Department of Defense was fully represented over a period of weeks in the discussions within the government relative to the invasion of Cuba by the Cuban exiles.

"Secondly, the Joint Chiefs of Staff or their representatives and I represented the Defense Department in those discussions.

"Thirdly, as Secretary of Defense I am responsible for the operations of this Department, and I am responsible for the actions of all the personnel in the Department, both military and civilian. Any errors, therefore, are my errors. They are not to be charged to others. Whatever deficiencies are chargeable to the Department are chargeable to me.

"And fourth, with specific application to the question, the Joint Chiefs are intelligent, experienced, dedicated men, and I consider it a great honor to be associated with them."

It was not enough. The Administration made it known otherwise that it was disappointed with the performance of the Chiefs. And the Chiefs in turn believed they had been badly used. Their advice indeed had favored the operation, but it had been tied vaguely to a number of conditions, including the possible use of air support for the invasion. One of them later conceded that their advice had been murky, but insisted, "What we had to work with was murky. We had to base our judgment on what was passed on to us from the White House, and we did not know until later just how much was withheld."

However the responsibility should have been shared, McNamara felt his own failure deeply. Almost seven years later, as he prepared to leave the Department, he brought the subject up for a *mea culpa* on a national television broadcast. In retrospect the Bay of Pigs operation seems preposterous, but only a few saw it that way at the time. In any case, as Secretary of State Dean Rusk put it, there was blame enough to go around. The new Administration fell victim to its own inexperience, to frustration and vacillation among its military advisers, and to the self-delusion of the CIA. In McNamara's case, it was a display of action without rational consideration—of weaknesses repugnant to him, inexperience, and ignorance—in a situation with far-reaching implications for the way other nations would judge the new Administration.

The Bay of Pigs was primarily a political crisis. From the beginning Kennedy had ruled out overt American participation, though many involved in planning thought he would intervene in the end to save the operation. The caldron of Southeast Asia presented crises demanding both political and military decisions.

By 1961 the Communist Pathet Lao forces in Laos, inspired

from Hanoi and supported from Moscow, were edging toward control of the country. Their cause was aided immeasurably by chaos in what passed for a formal government structure and gross contradictions in American policy. The United States had poured $300 million in military aid into a country of less than three million population. The money was largely wasted.

Kennedy came down quickly for a neutralist coalition as the only reasonable political solution. At first the Communists were too encouraged by success to be interested. U.S. leverage was limited, for the President received discouragingly open-ended alternatives from the Joint Chiefs of Staff. They laid out a sequence for intervention that led through the commitment of as many as 60,000 men to the use of tactical nuclear weapons—in a land which then contained total armed strength of something like 50,000 men, friendly and hostile.

Kennedy rejected the open-ended commitment. He finally decided on limited direct intervention—though there is disagreement on this among former aides even today. At any rate he alerted U.S. forces in the Pacific, including Marines in Japan and Okinawa, and let the Soviet Union know it.

McNamara, however, was painfully aware of the limits of American power—and he so advised the President. Then as now, the role of tactical nuclear weapons in the spectrum of warfare was unclear. To keep the nuclear threshold at an acceptable level, the United States would require several divisions for Laos, McNamara warned, and they were unavailable. Finally Nikita Khrushchev, apparently convinced Laos would go Communist in any case, and uncertain of American intentions, let the tension slide into a new round of Geneva negotiations. The tactic blunted the crisis for the time being.

The deteriorating situation in South Vietnam at the same time was becoming more demanding. After several years of progress following the 1954 Geneva Accords, the government of Ngo Dinh Diem was faced with steadily increasing pressure from guerrillas, both locally recruited and infiltrated from North Vietnam. As the challenge grew, Diem turned more and more suspicious, oppressive, and dependent upon members of his immediate family.

Here, too, the United States had to make fundamental decisions: not, at this stage, on direct intervention, but on whether its involvement in South Vietnam was worth preserving. A series of reports from the scene convinced the President it was.

Kennedy agreed to increase economic and military aid, but left open the question of direct, unambiguous intervention. The decision to pursue the commitment, needless to say, was one of the critical points in that first year, though it was just one of the treacherous crossroads encountered in the Vietnam involvement.

McNamara did not develop as a primary policy-maker on Vietnam in those months. He was more concerned with the organization of his Department, though he fully agreed with the decisions on Southeast Asia. It was noteworthy, nonetheless, that the White House staff and the Defense Department were more visible than the State Department in these decisions.

The Secretary of Defense finally began to come to the surface in military and political policy, however, with the Administration's next foreign crisis of the year. Beside Berlin, the humiliation of the Bay of Pigs and the chronic nagging of Southeast Asia faded into the background.

For months before the President's trip to Europe in early June, the Soviet Union had been rumbling once more against the enclave of West Berlin. Twice before since World War II, the Soviet Union had threatened the Western position in the city. The former German capital had become a natural pawn in the Cold War under the terms by which the Allies ended the conflict in 1945. The great disadvantage, of course, was that Berlin was 110 miles inside the Soviet zone of East Germany.

At Vienna the Soviet leader threw the challenge again in most explicit terms. His government, he told Kennedy, would sign a treaty with East Germany by the end of the year, proclaiming East German sovereignty and giving it control over access to Berlin. The United States must adjust accordingly.

Precisely why Khrushchev calculated as he did remains uncertain. The behavior of the United States on the Bay of Pigs and Laos must have encouraged him. It is quite possible that Moscow simply saw an opportunity to give the new Administration a controlled test. Kennedy hardly left an impression of strength with Khrushchev, and the Soviet leader apparently felt he was dealing with little more than a spoiled youth. It was a serious miscalculation, of course. More than Berlin was at stake, though that was enough: the broader challenge was to the bedrock position of the United States as a world power. The Kennedy Administration had revealed itself as one acutely sensitive to its world role. Flexible response was not a passive doctrine like that of massive retaliation. A case could be made, in fact, that the Administration was inclined to equate the capability for flexible response as a mandate for action. This was hardly a perception of June, 1961, however.

Kennedy immediately began to recast a European review already under way. Dean Acheson, Secretary of State under Harry Truman, had been at work since spring on the American stance toward the North Atlantic Alliance and Germany. His primary aim was to develop the option of conventional warfare early in a European conflict and thus delay, at least, nuclear confrontation. For the long run, the Administration hoped the insertion of more conventional forces into the NATO line would serve both the obvious military purpose and as a demonstration of political will. But with the new crisis gaining momentum, McNamara reminded the White House that formal contingency planning still looked to nuclear war early in a conflict over Berlin. Kennedy quickly asked him to revise the plans.

As time began to run out, McNamara, leading a special Berlin Task Force, came into his own. Working shirt-sleeved even longer hours than usual, he set a rising tempo in the Pentagon. What emerged was a careful balance between military and political goals that had been somewhat conflicting.

Acheson had originally wanted a major show of force, with

strengthening of both conventional and nuclear forces on the continent, and declaration of national emergency. General Lauris Norstad, the NATO commander, could see long-range problems in a sudden, heavy reinforcement of troops: the Europeans would be reluctant to match the effort, yet they probably would see the subsequent withdrawal of the extra Americans as a U.S. retreat. Beyond that, there were operational problems in the blossoming strategy. Norstad could imagine a situation in which his tactical air forces might be depleted by nonnuclear combat—say, in support of an infantry and armored drive toward Berlin—just before a sudden turn to nuclear weapons. In July McNamara flew to Europe for a personal examination.

What resulted, as a participant in the debate recalled later, "was the first compromise between the hawks and the doves of the sixties." McNamara, balancing the appeals of those who favored negotiations—though it was never quite clear what was to be negotiated—and those who wanted a no-nonsense show of force, surfaced as the first "dawk." By July 25 his military response was ready.

That night the President appeared on television to assert American determination to hold fast in Berlin. Once again he asked for more money, this time for $3.5 billion almost exclusively for conventional forces. Berlin had pre-empted the orderly approach to a nonnuclear buildup. McNamara had drafted plans to raise the Army from 875,000 to 1,000,000 men, to increase the Navy by 29,000 and the Air Force by 63,000. Kennedy asked Congress for special authority to summon National Guard and Reserve forces without declaring a national mobilization. The object, as McNamara saw it, was to convince the Soviet leaders of a critical truth: the United States was prepared to take the ultimate risks, first with conventional forces, then to go to nuclear war if necessary, to protect its vital interests in Europe. Acheson's proposals had been modulated considerably to convey what Kennedy and McNamara hoped would be regarded as firmness rather than bellicosity.

About 40,000 troops, plus 11 air squadrons, were sent to flesh out Norstad's forces, a volume he could be comfortable with. At home the services grew steadily. By mid-November 156,000 National Guardsmen and Reservists had been called for a year of active duty, dislocating, as Kennedy had warned, many careers and family plans. A background chorus of anguished complaints arose from Congress. The limited mobilization was controversial even among the Joint Chiefs. Some of them felt the essentially political purpose—to demonstrate American will—could have been accomplished better with forces already in being during a more measured buildup.

At the policy level there was agreement that the Reserve mobilization meant little in terms of quick "usable power," as McNamara put it. He was certain, however, it was the most powerful device readily available to convince the Soviets of American determination.

In the face of the U.S. reaction, the Soviet Union found its own solution, though it was not recognized as such at the time. On August 13, Communist forces choked off traffic between East and West Berlin and began construction of a wall to divide the city. The move ended the greatest threat West Berlin presented to the East: refuge for the cream of East German youth, science, and education. It had been flowing westward at a rate that finally reached 50,000 persons a month. The wall stopped the flow. There were still moments of high tension ahead, but by the end of the year the Berlin crisis had begun to fade. Khrushchev himself finally recast the date of his treaty with East Germany into the indefinite future.

For McNamara the months had been a grinding test of strength and adaptability. On balance he felt his management of the Department had proved itself, a view enthusiastically shared in the White House. Congress had provided the extra $6 billion he requested, and much of it was being converted rapidly into usable power.

The Berlin crisis, he felt, had provided preliminary justification for flexible response. It was a view not universal in Washington. The emphasis on conventional forces in the buildup had made Senator Margaret Chase Smith of Maine nervous. Taking the floor of the Senate, she charged that the Administration had practically told Nikita Khrushchev "we do not have the will to use that one power with which we can stop him; in short, we have the nuclear capability but not the nuclear credibility." McNamara thought that was nonsense. Citing the new plans for strategic forces, he said, "It is absurd to think that we would have unbalanced the budget simply to strengthen a weapon we had decided never to use under any circumstances."

A stiff current of criticism developed in Congress, some of it from unhappiness over the calling of Reserves, some over the Secretary's denial of additional bombers, some over his muzzling of the military. It is fair to say, however, that under the circumstances of massive change, it was muted. The military services, mostly as a result of the Berlin crisis, had gained about 300,000 men in the second half of the year. If necessary, the United States could respond to more than one nonnuclear challenge at a time—which it could not have done six months earlier.

McNamara had won every important struggle in Congress. In the process he spent eighty-nine hours testifying, and he estimated that three to four hours of preparation were required for each hour of testimony. The total would be a substantial portion of a year's work for most mortals. His military advisers accompanied him to Capitol Hill, but usually they had little to do.

Most important, the President let it be known that he regarded McNamara as his most valuable Cabinet member except for his brother Robert. Already McNamara was the most effective Secretary of Defense in history, in that the system responded when he commanded.

In the military particularly the reaction was a peculiar one of mixed admiration, doubt, and frustration. Those most concerned at McNamara's iron assertion of civilian control nevertheless bowed for the most part to his rules. The Secretary himself recognized the mixed emotions as part of "an additional and inevitable

human problem," as he put it later. His reforms "would necessarily change traditional ways of doing things, and limit the
customary ways of spending defense money. It is inevitable that
people will take more easily to suggestions that they should have
more money to spend . . . than to suggestions that they must
spend less or that they must abandon established ways of doing
things."

Yet despite their differences, McNamara and the Joint Chiefs
were working more closely in harmony. The Chiefs had learned
to make their system respond with greater speed to McNamara's
lust for facts. They had learned also to live with the Secretary's
disconcerting ability to return from, say, a Honolulu conference
on Southeast Asia and repeat from memory the pertinent economic, military, and political data on every country in the area.

There were even signs that the Secretary was beginning to relax
socially. He and his wife accepted more invitations to dinner—
though he easily avoided most cocktail parties because of his
working schedule. Hostesses discovered, as had a dedicated circle
of McNamara friends in Michigan earlier, that the Secretary of
Defense away from the job, with people who engaged him intel-
lectually, could be a warm, wryly humorous guest and host.

McNamara was settling in. In December he and Mrs. McNamara paid $127,000 for a comfortable sixteen-room stucco house
at 2412 Tracy Place in Northwest Washington. The lease at
Kalorama Circle was about to expire, and McNamara had promised to remain as long as he was needed.

Directly or indirectly that first year had provided a taste of
every important issue that would arise in national security for
the next six years. It also had revealed the Secretary of Defense
sufficiently to suggest that when he made mistakes, there would
be nothing minor about them. They would be memorable.

5

Building a Strategy

I T all began to come together, for perhaps the only time it all came together with any certainty, the night of October 15, 1962. The McNamaras were host to a "Hickory Hill Seminar," a freewheeling discussion group named informally after the home of its founder and dean, Robert F. Kennedy. While the Secretary of Defense argued happily with friends, officers deep within the Pentagon leaned tensely over films exposed a day earlier over Cuba. The evidence was compelling to the trained eye: the Soviet Union had begun rapid installation of missiles capable of reaching the vital centers of the Eastern United States. A quick telephone call alerted Roswell Gilpatric, and he began calling other key figures in the Administration.

Along with the rest of high officialdom, the Secretary of Defense had misjudged Soviet intentions in Cuba. Late in September he had told friends privately that the danger from the island was less than it had been a year before. Even after the evidence of Soviet missiles became a certainty, McNamara rejected arguments that the Soviet Union had set out to shift fundamentally or redress the balance of power. It made no difference, he said, whether one was killed by a shorter-range missile from Cuba or an ICBM from the Soviet Union. These were, after all, "soft"

106

missiles, easily targeted from the United States, suitable only for a deliberate first attack, and no one believed the Soviet leadership mad enough to go to that extreme.

For months Moscow had been arming Cuba, more recently at a faster pace. The possibility that offensive weapons, capable of reaching the United States, might be installed had been kept open in Washington, though Soviet leaders earnestly disclaimed that intention. The Russians had been warned repeatedly. High above the island, U-2 reconnaissance planes watched through their cameras as the weather permitted. Suddenly there they were, telltale slashes in the earth seen before only in the Soviet Union. Most of official Washington understood immediately the vast political implications of the weapons, should they be flaunted brazenly just off the American coast, as the two nations competed before an uncertain world.

It was McNamara and Ros Gilpatric, over lunch as the Administration searched for its response, who worked out the blockade of Cuba. The option of doing nothing had faded early in the White House deliberations. At the other extreme, an attack on the missile sites inevitably would kill Russians, and thus quite possibly start the process of escalation. The blockade was an exquisitely tuned option between impotence and holocaust, leaving Moscow an avenue for escape.

It was McNamara, red-eyed, hoarse, sleeping in snatches, who orchestrated the planning and supervised the blockade in detail once the United States had confronted Moscow with its evidence. His close direction of Navy operations led to his famous collision with Admiral George W. Anderson, the Chief of Naval Operations, in Navy Flag Plot on October 24.

Both men were under heavy strain. What was this ship doing here? McNamara wanted to know. How did the Navy plan to intercept Soviet vessels? Were there men who could speak Russian aboard the U.S. ships? Exasperated, Anderson invited the Secretary of Defense to return to his office and let the Navy run its blockade. McNamara, finally satisfied with the way things were

going, did just that. But Gilpatric knew the two men could never
again have a sound working relationship. He dropped the word
quietly in the White House. Anderson left to become Ambassador
to Portugal when his two-year term expired eight months later.
As a parting shot, he decried in a Press Club speech "the lack of
trust and confidence between military and civilian echelons" in
the government.

McNamara had no patience at all with the Navy view that this
had become a classic military operation. Despite his uncertainty
over Soviet intent, he knew the challenge and response were first
of all political. In execution, he treated them as such.

Even with his preoccupation, he managed to steal away at
times during those days of keening crisis. Once he went home to
help his son Craig with his homework. "If you can't explain the
problem fully," he told Craig firmly, "then you don't understand
it yourself."

As a military exercise, the Cuba crisis fortunately was short of
a total test. The United States, moreover, was operating close to
home base. Strategists differed as to whether nuclear power alone
was responsible for the Soviet retreat. McNamara knew the nuclear threat, under the circumstances, was vital. He gave greater
weight, however, to the obvious readiness of the United States to
invade Cuba and to destroy the missiles with conventional bombs
if forced to do so. Troops and planes had been mobilized to do
just that, and the Soviet leaders knew it. The retreat was total:
there was no counterpressure even on Berlin, the exposed nerve
that presented the greatest opportunity for a Soviet diversion.

McNamara had come to accept fully the broader implications
of the Soviet gamble before United States policy in the crisis was
resolved. The following January he publicly joined that group
which saw Berlin as the motivating goal of the Russians: "The
psychological if not the military threat that those missiles would
have posed to our own homeland was apparently the trump card
which Mr. Khrushchev intended to play in the next round of
negotiations on the status of Berlin."

Others felt the reasons for the Soviet undertaking were even more fundamental: nothing less than an effort to offset the U.S. strategic advantage until long-range missiles could be deployed in Europe and Asia. Khrushchev later would claim that he intended simply to protect Cuba from another, this time better-planned, invasion attempt. Whatever the reason or combination of reasons, the weapons race at that time had reached a point largely unrecognized. At the end of 1962 the United States had about 650 long-range bombers on fifteen-minute alert. About 100 Atlas and Titan missiles were on their launching pads. Polaris submarines were armed with some 150 missiles. The Pentagon was pouring $15 billion a year into strategic forces. Measured against slower Soviet development, this was a force of such power that the United States, as Moscow may have seen it, might be tempted to launch a pre-emptive strike. The missile gap was all in favor of Washington.

How another Administration at another time might have met the crisis could only be guessed. McNamara, in any case, saw it as vindication, however preliminary, of almost two years of work in the development of a flexible, selective response to aggression as the foundation of strategy.

Of all the problems the new Administration had faced in 1961, none was cloudier than that of fixing a national defense policy. Nor was any likelier to captivate Robert McNamara. To a man of his nature, here was something approaching the ultimate intellectual exercise, part pragmatic, part theoretical. To one who thrived on challenge, this was challenge supreme with infinite stakes. In the management of the Department of Defense, McNamara's experience could be applied instantly. In the forging of the tools of war, and the policies to direct their use, it was of uncertain value. His own military years, however sparkling his performance, were limited preparation.

High strategy was a semantic puzzle in which the tilting of a nuance by a few degrees was magnified along the train of thought. Any generality became almost automatically an overstatement.

With the birth of nuclear weapons there were no longer any experts, only amateurs and professionals. McNamara arrived as an amateur, to become an instant professional.

Even the tools for analysis had changed. "You still have to wargame a problem," a RAND Corporation professional once remarked. "The difference now is that instead of a sandbox and game board you need computers and slide rules." The secret war games building at Fort Leavenworth, Kansas, complete with display screens and electronic data-processing center cost $300,000. Its students, including much-decorated generals, indeed work with computers. The more pertinent distinction for the layman in the new strategic thinking, however, is that nuclear weapons, translated into megatons and megadeaths, have been added to the historic components of armies and navies and, the interim development, air forces. It is not an easy discussion to follow.

John Kennedy accepted naturally the strategic pillar of deterrence; there was no rational alternative to that. Around it, his security platform was dominated by a broader theme. The nation must have a greater choice than surrender or all-out nuclear war, and this, he suggested, was the legacy of his predecessor. To create choice, the United States would have to build its nonnuclear power. The theme was something of a political exaggeration, of course. Yet there could be no doubt that U.S. ground forces at the time were unimpressive if their tactical nuclear weapons were discounted. There was in fact brisk debate over the strategic distinction between long-range and battlefield nuclear weapons. Any nuclear weapon, once used, might begin an unstoppable process of escalation.

At every opportunity during those early days McNamara underscored the instructions he had received from Kennedy: to determine the arms the nation needed, costs aside, but to provide them as economically as possible once the determination was made. There was a built-in exaggeration here, too. Any notion that cost would not weigh heavily on the outer limits of military hardware was nonsense. What had changed, however, was the element of readiness to spend, the scale of priorities, and receptivity to change itself.

Kennedy had long since accepted the outlines of flexible response as well. In McNamara he found a kindred spirit. With the "quick fix" of the spring, McNamara strengthened the strategic forces even as he destroyed the myth of the missile gap. Yet a missile race was very much under way, and it was far from clear what forces would make a credible deterrent or how they would be used. Whatever they might be, he believed the nation had some distance to go.

Despite the immediate emphasis on nuclear weapons, the conventional forces fell into place first. The Berlin buildup had overtaken the slow, deliberate approach. With the addition of hundreds of thousands of men, the need for reorganization stood out glaringly.

The Army came out of the Berlin crisis with sixteen divisions instead of the fourteen inherited from Eisenhower. Kennedy himself ordered the additional two—McNamara was still unconvinced—to replace National Guardsmen discharged from crisis duty. Three regular divisions being used for training were converted to combat-ready status. The other services grew accordingly.

More important than manpower levels, however, was the overhaul in organization and weapons. By far the greater amount of additional money was spent in this area as the defense budget rose almost $8 billion a year above the plans inherited from Eisenhower.

Slowly the Army was recast to lessen its reliance on tactical nuclear weapons. Its divisions were redesigned for flexibility. Each division would be made up of three brigades, and each brigade would command whatever number of battalions was necessary for a specific mission.

With the fading of the Berlin crisis, McNamara returned to a project he had adopted from Eisenhower and modified: reorganization of the politically sensitive Army Reserves and National

Guard. Shrieks from Capitol Hill and state governments had caused the previous Administration to retreat. Several times McNamara was rebuffed as he set out to give priority Reserve and Guard divisions quickly usable combat status, and in the process cut their total numbers. He persisted doggedly. By 1967 he had reached most of his goals through an interplay of executive action and fringe legislation that drove some members of Congress to near fury.

But it was the problem of nuclear weapons that set the tone of the McNamara strategy.

The first considerations naturally were primitive. Political and moral questions aside, the nation that held a monopoly could prevail by obliterating enemy forces with few if any losses itself. That choice for the United States passed in the late 1940s as the Soviet Union became an atomic power. Even with its monopoly, the United States had not used these weapons to break the Berlin blockade, to prevent the consolidation of Soviet power in Eastern Europe, or to meet other tests. The political and moral constraints were, in fact, prevailing.

Strategy now had to be directed at sustaining national goals while deterring nuclear war or, if deterrence failed, ending it on the best possible terms. The central questions of nuclear strategy then were related ones: What sort of forces were necessary for deterrence? How would nuclear war be fought if it nevertheless came? From these flowed the infinitely complex series of military, political, and economic considerations that had so engrossed and divided military and civilian strategists throughout the years since World War II.

When McNamara moved into the Pentagon, the extremes of nuclear discussion rested on the "newspeak" concepts of counterforce and minimum, or finite, deterrence.

Counterforce, carried out fully, implied an endless race in which U.S. power would be directed first against enemy weapons. American missiles and bombers would be trained on the potential foe's missiles in underground silos, bombers on their bases, mis-

sile submarines in port. The most obvious weakness of counterforce was that much of its effect would be wasted as long as the
United States renounced the use of nuclear weapons first—the
so-called first strike. If the enemy struck first, many of the targets
of American weapons would be missing, already destroying the
United States or on their way. Yet counterforce would require
covering all of them anyway, leaving it up to the enemy, in effect,
to determine American force levels. Counterforce dictated a
classic arms race, with possibly unbearable drain on resources.

"Pure" finite deterrence suggested that a relatively small number of weapons, protected and targeted on the Soviet population,
would deter Soviet nuclear power and leave the resolution of conflict to other means. Nikita Khrushchev, in fact, seemed to fuel
this concept with his famous speech of January 6, 1961, promising support for wars of "popular uprising" as the conflict of the
future. The great weakness of finite deterrence, however, was in
its very inflexibility. It was an all-or-nothing strategy, and if deterrence failed, then there were no alternatives beyond a spasm
of nuclear exchange.

U.S. strategy at the time was an imprecise amalgam that leaned
toward counterforce. Massive retaliation still implied a cataclysmic war in which the United States would "win" once the flash-
point was reached. Given the natures of John Kennedy, Robert
McNamara, and the men around them, it was inevitable that their
path would somehow be found nearer the center of the maze.

McNamara accepted from the beginning the capability to
retaliate—but not necessarily massively—as the fundamental
need. Then he began to refine the alternatives. This was the kind
of exercise on which he thrived. When he was in town, he could
sit at his desk an entire day probing for options, if not strategic,
then on hardware or personnel. His schedule for February 26,
1962, chosen at random, recorded his arrival at the office to read
papers at 7:10 A.M. Appointments followed at half-hour intervals
throughout the day except for "lunch at desk," recorded precisely
at 1:50 to 2:00 P.M. He headed for home at 7:30 P.M.

He saw early that somewhere there was a limit beyond which it was pointless to deploy more nuclear weapons. The world could be destroyed only once. Requirements would vary with circumstances, of course, but the implication was obvious. If the Soviet Union pushed ahead with its own missile program, a state of parity or nuclear stalemate was somewhere on the horizon. McNamara was not yet ready to confront Congress with this unvarnished prospect, however: he spoke steadily and confidently of U.S. superiority. Nonetheless, the hints of eventual parity appeared early, even as McNamara expanded American nuclear forces. Congress, for some time, seemed not to be listening closely, even though some concerned Air Force generals were talking of the need for several thousand missiles.

To prevent war by accident, the United States developed elaborate safety devices and rituals for arming and firing its nuclear weapons. To prevent war by miscalculation, it sought greater protection for its missiles—"hardening" in underground silos—so American decision-makers would have time, and enemy decision-makers would have reason, to think before acting. To hold open at least the hope of limiting war if it erupted, command and control systems were constantly refined. Over it all, McNamara and his band tried to impose a body of rational doctrine.

The nuances of the new strategy began to emerge in 1962, at times in contradictory form. McNamara first began carefully to warn U.S. allies that their heavy reliance on nuclear weapons stemmed from a dangerous delusion. In March he laid his theories out even more clearly before shaken and silent delegates at the spring NATO meeting in Athens. Then, in June, he put many of his ideas into a now-famous commencement address for the University of Michigan at Ann Arbor.

On basic nuclear strategy, he said, the Administration had concluded that primary military objectives "should be the destruction of the enemy's military forces, not of his civilian population." The strength of the alliance made it possible to "destroy an enemy society if driven to it," he elaborated, but "we are giving a possible opponent the strongest imaginable incentive to refrain from striking our own cities."

The outcry was prompt, sharp, and apparently a surprise to McNamara. Within the extremes of counterforce and finite deterrence, he had leaned toward the former. Though he later would insist that he never intended to close any alternatives, he would concede that he probably had tilted the emphasis too far at Ann Arbor. A former McNamara aide was perhaps closest to the mark: "The Ann Arbor speech was an aberration. Bob still wasn't thinking for himself. He was listening to his Whiz Kids and accepting too much of what they said at face value. In any case, he should have known there could be no such thing as primary retaliation against military targets after an enemy attack. If you're going to shoot at missiles, you're talking about first strike."

In fact, McNamara soon moved back toward the center of the strategic debate. He began to mention more frequently the outer limits of nuclear deployment. At one point he snapped at an Air Force general, "Damn it, if you keep talking about ten thousand missiles, you are talking about pre-emptive attack. Why don't you just say so?" The path the United States would follow if the Soviet Union caught up and kept building was not well lighted. Learning as he lectured Congress and a confused public, McNamara was not eager to put bluntly the outlook for nuclear parity. Americans did not like to think of themselves as being stalemated. There is no question that for a time McNamara deliberately obscured the outlook for an eventual nuclear standoff, long after he understood the prospect himself.

He edged steadily closer, however, during the summer and fall. During a television appearance in September, 1962, he acknowledged that "The value of our nuclear security may decline over time. We can, for a long time to come, we believe, maintain nuclear superiority over any possible opponent. What is doubtful, though, is that we can maintain the kind of superiority we have now and will have for at least the next few years."

In a November interview with Stewart Alsop of the *Saturday*

Evening Post, he voiced something approaching the ultimate heresy for the times. Asked whether the Soviets also would reach full retaliatory power, he answered, "Indeed, yes." He seemed, in fact, to think it was a good idea. "When both sides have a sure second-strike capability," he said, "then you might have a more stable balance of terror. This may seem a rather subtle point, but from where I'm sitting it seems a point worth thinking about." To put it another way, the Soviets, secure in the knowledge they could retaliate after an American attack, would not be tempted into the folly of a pre-emptive first strike.

By the following January McNamara was ready to outline his ideas in more detail. A year earlier he had delivered to Congress a statement setting out the Administration's views on every major international issue and projecting military capability over the next five years. In this second "posture statement," his shift back to a complete range of options toward the Soviet Union was pronounced.

In fact, he told Alsop in another interview, too much had been made of his remarks on avoiding populations in his speech at Ann Arbor.

What the United States had to have, he said, was the capability to hit the Soviet military-urban complex all at once, or to destroy as many military targets as possible first and then, if necessary, "strike back at the Soviet urban and industrial complex in a controlled and deliberate way." The pattern now was set. McNamara had rejected the rigidities of both counterforce and finite deterrence. He would claim the capability to inflict massive retaliation if necessary, or less if possible, with the strong suggestion that a vast number of weapons was unnecessary.

Soviet leaders had shown no signs of accepting the notion of limited nuclear war. In fact, their public utterances all assumed total nuclear exchange if war came. McNamara concluded this would be their position as long as their missiles remained vulnerable. But "even if we were to double and triple our forces we would not be able to destroy quickly all or almost all of the hardened ICBM sites," he said.

In short, McNamara told Congress, there was no way to win nuclear war within the normal definition of victory. "We would win," he explained, only "in the sense that their way of life would change more than ours, because we would destroy a greater percentage of their industrial potential and probably destroy a greater percentage of their population than they destroyed of ours."

Even this late, he sometimes got carried away into language that overstated his fundamental position. At times he still talked of "superiority" over the Soviets without the leavening that placed a ceiling on the arms race. "I don't believe that any time in our lifetime they will reach parity with us in the total power of their system versus ours," he told Congress in 1963. He was wrong, of course. His language was misleading, surely by choice, and the public could be forgiven for overlooking nuances when such testimony was converted into headlines like, "Lifetime Lead for U.S. Predicted by McNamara."

For a time Congress simply refused to translate what McNamara was saying into the logical consequences. When later he was accused of deception, he could point back to statements in which the implication of a nuclear standoff was quite clear. McNamara suspected that many in Congress simply did not do their homework. In 1963 and 1964, however, as he continued to cast aside the assumptions of years, the reception was increasingly anguished.

Part of it was personal. From the beginning McNamara had refused to use the customary oratorical flourishes to woo the distinguished members. "I don't believe in throwing bouquets," he told aides, instructing them to remove frills from prepared testimony. During hearings, critical queries disappeared under an avalanche of facts, knit together in precise one-two-three order. The Secretary was seemingly master of every detail in his vast organization. He knew about pay scales, helicopter production, reserve forces, even minor facts about management of the Pentagon—such detail that even friends suggested he was spreading himself too thin. What was self-confidence to his admirers became arrogance to his detractors. Military men were wounded when he rejected their professional judgment and accepted that of his civilian advisers. "There's less and less opportunity to question his decisions or to give the Secretary detached criticism," a general remarked. "Mr. McNamara shows an inclination to hog the stage and to give the impression that the Defense Department is a one-man show."

"He doesn't have much humility," a close friend of McNamara conceded dryly. "Bob's very brilliance tends to make him intolerant of those with less talent. His obvious superiority rankles some of his supposed equals a bit." The *Wall Street Journal* quoted anonymously a high officer who spoke with reluctant admiration: "Mr. McNamara is not subject to the family, socialite, and public-figure consciousness of Neil McElroy. Nor is he subject to the Ivy League inhibitions and investment-trust dignity of Thomas Gates. Mr. McNamara simply is not susceptible to any pressure—social, military, intellectual, or editorial."

A service magazine suggested that the Secretary and his civilian team lacked "a certain visceral comprehension . . . which goes beyond what the completely rational man can 'understand.' But high intelligence does not guarantee its acquisition." The article went on to mention special characteristics of armies, "their capacity for deep, prolonged, sustained continental war around the globe." What the Army needed, it concluded, "is understanding leadership." If the suggestion here was that some mystique should set aside objective evidence, obviously McNamara would reject it.

In the House, conservative Representative Leslie C. Arends bitterly accused "I-know-all-the-answers McNamara" of substituting "civilian judgment for military judgment in matters strictly military." McNamara assured Congress that he wanted to push the decision-making process down to the lowest possible level. Yet lower-level executives, he said, could not make intelligent decisions until they had a framework of basic policy—and that he was providing.

Given compelling evidence, he said, "I have no hesitance whatever in presenting a recommendation to the President that may differ from the views of the Chiefs." Until new basic policy was translated into balanced forces, the services singly could not make decisions affecting the entire defense establishment on their own. "This isn't because I like to make decisions," McNamara added. "And I don't happen to like to work six or seven days a week, twelve hours a day, but I don't know any other way to do it when passing through this transitional period."

He felt Congress was reacting with emotion rather than reason to the prospect of exotic new weapons. "You can never substitute emotion for reason," he told an interviewer. "I still would allow a place for intuition in this process, but not emotion. They say I am a power grabber. But knowledge is power, and I am giving them knowledge, so they will have more power. Can't they see that?"

Many of them couldn't. Much of the criticism flowed from arguments that the Secretary was neglecting human factors, and S. L. A. Marshall, the prominent writer on military affairs, asserted that McNamara had lost the confidence of men in uniform. Hanson Baldwin, the military editor of the *New York Times,* accused McNamara of overlooking "the importance of the human being to the military services in the nuclear age."

The controversy over the McNamara strategy had less to do with the Secretary's strong rule and with strategic theory than with the means to fulfill the theory. At one point in 1963, grumbling at McNamara's cancellation of costly weapons systems, Representative F. Edward Hébert wondered whether Congress had given the Secretary of Defense too much power over weapons. "I disagree with the philosophy that we depend on the Minuteman and the Polaris," he said.

It was a valid point, seen from the position of Congressmen

accustomed to accepting military recommendations on hardware. McNamara had settled on Polaris and Minuteman as the heart of the strategic force through the sixties and beyond. Inherited from the Eisenhower Administration, the two missiles promised relative accuracy and reliability. Above all, they fit into the maturing McNamara strategy, which included absolute power to retaliate, or, as he called it, "assured destruction," beyond all other considerations. Hébert and others argued for greater variety in the arsenal of superweapons.

Two chronic arguments over specific weapons illuminated the fundamental differences between McNamara and his critics in both Congress and the military on strategic policy. These turned upon the proposals for an advanced manned strategic aircraft (AMSA) and an antiballistic missile (ABM) system. He inherited the strategic bomber and ABM controversies, and they were still climbing the scale of intensity, though the context had changed, as he departed.

McNamara had all the best of it objectively in his first brush with the strategic bomber, for it concerned the doubtful B-70. Conceived in 1953 as a replacement for the B-52, the B-70 was supposed to fly at three times the speed of sound in high-level attack.

Skeptically, McNamara downgraded the project by asking for more development. Back came the Air Force with a plan to convert the B-70 into an RS-70, a reconnaissance-strike vehicle which would loiter outside an area of nuclear attack and find new targets for the missiles it carried, or targets which ICBMs had missed. Harking to General Curtis E. LeMay, the new Air Force Chief of Staff, the House Armed Services Committee wrote the defense appropriations bill to "direct" the Executive to spend $491 million toward deployment of the aircraft.

LeMay, the brilliant architect of the Strategic Air Command, was a hard-liner dismayed by the subtle new theories and passionately convinced the Air Force needed a new strategic bomber. McNamara was willing to keep open the possibility. But he was unconvinced that the bomber had a role in the strategy of the next decade. The action of Carl Vinson's committee, however, had cast the debate into a different context: a test of the relative powers of the executive and legislative branches of government.

The confrontation faded in March, 1962, only after President Kennedy took Vinson for a famous walk in the White House Rose Garden and persuaded him to withdraw the mandatory language. In return, Kennedy promised a thorough review of the B-70 program.

What came of the review was hardly comforting to the Air Force. In May, McNamara produced a detailed analysis that disposed of both versions of the B-70. The plane, he said, lacked the advantages of a missile and had the vulnerability of a bomber. The RS-70 required new technology that might prove unsolvable, and it promised to cost at least $10 billion.

Besides, McNamara reported solemnly, the Air Force was getting a bit carried away with its arguments. On the one hand, it was asking for a new plane because missiles were undependable. On the other hand, some of its theater commanders were asking for nuclear-armed missiles to replace their aircraft. At the same time, it was advocating an aircraft that depended for its attack capability on highly sophisticated missiles.

This came close to suggesting that the Air Force wanted a bomber just for the sake of having one. McNamara converted the entire program into the production of three experimental B-70s at a total cost of $1.3 billion. Even most of the Air Force seemed resigned, with the notable exception of LeMay. The bomber advocates retired to prepare a new approach.

The issue ran to the heart of the strategic debate, though McNamara tried to discount the extent of his disagreement with the Air Force. With varying support from the other services, LeMay insisted a new bomber was needed to vary the arsenal, to mop up after missile attacks, to force the enemy to reckon with more than one threat. To McNamara none of these arguments was persuasive: the bomber was vulnerable on the ground during those precious minutes before takeoff and, in relative terms, slow after it was airborne. "Missiles will be able to do anything bombers can do—cheaper," he told associates.

He also ruled out, in one of his first important strategic decisions, the production and deployment of the Nike-Zeus ABM system. Its mission, to intercept and destroy or neutralize incoming missiles, was spectacular. American scientists likened it to intercepting one bullet with another, actually an understated analogy. Nikita Khrushchev later put it well when he claimed, though without justification, that his experts could hit "a fly in space." The Nike-Zeus had picked up impressive support, with General Maxwell Taylor, among others, strongly urging plans for deployment. McNamara's reasoning at the time could almost be cited as an introduction to one of the great strategic debates.

Obviously, he told the Senate Armed Services Committee in 1961, a rocket that could meet and destroy another would be a great achievement. But there was serious doubt that it would work. Even if it did, it could have a contradictory strategic effect. While it would force an enemy to spend more on offense to compensate, it could nevertheless be overwhelmed by sheer numbers of less costly offensive missiles. McNamara proposed to continue development of the system, but ruled out production.

Two years later the search for ABM defenses took a significant turn. What scientists called "Penaids" (penetration aids) for offensive weapons were being developed rapidly. These were devices to confuse missile defenses—decoys, electronic jammers, and the like—and thus increase chances that offensive warheads would reach their targets. There was every reason to believe the Soviet Union was hard at work in the same area.

It also now seemed possible vastly to improve the ABM. New, incredibly sophisticated radars showed promise. An ABM system with two missiles, one (Spartan) to make long-range interceptions, the other (Sprint) to destroy missiles that penetrated the outer defense, seemed feasible. McNamara turned the emphasis on the

Nike-Zeus program into the search for a new Nike-X, focused on new technology. If successful, it would be the most complex system in an increasingly complex arsenal.

There was no doubt where McNamara was heading with his own ideas. Even as he blocked the B-70, held out firmly against a follow-on bomber, and made clear his worry at the consequences of an imperfect ABM system, he pursued offensive missile power —with limitations. As early as 1962, he set a goal of forty-one Polaris submarines as the undersea attack force necessary through the decade and into the next. The Minuteman program increased steadily, even as the missile itself was improved. By 1964 the Secretary put a ceiling of 1,000 missiles on Minuteman, dropping 200 from his own earlier plans and frustrating Air Force officers who had never gone below 1,800 in their independent projections of need.

He was not always consistent in his arguments. This was an area in which nuances were critical. The ABM discussion had a peculiarly political character. McNamara seemed satisfied with the state of ABM development as a card for negotiations with the Soviet Union, but discounted it in talk of deployment.

At the mid-sixties his basic strategic concept and his plans to fulfill it were essentially complete. He aimed to guarantee—and this required convincing the Russians—that the United States could inflict unacceptable damage on the Soviet Union even after a Soviet attack. In the end, he had rejected both counterforce and finite deterrence, as they usually were defined, and had taken a stance spanning both.

Along the way he had beaten back repeated efforts in Congress to adopt a new bomber and an ABM system, although General LeMay and those who shared his worries wielded vast influence on the Hill. In the Presidential campaign of 1964, Barry Goldwater had accused the Administration of planning "unilateral disarmament" and a "no win" policy rather than victory over Communism. Goldwater's matter-of-fact reliance on nuclear weapons chilled even most Republicans, however. After Lyndon Johnson's decisive re-election, the nation seemed briefly to be moving toward strategic stability.

McNamara had settled on a simple structure at the heart of his deterrent. Yet that did not mean the weapons themselves were unchanging. Over the years the Polaris missile was actually several missiles, from the A-1 to the A-2 to the A-3, and at the end, the Poseidon. The Minuteman evolved from the Minuteman I to the Minuteman II to the Minuteman III. Each evolutionary step represented a substantial, and costly, increase in range, accuracy, and destructive power, until finally the nation was faced with MIRV. The acronym stood for multiple independently targeted re-entry vehicle, which meant one rocket would be able to lift several warheads which would separate in space and proceed to individual targets.

These improvements in offensive missiles, as McNamara saw it, were dictated by his aim to maintain assured destruction capability. To his mind, they were in a different category from the ABM system, which, even if it worked, threatened yet another cycle in the arms race.

Yet it is easy to forget that McNamara spared nothing in development of the Nike-X. By 1966 he was spending $500 million a year on the system and more than $2.5 billion had been invested in ABM research and development. In scope, intensity, and in strategic implications it far overshadowed the debate over the bomber which, to the end, remained with him. But to the end, also, he resisted deployment of the ABM.

It was a struggle he lost, though the losing was left ambiguous by the public evidence. McNamara had held open always the possibility of ABM deployment, just as he had kept open the option of eventually producing a new strategic bomber. But there was no doubt in the mind of anyone where he stood on both. To change his thinking, advocates would have had to present compelling cases with greater certainty of success than either appeared —to him at least—to offer. Ultimately, the circumstances in which he lost developed in a gripping interplay of the forces at work on the second President he served.

For slowly the evidence grew that the Soviets were deploying their own ABM system around Moscow. Word filtered out of the Pentagon that a further, more elaborate system was being installed to protect other Soviet cities. In response, McNamara began unveiling highly secret evidence to sustain his own arguments on American security.

What emerged were dry statistics of horror almost incomprehensible to the layman. Even if the United States went for maximum ABM defenses and the Soviets failed to expand their offense, he said, a Soviet surprise attack would still take thirty million American lives. If the United States should attack first, twenty million Americans would die from Soviet retaliation. And these were the most favorable circumstances, for Moscow certainly would increase its offense to guarantee the death of ninety million Americans, even if the United States attacked first.

At this stage the Secretary was still in command of the strategic pattern. But his hold was slipping. In 1966 Congress rebelled with unprecedented ferocity. Again part of it was personal. The Secretary had silenced but alienated much of the military. He had eliminated the boondoggling military reserve units composed of Congressmen and their employees on Capitol Hill. Any hope of rapport between such a man and Mendel Rivers of South Carolina, who had succeeded Carl Vinson as chairman of the House Armed Services Committee, obviously was wasted. Rivers was an old-style politician who believed in the pork barrel as a source of good things. And he supported the military on most of the issues on which it collided with McNamara. The Secretary, moreover, persisted in closing military bases he judged to be wasteful, and military bases were important symbols of influence to members of Congress. "I don't trust that man," he said of Rivers. "He'll stab me in the back the first chance he gets."

But the criticism went beyond the personal. The Administration's miscalculations and misrepresentations on the war in Vietnam had helped create what became known as a "credibility gap." McNamara tended to overstate his own case frequently and to understate the degree of internal opposition in his Department. When he was caught short, the critics were not unhappy. More important, these personal influences combined with genuine concern over management of the war and strategic policy to cause what one senior general called the "damnedest catfight I've ever seen." For McNamara finally began fighting back in kind.

At the bitterest stage no less than five Congressional investigations were under way into McNamara's stewardship of the Pentagon. Representative Hébert of Louisiana proclaimed shock at McNamara's resistance to the strategic bomber and accused him of understating military support for the aircraft. A Pentagon spokesman promptly snapped back at an Hébert subcommittee's "digression into trivialities, insinuations . . . and failure to deal adequately or objectively with the future needs of the U.S. strategic offensive forces." Hébert returned the compliments. The McNamara response, he said, was an "insulting indictment" of a Congressional committee, "impugning its motives." To say that nerves were raw would be a monumental understatement.

Out of the storm, the pressure on the Administration grew. The Nike-X, with almost $4 billion invested in a decade of work, had reached a point in development that made it difficult to delay further basic decisions on deployment, go or no go. Congress set aside $167.9 million for procurement.

Lyndon Johnson now was being whipsawed. From liberals on the Hill came a growing cry against the war in Vietnam, but only stirrings of opposition to deployment of ABM. From the conservative side the clamor for ABM and the strategic bomber was unrelenting, along with the customary demand for a tougher policy in Vietnam. The Joint Chiefs favored going ahead with Nike-X and wanted to move more rapidly than McNamara on the bomber.

McNamara was furious at the appropriation for ABM procurement. "What the hell are we supposed to do with it?" he de-

manded privately of a committee chairman. "You don't even say
what kind of a system we're supposed to deploy." "I don't care,"
came the reply. "Just get it out there."

The Secretary summoned principal officers of Western Electric
Company, a primary contractor on the project, and asked for
their private judgment. Don't deploy, they said reluctantly, it's
not ready. McNamara regarded the self-denying recommendation
as a historic act of industrial statesmanship.

"Hold off," McNamara pleaded with the President at a series
of meetings in late 1966 at the Texas White House, "at least let
us try to get the Soviet Union to turn this thing around." For a
time Johnson agreed. He coupled a plea to the Soviets for negotiations on strategic weapons to a request to Congress for $375
million. The money was for "possible" ABM deployment in case
the political approach failed.

The arms race meanwhile was proceeding into a new phase
with little public awareness. One of McNamara's principal goals
was to push backward the date by which he would have to favor
ABM under his own guidelines. To achieve it he relied upon
greater and greater offensive power. In 1966 he set out to substitute Minuteman III for some of the earlier missiles. The following
year he announced plans to replace most of the Polaris missiles
with Poseidons.

The critical distinction of these weapons was that they could
be fitted with multiple warheads, as soon as MIRV was ready, in
addition to new penetration aids. They had greater accuracy and
range. With the deployment of MIRV, numbers of rockets as such
would lose even more of their validity as a strategic yardstick.
McNamara had never cared for the relative numbers game anyway. To him numbers were significant primarily in terms of
maintaining the power to retaliate. Some of the nation's leading
strategic analysts felt he lost perspective on the issue.

"He was so determined to build his case against the ABM, that
it wouldn't work, that he went for MIRV," one argued privately.
"He didn't notice that this might restore first-strike capability,

which he was avoiding. The Air Force thought MIRV was a splendid idea; it understood the implications fully."

McNamara himself saw no inconsistency in his course. To him the strategic differences between offensive and defensive weapons were decisive at this stage. He had long since concluded with regard to the Soviet Union that "the destruction of one-fifth to one-fourth of its population and one-half to two-thirds of its industrial capacity would mean its elimination as a major power for many years." It remained, of course, to convince Soviet leaders to accept that judgment, understand U.S. power to inflict it, and thus be deterred. For enforcement, McNamara's revised plans into the 1970s included the raw framework of 1,000 Minutemen, 496 Poseidons, 160 Polarises, 54 old Titan II missiles, and 534 B-52 bombers whose lives had been extended by rebuilding and the addition of new weapons. The number of warheads, however, would be rising with the installation of MIRV.

McNamara began to draw upon the early nuclear thinkers to remind critics of the ambiguity of numbers in the strategic debate. As early as 1946, he recalled, Bernard Brodie had observed that "superiority in numbers of bombs is not in itself a guarantee of strategic superiority in atomic bomb warfare. . . . If 2,000 bombs in the hands of either party is enough to destroy entirely the economy of the other, the fact that one side has 6,000 and the other 2,000 will be of relatively small significance." A decade later, Charles E. Wilson morosely forecast a condition in which "two parties could, as a practical matter, destroy each other." At the same time Air Force Secretary Donald Quarles looked to a time when "mutual deterrence" would prevail.

Finally, however, the numbers game took a turn that threatened to bring down the McNamara strategy in 1967.

By the end of 1966, as they built their ABM system, the Soviets had suddenly opened a parallel expansion of their ICBM force. Even as McNamara reported this publicly, he assured the nation he had taken into account just such "greater than expected" threats. But a year later he had to announce that the Russians had more than doubled their ICBM launchers—to 720—and that the number was rising. During that year his campaign against ABM had been compromised in almost bizarre fashion.

His last remote chance to relieve the pressures on Lyndon Johnson, and thus further delay ABM deployment, came in June, 1967. The occasion was the meeting between President Johnson and Premier Aleksei Kosygin at Glassboro, New Jersey.

McNamara rushed to Glassboro armed with a swiftly updated outline of variations on the possible consequences if the two governments continued the arms race. Though the statistics varied, it was essentially the prospect he had held out to Congress and the public earlier in the year. In effect, McNamara urged the Soviet Premier to apply the brakes and negotiate: neither nation, he argued, could hope to gain decisive superiority over the other. The ABM, he said, would change nothing.

Kosygin twitted McNamara about being an "arms merchant," and somewhat loftily proclaimed Soviet interest in defense rather than offense. He listened closely, but Moscow was not yet ready to accept—as it would later after McNamara, though not Johnson, had left—the offer to negotiate strategic weapons.

With that there was little for McNamara to do except make his peace with compromise. The political pressures on the President finally had become unbearable. Two themes descended clamorously from Capitol Hill: on the one hand, the military committees cried for ABM and a strategic bomber; on the other, the antiwar forces, concentrated in the Senate Foreign Relations Committee, demanded changes in American policy in Vietnam. Mr. Johnson knew or suspected at the end of that summer, as enemy strength continued to grow, that the greatest trial of the war was yet before him. McNamara's own disillusionment over the war had mounted, and his latest recommendations to the President on its conduct were hardly what Mr. Johnson hoped to hear. Thus there was a growing element of disenchantment in the relationship between two men who had observed total loyalty toward each other. The President told McNamara to yield on the ABM.

The Secretary did so in one of the remarkable utterances of an anguished period. As his vehicle, he chose a speech on September 18 before editors and publishers in San Francisco. What developed was, first of all, a plea against the arms race.

The nation's policy had been and must remain one of deterrence, he said. Deterrence would continue only through the capability to destroy any combination of aggressors. The United States had such power in abundance, he declared, and would retain it. But so did the Soviet Union. "There is, of course, no way in which the United States could have prevented the Soviet Union from acquiring its present second-strike capability," he said, "short of a massive pre-emptive first strike on the Soviet Union in the 1950s."

Unable to judge Soviet intentions, the United States had built a larger nuclear arsenal than it needed. The Soviets in turn, perhaps fearful the United States was attempting to reach the first-strike level, had responded in kind. "It is precisely this action-reaction phenomenon that fuels an arms race," McNamara said. It was high time for an agreement, first to limit, and then to reduce, strategic forces.

As for the ABM, the Soviets were wasting their money on a system against U.S. missiles. And the United States would be wasting its money on a system against a possible Soviet attack. Each, he said, could overcome the ABM by a much smaller investment in more offensive power. Up to this point, it was classic McNamara.

Then, abruptly, he turned to China. Apart from a massive ABM defense against the Soviet Union, he said, a lighter defense might be erected to protect offensive missiles or against the "modest" ICBM force China might have in the mid-seventies. The United States had total first-strike capability against China, that is, the power of absolute destruction at no risk. There was "ample evidence that China well appreciates the destructive power of nuclear weapons." Yet Peking might miscalculate, and thus there was "marginal" ground for proceeding with a light ABM deployment. "After a detailed review of all these considerations, we have decided to go forward with this Chinese-oriented ABM deployment," he said, "and we will begin actual production of such a system at the end of this year."

It was one of Robert McNamara's bitterest moments. "Bob had been whipped on the ABM," remarked one of the nation's leading strategic analysts. "But he was determined to give it the least possible chance for expansion. He chose deliberately the worst credible rationale for its deployment."

It was at once an eloquent and contradictory performance. McNamara for several years had considered the possibility that Chinese weapons might force ABM deployment eventually. Just recently, however, he had publicly judged that date to be well in the future, and little had changed in the meantime. It was the Soviet momentum, not the Chinese, that had forced the President's hand. Nonetheless, McNamara chose the Chinese rationale, hoping to curb domestic enthusiasm for a broader system and to give the Soviets an excuse against reaction if they would take it.

Far more important than the estimated $5.5 billion cost of the limited system, which the Administration called Sentinel, the breakthrough eroded barriers to another cycle in the arms race. Concentration on offensive missiles, penetration devices, multiple warheads, "hardening" of launch sites, all had carried McNamara's action-reaction phenomenon forward. He deemed these manageable so long as he held to his basic framework. Even if MIRV were installed, he felt, either side could come close in its estimate of the warheads it faced. Coming close on offensive missiles at least would leave greater stability than escalation into even more exotic weapons.

In any case, the distinctions among the various rationales for ABM deployment were more apparent than real.

This became obvious when the Nixon Administration later reoriented the system. Its name was changed from Sentinel to Safeguard. It was supposed to place greater emphasis on protec-

tion of offensive weapons, and thus preserve the power to retaliate. ABM thus became publicly more Soviet-oriented, assuming
its true colors. The Nixon plan, to protect missiles, would move
the first ABM sites to the thinly populated West. Still, as a sort of
final irony, maps of relative coverage showed that Sentinel and
Safeguard would provide essentially the same light shield over the
entire United States. The difference in coverage was slight.

McNamara, meanwhile, had lost an important fight. He would
not concede that the ABM compromise invalidated his ideas on
the kind of forces needed, however. In the larger sense, it did
nothing to the basic strategy of deterrence with flexible response;
it did threaten to make maintenance of that strategy infinitely
more costly and complex.

Ironically, the decision caused a significant turn in Congressional sentiment. Congress had polarized at conservative and
liberal extremes for and against a tougher course in Vietnam. The
conservatives, with their greatest strength in the military committees, also had represented the cause of more and bigger weapons. With McNamara's forced endorsement of the ABM, the
liberal corps suddenly came to attention and, as he departed,
began to resist the new dimensions in weaponry. It was an issue
that divided the scientific community as well as Congress. The
course of the arms race, despite Lyndon Johnson's short-term
capitulation, remained far from certain.

6

The Flying Malaprop
and Other Objects

To the innocent eye and untrained ear, October 15, 1964, seemed a day of rejoicing in the huge plant of the General Dynamics Corporation at Fort Worth, Texas. High government officials, bemedaled generals, and industrial titans gathered to look with admiration on an airplane. The occasion was the unveiling—the "rollout ceremonies"—of the first completed F-111A, a plane whose design translated advanced knowledge into practical application.

Robert McNamara, the principal speaker, greeted the rollout with an air of vindication. "This aircraft is a weapons system which some said could never be built," he said. "But it will be built and its contract will represent the largest single airplane production contract in the history of this country or any other country."

He praised the Air Force, the Navy, and the many contractors for meeting unprecedented specifications. By doing so, he said, "they have made the greatest step forward in combat aircraft design in the last several decades. The F-111 is not only a major advance in technical aircraft design but is unique in a number of respects. It's an aircraft in which we have combined a very agile fighter and pursuit plane and an aircraft with the carrying capacity of a bomber and a transport.

"It is also unique in that it is the first combat aircraft ever designed to solve the requirements of two of the services. By jointly conducting its design and development program, these two services have each acquired a highly advanced airplane tailored to their missions while spending approximately one billion dollars less than would have been spent had two separate weapons systems been pursued."

Nor was there any great restraint in the remarks of Paul H. Nitze, who was by then Secretary of the Navy: "The Navy is firmly committed to the success of this program. . . . Today's F-111 rollout gives us confidence that the joint Air Force–Navy team, working with General Dynamics, Grumman, Pratt & Whitney, Hughes, and many other contractors, will give us the finest weapons system ever produced for the achievement of air superiority. The F-111 provides the final line in our carrier weapons system armor and will help to insure that our carriers can fulfill their vital roles in the 1970s and the 1980s."

The object of all this attention was an odd-looking machine by familiar standards, and odder according to when one looked. For the F-111 was the first production model plane with wings that could be swung forward and backward from their roots in the fuselage during flight. Beyond that, it looked like a fighter but seemed big enough to be a bomber. Its cockpit, with the two-man crew sitting side by side, gave it a slightly humped appearance.

Despite the rhetoric in Fort Worth, the F-111 was a creature of trouble. Its tortured past had inspired McNamara's attitude of vindication. Yet its future remained uncertain enough even in late 1964 to make any optimism premature. The rollout fanfare at Fort Worth proved to be only a pause in the storm.

Almost every claim McNamara made for the F-111 that day was in smoldering dispute. The Air Force and Navy indeed had worked on the plane together, but it was a shotgun marriage with McNamara holding the gun. The controversy plumbed old issues of interservice rivalry, of civilian control over the military, of executive-legislative prerogative. It sharpened, and left largely unresolved, the questions raised by Dwight D. Eisenhower about the multibillion-dollar military-industrial complex. For almost seven years the furor over the F-111 tested McNamara's awesome abilities. Even more, however, it dramatized his weaknesses. For that matter, few who touched the F-111 would walk away with their image enhanced.

McNamara first encountered the idea for an especially versatile fighter-bomber before he had been in the Pentagon a month. It had been left unresolved by his predecessor, both because the necessary technical advances were quite recent and because Eisenhower did not want to commit his successor to an expensive weapon.

In the Air Force's Tactical Air Command, General F. F. Everest was looking for a fighter-bomber to do things fighter-bombers weren't supposed to be able to do: fly both very high and slow, and also very low at supersonic speeds. His ideal plane also could fly across the Atlantic nonstop. It then could be flown from short, unfinished European fields—glorified cow pastures—and thus escape the nuclear attack that surely would fall upon conventional airfields if war came. It all sounded as if General Everest were asking too much, except that he knew of technical progress outside his command. While he was charting his requirements in 1959–60, others were working independently on the designs that would meet them. At the Langley research center of the National Aeronautics and Space Agency, a team headed by John Stack, a pioneer in flight engineering, solved the problem of the variable-sweep wing.

Little knowledge of aerodynamics is required to understand the advantage of a wing that can be moved in flight. For slow flight, and particularly slow high-altitude flight, maximum extension of the wing is required to obtain the greatest lift from the thin air. For supersonic flight, especially fast low-level flight, the opposite is true; the plane must be more rugged to withstand the buffeting of the air, and the ideal shape is something like that of a child's delta-shaped paper airplane. Stack's wing could be extended for takeoff from short, rough fields, for slow flight which would keep the plane in the air for long periods. It could be swept back during flight both for high-speed, low-level bombing runs beneath enemy radar and for aerial combat. The aircraft design that included General Everest's requirements, along with the variable wing, was called the TFX—for Tactical Fighter, Experimental.

All the while the Navy had been searching for its own next plane, to perform what it called the fleet defense role. The mission required a plane that could loiter at high altitudes over its ships for hours, guarding them with a sophisticated missile system against aerial attack. As originally conceived, this would be a subsonic aircraft, carrying a huge radar system in its nose. In the final months of the Eisenhower Administration, the Navy began to think of greater versatility in this aircraft, including supersonic speed.

Both the Navy and Air Force projects were suspended, however, with the approach of a new Administration. Defense Secretary Tom Gates wanted to avoid committing his successor to major weapons systems.

All these elements were waiting when McNamara took office. The new team had hardly found its desks when Paul Nitze's study group on limited war—one of the four basic analyses McNamara ordered immediately—recommended a multiservice fighter-bomber program. As a colleague described McNamara's reaction: "His eyes lit up like a pinball machine." For one determined to build both conventional and nuclear forces at the same time—while saving money—commonality had a ringing appeal.

McNamara's first reaction was to order studies of the feasibility of building a single basic fighter-bomber, based on the TFX, for all tactical missions—including ground support of troops. He soon yielded on the ground-support role in the face of unanimous opposition. But the Air Force and Navy, especially the latter, also balked on the concept of a joint fighter-bomber. Their missions, they argued, were too far apart to be resolved in a single plane. The Navy wanted a light plane that could operate easily from its carriers; it did not, its spokesmen argued, need the weight, size, range, and ruggedness demanded by the Air Force. The Air Force wanted a plane that weighed no less than 75,000 pounds, the Navy one that weighed no more than 55,000.

Faced with a deadlock, McNamara began to move in the summer of 1961 toward his first critical decision. Behind all the technical arguments, he faced historic forces of interservice rivalry, and he knew it. In May Navy Secretary John B. Connally warned him that compromise designs were still "too large and expensive, and we neither need nor want them on our carriers."

If the joint plane was absolutely necessary, Connally went on, then the Navy should be in charge because of its stricter requirements. McNamara was unpersuaded. In June he ordered Air Force Secretary Eugene M. Zuckert to develop the TFX as the successor to the Air Force's F-105 and the Navy's F-4.

The services haggled, appealed, compromised slightly, tried to reverse the decision for commonality. In August they were still deadlocked. Finally, in a memorandum of September 1, McNamara took the issue out of their hands. "A single aircraft for both the Air Force tactical mission and the Navy fleet air defense mission will be undertaken," he ordered. "The Air Force shall proceed with the development of such an aircraft." Then he decreed the technical outlines—of weight and dimensions—on which the services had stalled. Finally he ordered that changes in the Air Force version to accommodate the Navy be held to a minimum.

The shotgun wedding was thereby performed. McNamara was showing increasing impatience with the intransigence of the services. Their resistance to a common plane, "based on years of going separate ways, was understandable," he commented with calm certainty later. "I did not consider it a realistic approach, considering the versatility and capabilities that could be built into modern aircraft." Thus the burden of conflicting civilian-

military judgment, as well as interservice rivalry, was added to
the weight problems of the TFX.

These proved to be major but unmeasurable factors in the TFX
controversy. The services saw forced commonality as a threat to
their separate identities. Weapons development was an area in
which military judgment must prevail—but here was the new
Secretary of Defense, with ultimate arrogance, making these decisions for them. There were other, more important ones to come.
If commonality was a controversial decision, McNamara's choice
of a contractor had greater immediate impact—though he declared bluntly that "the first was far more important."

Defense Department procedure called for bidders on a major
weapons system to go through an elaborate screening process.
Pentagon evaluation groups studied the proposals from aircraft
builders and submitted their own findings to a Source Selection
Board. Gradually the recommendations worked their way up to
the Secretary of Defense. Early in the competition for the TFX,
the choice came down to two contractors, the Boeing Company
and the General Dynamics Corporation. The latter proposed to
develop and build the plane with Grumman Aircraft as primary
subcontractor.

Four times in late 1961 and during most of 1962 the two firms
submitted, revised, and resubmitted their proposals. Military
analysts showed an early preference for Boeing, which had started
a year ahead of General Dynamics in meeting the variable-wing
challenge. At one point the Navy, using to the fullest its limited
veto power, almost got the program killed: McNamara saved it
by authorizing changes in the plane to meet Navy demands.
Finally, with the fourth competition, both companies produced
what the services agreed were acceptable designs.

Yet unanimously the military agreed that the Boeing designs
were superior, offering more airplane for less money. Unanimously its leaders recommended accordingly.

On November 21, 1962, the thunderbolt struck. The Pentagon
announced that a $439 million contract for development of

twenty-two prototype TFXs—now the F-111—would go to General Dynamics. McNamara, backed by Zuckert, Navy Secretary Fred Korth, who had succeeded Connally, and Deputy Defense Secretary Roswell Gilpatric, had overruled one colonel, four major generals, six lieutenant generals, five generals, five rear admirals, one admiral, and literally hundreds of lesser rank. He went ahead with the contract though he soon knew he was heading into even greater controversy. Only hours before the first commitment went to General Dynamics from the Air Force, the Department received a request for delay from Senator John L. McClellan of Arkansas. McClellan was chairman of the potent Permanent Subcommittee on Investigations, which, he said, planned an inquiry. Gilpatric, acting for McNamara, refused to hold up the contract.

Without question the award to General Dynamics was McNamara's responsibility; the support by his service Secretaries was a bonus. The immediate question in Washington was: Why?

There were obvious political implications. The Vice President, the former Secretary of the Navy, and the new Secretary were all Texans. General Dynamics would build the F-111 at its Fort Worth plant. Texas and New York—where Grumman would participate—commanded electoral votes (sixty-nine) far surpassing those of Washington (nine), where Boeing made its headquarters in Seattle, and Kansas (eight), where the F-111 would have been produced at Boeing's Wichita plant. Both Texas and New York went to Kennedy in 1960; neither Kansas nor Washington did. General Dynamics was facing serious economic trouble: it was ending production of the B-58 bomber, and it recently had taken a severe $425 million loss on commercial jets.

"Neither so-called nor actual socioeconomic factors entered into it," McNamara said firmly. Later he would respond, "Absolutely none," when McClellan asked him if Vice President Johnson's Texas origin had any bearing. Kennedy himself told reporters flatly that the choice of a contractor was a Defense Department decision.

Yet the political signs were there. The obvious need for the

President to know of such a massive contract contributed to them. At one point early in the TFX contest, McNamara sent Zuckert and Korth a memorandum of a single sentence: "I have told the President that we propose to discuss with him our recommendations regarding the final award of the TFX contract before the contract is let."

Zuckert also revealed, after McClellan's subcommittee investigation got under way, that McNamara had told the President before evaluation of the fourth round of proposals that "it looks as if General Dynamics would be chosen." Kennedy might easily have been looking at both the economic and political considerations as the contest progressed. The faintest hint from him that, other things being equal, an award to General Dynamics might be desirable obviously would have influenced McNamara. In any case, McNamara visited the White House to tell the President of the pending decision on November 13, eight days before the announcement was made. That Kennedy approved the choice is certain. It may be significant that some former members of White House and Pentagon inner circles are convinced that he at least indicated his preference.

"Only two men ever really knew the answer to that," one of this group commented, "and one of them is dead." McNamara, understandably, simply would not discuss the point.

It is unquestionably true, however, that the reasons he cited for the award to General Dynamics were precisely the sort that would appeal to him, politics aside.

With the fourth evaluation of the Boeing and General Dynamics proposals, the services had agreed that both contractors were capable and had submitted designs suitable as starting points for the TFX. General Dynamics had even registered slightly higher in the weighted scoring system. But Boeing had included more technological innovations and promised better performance at less cost. Military men therefore opted for Boeing.

Air Force analysts recognized that cost estimates by both companies were unrealistically low—that industry once again was "inserting the thin edge of the wedge." Their own revisions projected a total cost of $7 billion, against estimates of $5.455 billion by General Dynamics and $5.364 billion by Boeing.

McNamara did not believe the F-111 needed the performance or advanced features proposed by Boeing. The plane already was enough of a challenge with the very minimum of innovations. Boeing, he concluded, had too little experience with lighter planes, while General Dynamics, after all, had produced the supersonic F-102 and F-106 fighters and the B-58 bomber. Besides, General Dynamics offered greater commonality between the Air Force and Navy planes.

Equally important, McNamara argued that General Dynamics had shown a more realistic sense of costs, though even its estimates were too low. In essence, then, McNamara's position was that he was fitting the F-111 realistically into overall defense needs and resources, while the military was focused on its parochial interests in a single area.

At $7 billion, the F-111 program would be by far the biggest such project the United States had ever undertaken. The company that developed the plane would, of necessity, build it in volume. The services were thinking at the time of about 1,700 planes, 1,400 of them for the Air Force. McNamara knew it would cost even more than the Air Force estimates—but he did not know how much more. He was certain, at least, that the cost variables were great enough to render irrelevant the differences between the Boeing and General Dynamics proposals. It was a difficult argument to sustain, however. By accepted standards, if bid figures and estimates were not relevant, then what was?

At the same time McNamara was trying to develop a contracting system that would prevent deliberate underestimates on major new weapons. The familiar and much criticized cost-plus-fixed-fee contract had been used most often in the past. As defense challenged the outer reaches of science, there were too many unknowns for industry to be able to finance development; the risks were too vast. Instead, it had spent what was necessary, its fee was fixed, and the government picked up the tab.

For the F-111 program, McNamara planned a fixed-price-incentive-fee arrangement. A target price was fixed. A higher figure was agreed upon as the ceiling, and the contractor's profit would vary as he remained below (wishful thought), met, or went above the target price. Above the ceiling, he would be totally responsible for overruns. There was an obvious major exception, one which proved to be sadly applicable in the F-111 program: the government would pick up the tab for any program changes it ordered.

McNamara's decisions had a galvanic effect on the McClellan subcommittee, already once rebuffed by the Pentagon. The crusty Arkansas Democrat was chairman of both the Senate Committee on Government Operations and the offspring Subcommittee on Investigations. One of the subcommittee's more prominent members was Henry M. Jackson, Democrat, of Washington, who had an interest of long standing and had developed expert knowledge in issues of national security. Senator Jackson, who had just watched his constituency lose a sizable portion of at least $7 billion, asked for an investigation. On the basis of the bid figures alone, he had little choice.

McNamara thought he had smoothed over McClellan's irritation at the refusal to delay the initial contract award. In a talk with the chairman, he explained his reasons for choosing General Dynamics. McClellan, apparently convinced, suggested that his hearings would last only a few days. Through it all ran the strong implication that things would quiet down once Senator Jackson had done his duty for his constituents. In that light, McNamara elected to delay presenting his own case until the final stage of the hearings. Even when they formally opened on February 26, 1963, McClellan remarked that "We anticipate the committee will be occupied with this investigation for some five or six hearing days."

From the viewpoint of the Pentagon's civilian leaders, the closed proceedings immediately turned sour. The committee had made special arrangements to give reporters censored testimony daily. Inevitably, the first five hearing days produced a flood of evidence from those who had favored the Boeing plane. News accounts thus ran heavily against the choice of General Dynamics. For most of the public, this was the first exposure to the controversy. On the face of it, the facts hinted scandal: potential contracts for billions of dollars awarded against unanimous military advice.

The hearings might still have been rescuable from McNamara's standpoint. There is some evidence that McClellan already felt he had been misled on the facts by the Secretary of Defense. Some officials sympathetic to McNamara believed the Administration should have conceded that local economic conditions and the need to preserve the General Dynamics production base had tipped the balance. In fact, McClellan even told a reporter for *Aviation Week* magazine that he could accept the decision if McNamara would admit the government wanted to keep the almost idle General Dynamics plant open in the interest of national defense. But McNamara, with customary stubbornness, remained adamant: the best design had won, he insisted, though it had been close. Instead of conceding, he counterattacked.

The first assault came from Arthur Sylvester, the vinegary Assistant Secretary for Public Affairs. Sylvester was a former journalist, with a quick temper. In a briefing for reporters on March 8, he snorted that "obviously, you will hardly get a judicial rendering by a committee in which there are various Senators with state self-interest in where the contract goes. So there is only one Senator I have seen on the committee, Senator Muskie, who hasn't got an interest in it." Sylvester was not only indiscreet; his remarks were unprovable.

Subcommittee members were furious, and McClellan "invited" him in to testify. Sylvester wrote a letter which some of those offended chose to interpret as an apology. But when he testified the following week, he hardly sounded repentant. Indeed, he managed to make the argument that "a contract has been let, and an effort is being made by the disgruntled losers to knock the contract down."

McNamara's next move came the day after Sylvester's briefing.

The Secretary wrote McClellan a letter in which he argued sharply
that the committee was developing the TFX affair out of context.
"Neither the committee members nor the public have had an
overall framework in which they can put the testimony of individual witnesses in perspective," he said. "In my judgment, the
fragmentary release of portions of the testimony of witnesses, who
themselves are only familiar with part of the considerations underlying the decision in question, have needlessly undermined public
confidence in the integrity and judgment of the highest officials
in the Department of Defense." Then he claimed the right of an
injured party to submit a statement "of relevant facts" in advance
of his formal testimony. It covered familiar ground for all who
had been involved in the TFX affair. From McNamara's standpoint, however, it was the first public exposition of the aircraft's origins and his reasons for choosing General Dynamics to
build it.

The episode did nothing to endear McNamara to McClellan.
The committee chairman fully understood that the Secretary of
Defense was treating him as an adversary. In fact, it rapidly became clear that McClellan felt McNamara and his principal aides
had erred, at best, in their handling of the TFX. Objectivity was
a quality that quickly deteriorated whenever it cropped up in the
TFX imbroglio.

The Pentagon's third counterattack in rapid succession came
from Roswell Gilpatric. In another of those ill-fated back-
grounders, the Deputy Secretary conveyed the idea that the
McNamara team had been double-crossed into thinking the hearings would be perfunctory. "Pentagon Cries Foul Over TFX," the
Washington *Post* announced. This time Gilpatric was called in
for a roasting. Committee investigators began to dig more deeply
into his relationship with his former law firm in New York, and
their relations, in turn, with General Dynamics.

In the supercharged atmosphere every development made headlines. There was a flurry over the publication of an Air Force
report that charged that committee investigators had browbeaten

witnesses. McNamara, who said he thought all copies of the report were locked up, remarked that the leak "gave me indigestion." There was another when the officer charged with investigating the leak proposed to use lie detectors on the service Secretaries, among others. McNamara stopped that.

Near the end of March he still had hope of holding the noise level down in what he could see only as a needlessly divisive dispute. The responsibility for the decision was his, he said, for the reasons he gave, and that ought to be the end of it. In an appearance before the committee on March 21, he told McClellan he felt "tremendous harm" would befall many individuals as a result of the hearings. The exchange that followed richly represented his mood:

McCLELLAN: . . . I think that we had better go on and try to make a record here and get the facts on the record, so that there will be no further doubt about what the truth is.

McNAMARA: Mr. Chairman, I know that that is your desire and intention and I hope that that is the result. I don't believe it will be. Last night when I got home at midnight, after preparing for today's hearing, my wife told me that my own 12-year-old son had asked how long it would take for his father to prove his honesty.

McCLELLAN: Well, don't you think that is true with all of us in public?

McNAMARA: I call it harm and not good.

McCLELLAN: I feel strongly about it too. I have been charged with about everything, and I have the same sentiment and feeling as you. But I have a duty to perform, and I don't think that I ought to shirk that duty.

McNAMARA: I don't believe that you should, but I don't believe any good is going to come of it.

SENATOR JACKSON: Mr. Secretary, some of us, as you heard this morning, have been subjected to some rather serious charges from anonymous sources. I am sure you don't condone that sort of thing.

McNAMARA: I do not. I call it harm. I don't call it good.

JACKSON: That is what I am talking about.

McNAMARA: That is harm.

JACKSON: Of course it is, but if you have to get the truth and the facts out, some of these things happen. I have not accused anyone in the Department of anything and I don't know anyone in the committee has. I have not.

McNAMARA: I don't believe you have. But the press of this country has been fully implicit that I am either subject to political influence, self-interest, or stupid, and I call that harm.

Some of McNamara's staff would report later that the emotion was not entirely spontaneous. In any case the moment of near pathos passed quickly, though the same hardly could be said for the hearings. They ground on, revealing publicly the mountain of support that had accumulated within the military for the Boeing plane. The work statistics themselves were impressive: more than 200 specialists had spent 275,000 man-hours appraising the competing designs—and had opted for Boeing.

Both Admiral George W. Anderson, the Chief of Naval Operations, and General Curtis E. LeMay, the Air Force Chief of Staff, professed astonishment at McNamara's choice of General Dynamics. Neither, of course, had any fondness for the Secretary of Defense. He and Anderson had clashed during the Cuban missile crisis, and the McNamara-LeMay differences over strategic weapons were notorious. In far broader terms than the F-111, McNamara's assertion of control over the Pentagon had created a fundamental civilian-military cleavage.

Two of McNamara's principal aides proved also to be vulnerable in the psychological war. Gilpatric had done considerable work for General Dynamics as a partner in the New York law firm of Cravath, Swain and Moore before entering this latest tour in the Pentagon. Officially, he had severed his connections with the firm, but its insurance underwriters, at least, recorded him as being on leave of absence. And in the meantime Cravath, Swain and Moore had become principal counsel to General Dynamics. All this time, Gilpatric was drawing $20,000 a year under a severance agreement with the partnership. None of this had been a secret to the Administration—but it raised a clear question whether Gilpatric should have ruled himself out of the TFX decision. After grueling weeks of testimony and debate, the committee was divided about evenly on the question, with McClellan declaring Gilpatric should have disqualified himself. The Justice Department, however, ruled that Gilpatric was innocent of any legal conflict of interest.

The Deputy Secretary, out of presumed necessity, had insisted that his return to his former law firm was not a certainty. When he finally left the Pentagon in January, 1964, a year later than he had planned, he returned, of course, to Cravath, Swain and Moore as a senior partner. His case was a dramatic illustration of a chronic problem in government, especially defense: how to obtain qualified men for key positions without forcing them into preposterous fiction or into abandonment of their established careers. "I have full confidence in Roswell Gilpatric," McNamara said firmly. "His integrity and devotion to public service are unassailable."

Fred Korth's case held fewer ambiguities. A former Assistant Secretary of the Army, he had returned to the Pentagon from the presidency of the Continental National Bank of Fort Worth. At the very beginning he told Congress he intended to return to the bank after his government service. Korth retained $160,000 worth of stock in his bank, where General Dynamics had obtained a $400,000 portion of a larger loan during its lean months. The potential for embarrassment was glaring.

The Navy Secretary insisted firmly that as "a man of integrity" he was not influenced by these considerations. He was, in fact, irritated that Senator Karl E. Mundt of South Dakota persisted in calling him "Mr. Fort Worth" and "Mr. General Dynamics."

Unfortunately for Korth, he was a letter writer. Moreover, he was unable to subdue his interest in the bank's affairs. According to letters unearthed by the committee investigators, bank officials wrote Korth after he became Navy Secretary, thanking him for securing small accounts. His letters to former associates in Texas included invitations to come up for a visit aboard the Navy yacht

Sequoia, and some of these personal letters went out on his official stationery. It was all a bit too much for the Administration. The Justice Department saw no legal violation in the Korth affair either, but Attorney General Robert Kennedy suggested that a resignation was in order. Korth complied in October, citing the demands of private business.

Somewhat wryly, President Kennedy remarked that "I have no evidence that Mr. Korth acted improperly in the TFX matter. It has nothing to do with any opinion I may have about whether Mr. Korth might have written more letters and been busier than he should have been in one way or another."

From McNamara's standpoint, of course, these were burdensome digressions, and they were, indeed, largely irrelevant to the TFX debate. His own case already was difficult enough to make. He had changed the familiar rules, first by underscoring commonality, then by deciding, in effect, that performance which was not needed could be compromised to achieve it. His attitude on this point was summed up in a remark to an associate: "The military feels it has to have every bright, shiny new gadget that comes along, no matter how much it costs. I think we ought to buy what we need."

Yet he contributed to the difficulty of his own position. He had argued from the start that the decision for a single plane instead of two would save $1 billion. There was a minor sensation when Albert W. Blackburn, an engineer and former test pilot who had become a Pentagon expert on the TFX, told the committee the $1 billion was a hypothetical figure, generated even before the bidding had started. McNamara persisted in using it long after it had any possible relevance. The point was not that he was wrong —the savings from successful commonality might have been more or less or nonexistent—but rather that there was no reliable guide once the controversy developed.

In public relations terms, McNamara was even more vulnerable on another point of statistics—or rather the absence of them. He had acted upon experience in industry and, briefly, in the Pentagon when he ruled the Boeing, General Dynamics, and Air Force cost estimates to be unreliable. Yet he had nothing on paper to substitute for them. The atmosphere in the committee, as one witness recalled it, rippled with mixed satisfaction, frustration, and awe when Comptroller General Joseph Campbell and his aides testified that McNamara and Zuckert had acted on "rough judgment" rather than on independent cost analysis. "Both Secretaries told us they were relying upon their experience in the field previously," explained a member of Campbell's staff. "And that they were able to make rough judgments."

The McClellan investigation ventilated the unhappy TFX affair until November 20, when it was recessed routinely "subject to call." Two days later President Kennedy was assassinated and McClellan let it drop—though he would return to the attack often in other forums. The hearings had opened up many rivalries, suspicions, and questions of judgment—but they proved little. McClellan's "five or six hearing days" had expanded to almost nine months.

It is fair to say that the TFX itself never recovered from the hearings, even if the human principals did. Its difficulties, both physical and political, were tremendous. Hardly had development begun when engineers discovered that the already controversial Navy version would be even heavier than had been expected. Both the Navy and Air Force compromised their requirements, and still the Navy model was too heavy.

A reducing campaign went from WIP (Weight Improvement Program) to SWIP (Super Weight Improvement Program) to something called SCRAPE—which was almost literally that. Materials were substituted in some cases in order to lose only a few ounces. The greater the weight of a fighter, the greater the landing and takeoff speeds. The greater the speeds, the more constricting the limits of a carrier deck. When devices were installed to permit landing at slower speeds, pilots found the new angle of approach denied them a view of the deck. That called for still further correction.

Apart from the Navy's special problems, a mismatch of air intakes with engines caused loss of power in flight. More redesigning. And out of all this, the costs began to soar. Estimates for the Air Force model went to $5 million per plane; those for the Navy version, including its Phoenix missile system—which also encountered delays—went above $8 million.

When test planes began flying in 1965, there came the inevitable accidents that occur with every advanced aircraft. Though the Pentagon insisted the rate was consistent with previous experience, the history of the F-111 gave each accident a special significance. Ironically, the variable wing worked almost without a hitch in the early tests, though it, too, began to give trouble later.

Through it all McNamara proceeded with a total determination and surface confidence which was typical but which did little to improve his credibility. Early in the controversy he argued that, of the two decisions on commonality and choice of contractors, the first had worked out "to the satisfaction of everyone." It was, at best, wishful thinking. Unwisely, he cited the TFX as the sort of thing he was doing to avoid repeating the expensive mistakes of the past.

"All too often," he testified at one point, "large-scale weapons system developments, and even production programs, have been undertaken before we had clearly defined what was wanted and before we had clearly determined that there existed a suitable technological base on which to draw in developing a system." Now, he said, "we do our thinking and planning before we start bending metal." Congressmen have long memories on such remarks.

The problems persisted even after the F-111A, the Air Force model, went into production and prototypes of the F-111B, the Navy version, took to the air. McClellan and his supporters continued their periodic assaults. But McNamara, with apparent confidence, announced plans to create an FB-111, a bomber model to take over from the older B-52s, and an RF-111 reconnaissance plane. Unimpressed Pentagon cartoonists promptly created for private viewing two additional planes, a DDT-111 with spouts for crop-dusting, and a VTOL-111 which would land and take off vertically by flapping its wings.

As development faltered, McNamara stepped directly into the management process himself. His intervention was of questionable value. Some felt his talent more than offset the nervousness of subordinates aware that the boss was looking directly over their shoulders. Through most of 1966 McNamara summoned widely scattered aerospace executives and military specialists from throughout the nation for a series of Saturday morning seminars with a single purpose—to make the F-111 work.

The Navy model, Nitze said at one point during that period, "is a plane we must make work." In the Senate John McClellan cried, "Why? Why?"

In the military, generals and admirals developed a bewildering ambivalence. Stated requirements for the plane first went up, then down. There was even a period when the Navy's leading uniformed spokesmen seemed convinced their plane would perform from carriers—at weights they had once deemed horrendous.

As McNamara's tour in the Pentagon ended, however, positions had been sorted out in predictable fashion. The F-111A had performed moderately well in combat bombing tests in Vietnam, though three planes—and four lives—were lost through malfunction or pilot error. It no longer represented exuberant hope for a multimission fighter-bomber which would solve most of the Air Force's tactical problems for years to come. At best, it seemed capable of a limited role in the forces of the next decade.

The troubled Navy version, however, was doomed. Even when the Navy itself seemed anxious to save the plane in 1967, McClellan and his allies in Congress restricted production to seven test planes. Only a few weeks after McNamara's departure, Congress, with the Pentagon's concurrence, killed the production program entirely. But now the Navy was already planning its own successor plane, the F-14, which would draw heavily upon the experience with the overweight, underperforming F-111B. It promised to cost more than $13 million a copy.

Experience with the TFX had proved McNamara to be eminently correct on one point: his rejection of the original cost figures from both Boeing and General Dynamics. If the TFX case had not demonstrated the unreality of both estimates, the cost outlook for the F-14 did so.

It was cold comfort for McNamara, however. Commonality as he envisioned it had been abandoned. He had, in short, been defeated on the most important premise from which he had launched the project.

After it was all over, the reasons for the failure were frustratingly ambiguous. First the demand, then the compromises, for commonality had antagonized the services. They in turn had gained powerful support in Congress. McNamara himself, with his implacable certainty, had infuriated both. "If he had just been able to change his mind once it was made up," a senior general once mused, "how different it might have been. If he had been able to go to Congress and say, 'Gentlemen, last year I said it would have to be done this way. I was wrong. Now we must do it another way.'"

Others close to McNamara believed the Navy, with its tight requirements and its extensive experience in the field, might have saved the program if it had been in charge. Or if greater design concessions had been made to the Navy. Or if Boeing had been selected over General Dynamics.

The supreme irony of the TFX case, however, came in McNamara's own judgment after the fact. For he, too, believed the F-111 probably should not have been undertaken. Individuals thoroughly familiar with his views are certain on this point. At the end as at the beginning, he believed commonality was a valid concept, that it had been proved when the Air Force reluctantly adopted the Navy F-4 as a basic weapon in 1962. But the F-4, of course, had not had to survive the bickering of two masters from its inception. McNamara believed, moreover, that goodwill across the board, in Congress and in the military, would have saved the F-111 program as he planned it. With wry acknowledgment of political reality, he would concede that he possibly should have chosen Boeing as the contractor—because then the military, which favored Boeing, might have gone all out to make it work.

His final disenchantment with the TFX stemmed, however, from the fact that there had been no systems analysis at the beginning—that is, no civilian study as to what really was needed and how that need might best be met. "We didn't see the damned thing until it came time to defend it before the McClellan committee," one of McNamara's specialists reported with exasperation later.

McNamara himself ultimately concluded that the F-111, particularly the Air Force model, was undertaken without demonstration of a clear need. No one really knew, he felt, what its mission was to be, what was required to perform it, and what it would do that couldn't be done with existing planes. The F-111A was a good plane, he thought, but it did not add enough to existing capability to justify the project.

Needless to say, the premise for that conclusion was not shared widely within the Air Force. To the suggestion that his service had not really made a case for their original TFX, one general retorted briskly: "McNamara might not have understood what the plane was for. The Air Force did."

In any case, Alain Enthoven, the young McNamara protégé who became Assistant Secretary for Systems Analysis, recommended heavy reduction in the Air Force program soon after McNamara left and after the Navy plane had been killed. The bomber model should be abandoned, he said, and the fighter-bomber could well be cut back sharply.

At the end of the decade, final judgment on the F-111A was still pending. Once the total costs of the program were in, it would surely be recognized as a very expensive, very compromised airplane indeed—several billions of dollars for fewer than half the 1,400 planes originally planned.

McNamara himself felt he had learned something from the TFX. "It's not the military-industrial complex that represents danger," he remarked once. "That involves only money. I worry more about the military-Congressional complex. That involves the security of the country."

The TFX was an unhappy monument, at best, to the McNamara tenure in the Pentagon. It was by far the most visible weapons system—or "hardware"—development during his seven years. The Kennedy and Johnson Administrations presented nothing so publicly dramatic, so easily understood, as the introduction of atomic weapons, or of intercontinental rockets. Most of their hardware innovations, however important and complex, were in the nature of follow-on developments: multiple warheads, the Nike-X antimissile system, the introduction of nuclear power for aircraft carriers. McNamara, moreover, became embroiled in controversy on almost every important project.

The issue of nuclear power for surface ships was a spectacular example. Once again McNamara changed the rules. In the TFX case, he had failed to employ his management tools early enough by his own standards. The application of nuclear power to aircraft carriers, however, pitted McNamara along with his cost-effectiveness team for a time against almost everyone else in the military-Congressional complex.

Even the Navy came late to nuclear propulsion for its vessels. The Joint Congressional Committee on Atomic Energy practically had to force the nuclear-powered submarine fleet onto a reluctant Defense Department in the fifties. Technical director throughout was Vice Admiral Hyman G. Rickover. The Admiral, a slightly built, abrasive specialist, so offended his colleagues that he had to be saved from forced retirement by Congress. But Rickover was highly effective as a nuclear-propulsion advocate. When the Kennedy Administration came to Washington, the nuclear-powered submarine fleet, the big carrier *Enterprise,* the cruiser *Long Beach,* and the frigate *Bainbridge* were well along, and another frigate was almost ready for funding.

For a while the Navy was not at all sure it wanted nuclear power for other surface ships, however. The additional costs seemed astronomical. But as the new nuclear vessels came into service, their performance won over the last of the Navy diehards. While Navy enthusiasm grew, McNamara remained skeptical.

His doubts grew out of his mathematics of cost effectiveness, which were nonsense to Rickover and many others. Cost effectiveness indicated a declining role for the aircraft carrier. With the growth of the missile force, and given the vulnerability of the carrier, its utility for general war appeared doubtful. McNamara conceded the continuing value of the carrier for limited war —for flexible response—and he granted that the costs of nuclear power were being reduced. But he still judged them to be prohibitive. Against the unanimous recommendation of the Atomic Energy Commission, the Joint Committee, and the Navy, he ordered in late 1963 the construction of a carrier with conventional power.

Some commentators suggested that his decision was a factor in the resignation of Navy Secretary Fred Korth, who favored nuclear power, a few days later. In view of Korth's problem with the TFX affair, this seems most doubtful. In any case the decision once again put McNamara in the position of tilting against the inevitable.

Arguments that nuclear power represented "the best" impressed him not at all. "We would be fools" to buy on that basis, he said. "We would be foolish if we bought the best . . . in terms of speed and range and firepower when we don't need it." As for need and relative cost, he argued, conventional power was still the best buy. The Joint Committee, however, suggested strongly that he was loading the cost figures against nuclear power. It concluded that over the life of a carrier, nuclear power was only fractionally more expensive.

McNamara was particularly unimpressed by arguments that nuclear power provided great advantage by cutting down sharply on the need for supply ships. Nuclear carriers created a splendid image of self-sufficiency as long as they weren't fighting, he conceded. But when battle came, the logistics line of ships required for aircraft fuel and ammunition shattered the illusion. In any case, the carrier that became the *John F. Kennedy* was built for conventional fuel. It was the last.

Before he left office, McNamara spoke at the launching of the *Kennedy*. Caroline Kennedy was the sponsor—her mother the matron of honor—at the ceremonies on May 27, 1967, at the Newport News Shipbuilding and Drydock Company. The Secretary of Defense, by then beleaguered on many fronts, barely made it through his brief speech before emotion overwhelmed him. His voice faltered, the words slurred, before he turned away from the microphone, head bowed.

President Johnson himself signaled the change for later carriers even before the keel for the *Kennedy* was laid. On September 8, 1964, he announced development of "a new, very high-powered, long-lived reactor" which "will make nuclear power more attractive in the construction of aircraft carriers." Two of these, he said, could power a carrier, in contrast to the eight required for the *Enterprise* and the four considered for the *Kennedy*.

McNamara accommodated as gracefully as he could. When in 1966 he authorized the use of two-reactor systems for later carriers, he cited both the reduced reactor costs and the adoption of a new concept: the use of carriers as floating air bases, to which aircraft could be sent as needed. Thus a given carrier would not have on board its full complement of planes at all times, and thus the unit cost of the carrier would be less.

In one sense, McNamara regretted that the *Kennedy* was an oil burner. His affection for the late President was great. He would have preferred a more prepossessing monument. In management terms, however, he never lamented his decision. In fact, he later felt he had yielded too soon on the subsequent carriers. The evidence is strong that the President left him no choice.

It was an issue on which some of McNamara's normally ardent

supporters simply felt he was wrong. Even if he was correct in his initial judgment of cost effectiveness, one of them argued, "This was an area in which technical achievement, and all that this meant in crew and service pride, should have ruled. Bob didn't understand that. The cost difference was not all that great by anybody's estimate."

In the sum of McNamara's impact on the Pentagon, the furor over nuclear propulsion was only a tremor. With the carrier debate out of the way, nuclear power advocates turned to lesser vessels. By the end of McNamara's service, the Navy was working on a sizable fleet of escort ships which would comprise two all-nuclear task forces.

As with the TFX, McNamara was changing the familiar rules in his treatment of the carriers. He refused to consider any big hardware item in isolation. In theory, at least, he was determined to fit every major weapons system into overall defense priorities. Central to those priorities, of course, was the concept of flexible response in conflict short of general war.

Despite the noisier controversies, he was not always at odds with the military. There were times, in fact, when he marched hand in hand with military leaders—and Congress was the common foe. A community of interests developed over two major proposals for hardware of limited war—the massive C-5A transport plane and the Fast Deployment Logistics Ship, or FDL.

Once again McNamara was charting new ground. The nation had extensive commitments abroad but obviously could not maintain vast forces overseas forever. The solution seemed to him to lie in the capability to move those forces swiftly to trouble spots on demand. Fretful allies needed reassurance. The C-5A was a long-term step in that direction.

When he announced plans to develop the plane in late 1964, the Secretary reported it would "greatly reduce our reaction time" in meeting brushfire challenges. By far the biggest aircraft in the world, the C-5A would be almost as long as a football field. Its cavernous interior could carry almost any piece of Army equipment, or between 500 and 700 troops. Moreover, it supposedly was within "the state of the art," in that no technological breakthroughs were required for its development. That size alone would require an advance in the state of the art would not become apparent until later.

Equally important, the plane would be the first project assigned under the "total package procurement" concept. One contractor, in this case Lockheed Aircraft Corporation, would carry the project through from start to finish. The contract established a maximum the government would have to pay for the first fifty-eight planes. Beyond that, the price for a second buy of as many as fifty-seven would be based on Lockheed's actual costs.

Inevitably prices rose over the years. Critics suggested that Lockheed had underbid, perhaps hoping to recoup on the later sales. Inflation took its toll—as much as 25 percent between 1965 and 1969. Costs soared because of the war in Vietnam. The size of the plane was increased in mid-development, adding to the government's liability. By 1969 a program that had promised to provide 120 planes for $3.4 billion threatened to cost $5.25 billion. The Nixon Administration stopped buying at 81 planes. Lockheed was faced with a substantial loss unless the federal government agreed to assume a greater portion of the burden.

There were messier aspects to the arguments and investigations that erupted. An Air Force civilian analyst who disclosed the overruns ultimately was done out of his job. Evidence mounted that some Air Force officers had tried to conceal the growing costs.

Most of that controversy developed after McNamara left. He had begun to learn the magnitude of the overruns shortly before he left office. Yet from his standpoint the C-5A represented progress, however painful. By all accounts the Air Force had received a plane that exceeded performance requirements. The overruns, despite their breathtaking volume, were less in relative terms than those of past experience with major projects. "We made a start toward realistic contracting," McNamara remarked after he left the Pentagon. "That was about as much as we could expect."

The Fast Deployment Logistics Ship, or FDL, or "Fiddle," as it soon was called, was an eminently logical complement to the C-5A. As McNamara envisoned it, the FDL, 850 feet long, would be specially designed for long-term cruising with a heavy load of Army equipment. With a relatively high speed of 25 knots, it could move swiftly to trouble spots from U.S. ports, or lurk offshore as trouble brewed, waiting to supply the troops the big transport planes would deliver. When the time came, it could disgorge its 10,000 tons of military cargo with record speed.

In addition McNamara, anticipating the opposition, urged his concept for development of FDL as the potential salvation of the anemic U.S. shipping industry. Here, too, extended "total package procurement" would be used. Bidders for the billion-dollar FDL contract would agree to create highly automated shipyards for mass production. McNamara emphasized that FDL vessels would not compete with private cargo carriers—the nation would still need its civilian backup transport if sustained trouble developed. Besides FDL, the contract thus was supposed to create facilities for shipyards to build a new generation of civilian cargo ships.

Unhappily for FDL, operators of the antiquated private shipyards had neither the resources nor the inclination to participate. Only the aerospace industries were prepared to compete for the contract. Early on, the competition was narrowed to subsidiaries of Litton Industries, Inc., Lockheed, or General Dynamics.

This was one of the times McNamara, his civilian staff, the service Secretaries, and the military were in accord. Together they marched to Capitol Hill—and together they ran into a formidable coalition of opponents.

By late 1966 and 1967 even some of the traditional supporters of the military feared the United States had become too quick to intervene in peripheral wars. "No more Vietnams" was a cry heard outside the dovecote. As for FDL, Senator Richard B. Russell, chairman of the Armed Services Committee, grumbled: "If it is easy for us to go anywhere and do anything, we will always be going somewhere and doing something."

Russell noted that the C-5A was being built in his home state
of Georgia. "I suspect that there was at least a mild attempt to
coerce me," he said wryly, in the Pentagon suggestion that "if
one does not accept the necessity for a rapid deployment capability of the FDL type, the numbers of C-5As required might
have to be reduced." The C-5A, of course, was not so rigidly fixed
in its mission. An airplane can be used for other things than
transport of troops and their supplies into a crisis area. The FDL
was by definition a one-purpose vessel, and thus more directly a
symbol of intervention.

Shipbuilders and shipping companies mounted formidable opposition. The former had been left at the post in the competition,
and besides had to think of their relations with their clients, the
shippers. The latter were unconvinced that McNamara really had
their best interest in mind—and some claimed to be afraid of
FDL as competition. Most opponents thought greater federal
subsidy of an an expanded merchant fleet a splendid alternative.
Senator Russell's committee expressed concern "about the possible creation of an impression that the United States has assumed
the function of policing the world."

McNamara recognized this reasoning in his final statement to
Congress. By then it was clear that FDL most likely never would
be authorized. "One objection that has been raised to the FDLs
is, in fact, an objection to any kind of rapid response capability,"
he said. ". . . I want to emphasize that the FDLs, per se, would in
no way add to or subtract from our commitments. But as long as
we adhere to a policy of fulfilling our treaty commitments, we
should be prepared to do so with the minimum political and
military risks and the minimum cost in lives."

But the opposition was too great. FDL was stillborn. It had
been conceived as an impeccably rational tool for flexible response behind an outward-reaching policy. It fell victim to evolution of the policy, a disenchantment with involvement—and, more
prosaically, to intense lobbying.

As with any public man, McNamara's failures and the more

bitter contests tended to obscure the achievements. So it was in all those things that could be loosely grouped under the heading of weapons development, or, perhaps more justly, technical development.

While the TFX succumbed to a multitude of human and technical weaknesses, the nation's defenses leaped ahead. The debate over strategic needs aside, advances in rocketry—offensive and defensive—were spectacular. The 1960s lacked the high public drama of the 1950s in this area, however. For the layman, the vast distinction between the Minuteman I and the Minuteman III, and the Polaris and the Poseidon missiles, is for the most part lost—once you've seen one rocket, you've seen them all.

For that most complex of weapons systems, the individual soldier, the tools of his trade were, on the whole, vastly improved. Relative adequacy in battlefield arms is not the point; that subject will be in continuous ferment. The point is rather that there were steady and striking improvements in weaponry which received only passing public attention or none at all because they were not controversial.

There was considerable flurry for a time over the adoption of the M-16 rifle as a basic infantry weapon. Everybody, it seemed, liked the M-16—a rapid-firing, lightweight, souped-up .22 caliber rifle—except high-level Army traditionalists. Who ever heard of fighting a war with a squirrel gun? The shock and tearing action of the tiny, high-velocity bullet proved to be highly effective, however. McNamara and others who liked the rifle simply performed a neat end run around the Army leadership. They sent a small number of test rifles to Vietnam. Soon everyone in the theater was scrambling for the M-16, and most had them before the Army acknowledged that it was doing much more than testing the weapon.

Vietnam also elevated the helicopter into exalted status as a tool of the infantry. Air mobility, the concept of using helicopters to drop specially trained troops into battle, gained seemingly permanent standing. There were a number of questions still to be answered after Vietnam. Most of them turned on the uncertainties of the helicopter in more familiar infantry warfare rather than the peculiar infantry-guerrilla combination of Vietnam. How, for example, would Airmobile units fare if the enemy had planes? But the helicopter alone had guaranteed that ground warfare would never be quite the same again.

So had a number of less spectacular developments, some of them still highly classified. Even McNamara's costly and ill-fated effort to create a physical and electronic barrier between the two Vietnams to reduce enemy infiltration produced exotic results. His purpose, besides the obvious desirability of reducing the flow of enemy troops, was to help create conditions for stopping the bombing of the north. The enemy set out to make the construction effort costly in lives, and succeeded. Besides, enemy troups could always go around the barrier as necessary, since it would not be astride their main infiltration routes through Laos. U.S. military leaders never believed the barrier would work, and they behaved accordingly in building it. The most pungent criticism was voiced by John P. Roche, the White House scholar-in-residence. Roche asked politely whether the plan was to run the barrier all the way through Indochina to Burma. Then he suggested that perhaps the United States would like to buy the remnants of the Maginot Line, which France was putting on the market. His comments were not appreciated.

Nonetheless, the barrier program, which cost well over $1 billion, produced an array of new devices for limited war. Among them were acoustic and seismic detectors, which broadcast enemy movement with encouraging effectiveness after they had been seeded in the jungle.

Shortly before he left office, McNamara was asked by a member of Congress what ever had become of the so-called McNamara line. "The McNamara line is no longer called that," he replied with some bitterness, "because it is successful." It was a perhaps understandable overstatement.

In the end the bitterness and controversies had colored the

entire spectrum of weapons development during his Pentagon years. The mood, as well as the merits, had much to do with success or failure. Objective judgments were hard to find. With his unswerving commitment, come what might, once he had made up his mind, he had contributed vastly to the adverse mood. But he would agree that the weapons born in those seven years would not provide the true measure of his service. That would be found more in how he planned to use them—or not to use them.

7

Mr. Foreign Minister

IN one of his earliest interviews as Secretary of Defense, McNamara was asked about the decision to suppress a speech by Admiral Arleigh A. Burke. "Now what's the thinking behind that restraint on the Admiral's public statement?" wondered correspondent Martin Agronsky.

"Well, it's in line, Martin, with a very simple and strongly held belief of mine," McNamara said, "that it's inappropriate for any member of the Defense Department to speak on the subject of foreign policy. That's a field that should be reserved to the President, the Secretary of State, and other officials in the State Department."

Agronsky: "That goes for you then?"

"That applies to me as well as it does to all of the Presidential appointees, all of the military officers, and all of the high civilian officials in the Department," McNamara replied firmly.

Those who knew McNamara well might justly have hooted at such apparent modesty. But the first faint cries did not begin to radiate from the lower reaches of the State Department until late 1961. "Now what the hell is the Secretary of Defense sounding off on this for?" a worried desk officer in State demanded of Arthur Sylvester, McNamara's Assistant Secretary for Public

164

Affairs. McNamara had just commented on European developments in a way that sounded alarmingly like the privilege of
diplomacy. The offense was minor, but it was not the first time it
had happened. "I think you might as well get used to it," Sylvester told his colleague in Foggy Bottom. "You're going to hear
more and more of it."

Sylvester was never on sounder footing than in this opinion.
Given the nature of the issues and the interplay of personalities,
past and present, it was inevitable, whatever his intentions, that
McNamara would become more deeply concerned with foreign
policy than any of his predecessors except possibly Forrestal.
And given his standing with John Kennedy, and later with Lyndon Johnson, he would wield more influence than all of them. In
the end, his visible impact was even greater on many issues than
that of Dean Rusk, his counterpart at State.

There had been little room for assertive Secretaries of Defense
in political policy during most of the postwar years, even if they
had been so inclined. Dean Acheson and John Foster Dulles were
both strong-willed and confident men, each in his own way. It
was John Foster Dulles, not Charles E. Wilson, who articulated
the strategic policy of the Eisenhower Administration. After
Dulles, it was Christian A. Herter, a much milder individual, who
as a matter of course advanced the notion of a multilateral nuclear
force to the North Atlantic Alliance. Political and military policies were inseparable in foreign affairs. But it was the Secretary
of State who customarily spoke as the voice of the United States
Government beneath the President.

When McNamara moved into the Pentagon, he simply assumed
a different pattern. To him it was unthinkable that the Secretary
of Defense would be publicly passive or silent on the strategic
doctrine that controlled the weapons he created. Beyond that, he
was prepared to leave to State the foreign policy the military machine was in being to fulfill—as long as State produced. When,
to his mind, it failed, he took the short step across the line into
the political policy that dictated strategy.

"I have never taken actions bearing upon foreign policy without the complete concurrence of the Department of State," he once told a questioner at a press conference. That, in the minds of many at State, was part of the problem. Dean Rusk, as a diplomat put it, "let him get away with it."

The infighters at the Department of Defense always could produce what the bureaucrats called "a piece of paper," signed off by State, to support its diplomatic position. What was often overlooked was that the signature did not necessarily imply enthusiasm.

That Rusk had much choice in the matter is doubtful. McNamara's steadily increasing stature at the White House would have discouraged complaint. When McNamara was strongly combative, apparently without self-doubt, Rusk often appeared to the bureaucracy to be neutral or lacking in conviction. It was an erroneous impression, for Rusk held strong views. In style, however, they were vastly different. Each man drove himself relentlessly, but when McNamara moved he created a heavy wake. Rusk deliberately sought the opposite effect. The press found the Secretary of Defense infinitely more fascinating, as did most members and admirers of the New Frontier.

Yet no one ever detected bitterness in the relationship. On the contrary, a friend of both McNamara and Rusk described it as "an Alphonse and Gaston act. If something involving a point of privilege needed doing, Bob would say, 'You go ahead.' Dean would say, 'No, you go ahead,' and Bob would do it. The point is, it frequently was something the Secretary of State should have done without discussion."

A former senior policy-maker put the problem differently. "We had a Secretary of State who was skilled in the traditional arts of diplomacy, but who carried foreign policy around in his hip pocket," he said. "McNamara thought it absolutely essential that we have a public political base for the rationalization of the military structure. Rusk believed that doing nothing was sometimes the wiser course; McNamara felt that inaction was almost always a mistake. When Rusk appeared to leave a vacuum, McNamara filled it."

McNamara's public vehicle was what quickly became known as the annual posture statement, a report to Congress unprecedented in conception, length, and scope. The first, in its unclassified form, filled 112 pages; the last, 220. With these documents McNamara set out to define political issues and military threats, then explain how the United States proposed to meet them, from high policy down to such budget details as the cost of military retirement pay.

The first political summary was brief, though heavy with the Cold War rhetoric of the time in which words like "Freedom" and "Communist Imperialism" were capitalized. The nucleus of political policy was there as well, in McNamara's attention to such points as the threat of external support for subversion in undeveloped countries, and his insistence that the NATO allies must expand their nonnuclear forces.

By the following year his "Assessment of the International Situation as It Bears on Military Policies and Programs" had been considerably expanded. Touring the world, it ranged from assertion of a strong leadership role in NATO to an analysis of the Soviet economy and an examination of the American interest in every corner of the globe. It offered advice to the wayward: "It is our belief that both India and Pakistan must now recognize that they face a common enemy to the north in Communist China, that from this recognition must come the impetus for resolution of their differences. . . ."

Hardly anyone could argue with the substance, and indeed the substance had been cleared with State. But to professional diplomats there was a time for everything, not always every January. And the Secretary of Defense was hardly the source they would have chosen to state foreign policy. It did not help their frustrations to know that McNamara's then Assistant Secretary for International Security Affairs, operating what amounted to a small

State Department, was Paul H. Nitze, a man of formidable ability and experience in international politico-military affairs. Nitze had once headed policy planning in State.

"What happened over here," said a rare McNamara admirer in Foggy Bottom, "was that everyone went right up the wall. Everyone except the Secretary of State." One official reported that when he suggested to Rusk that the Secretary of Defense was poaching, with potentially serious consequences, "he just smiled and shrugged."

McNamara already had demonstrated between those two posture statements a tendency to leave considerable diplomatic wreckage in his wake. The Secretary of Defense, it turned out, had little more patience with the rigidities of allied governments than he had with those of Congress and the military at home. His approach to them was about the same, with predictable effect on their regard for him. Respect for his intellectual breadth and seething energy did not translate into acceptance of his ideas. Whether or not traditional diplomatic treatment would have been more effective was another matter.

The question was especially pointed with regard to Europe. In his management of the Berlin crisis in 1961, McNamara had brandished conventional forces to demonstrate political will. The Soviet Union, after its bellicose threats to Berlin, had backed quietly away. Here was affirmation, if McNamara needed any, for the concept of flexible response. The North Atlantic Alliance, he was convinced, must expand and improve its nonnuclear forces. Yet he found the allies anything but receptive.

Their reasons were varied, and in some respects quite understandable. Once before, when the Korean War appeared as a possible diversion before an attack on Europe, NATO had adopted ambitious goals for ground forces. American troops had poured back into Germany. But it eventually became apparent that Western Europe was unwilling to raise the thirty-five to forty regular divisions most strategists held to be necessary. Subsequent U.S. policy tended to justify that reluctance.

During the Eisenhower Administration the emphasis swung to massive retaliation in NATO as well as in American national policy. As tactical nuclear weapons were refined, hundreds, then thousands, were rushed across the Atlantic to the U.S. forces in Europe. The greatest threat, so the doctrine went, was from a massive Soviet onslaught with ground forces. It would have to be met, possibly after allied troops had slowed it long enough to allow Soviet second thoughts, with nuclear weapons.

Now here was the boundlessly enthusiastic new team in Washington, with McNamara taking the lead, trying to change the rationale again. European governments balked on several grounds. Nonnuclear forces were costly, and besides it was impossible, according to the current gospel, to match the supposedly unlimited hordes of Soviet forces. Somehow an expansion of nonnuclear forces came to be regarded as multiplying the risk. A conventional buildup, so ran the dominant European reaction—and that of some Americans—might convince the Russians that the West would not use its nuclear weapons against any nonnuclear attack. Even more fundamental was the suspicion, which Charles de Gaulle finally articulated, that the United States might not "go nuclear" against *any* kind of attack on Europe alone. Yet even as they resisted building their own forces, the Europeans became visibly and audibly nervous at any suggestion of an American troop reduction.

While there were glaring inconsistencies in these arguments, the fretfulness behind them was real. The American position, too, had not always been a model of consistency.

McNamara's solution was to open a sort of strategic school in which the pupils were the statesmen of Western Europe and the classrooms the historic halls in which NATO conferences were held. His self-imposed task was monumental. First he had to cut across the lines of historic European rivalries, which everyone was trying to obscure in the interest of Western unity. His first purpose, of course, was to reduce the risk of nuclear war, then any kind of war. In this he was burdened by the parallel needs to encourage the improvement of European armies and, at the same time, reaffirm the American nuclear deterrent. Many Europeans thought these were contradictory. Beyond that, he had adopted another equally forbidding assignment: an attack on the spread of small, national nuclear forces.

First at Paris in December, 1961, then at Athens the following May, he instructed NATO ministers on the illusions of nuclear power. First, he told them, NATO must build for itself a range of choices between holocaust or surrender. Second, while power for nuclear retaliation must be total, it must be done under central direction and control, guided by a single strategy. Along the way he challenged the popular assumptions of Soviet nonnuclear power. "It is important to realize," he said, "that the Soviet bloc forces are not unlimited, nor without their own problems." In other words, armies to counter a Soviet thrust were not beyond Western resources.

To prove it, McNamara took a fresh look at intelligence available on Soviet forces. His systems analysts surveyed the organization of the Soviet military and assessed what reasonably might be expected from the resources devoted to them. They found many divisions to be understrength and poorly equipped. Instead of 175 divisions, McNamara suggested, Moscow probably could put little more than the 22 divisions it maintained in the satellite countries into an attack without highly visible and time-consuming mobilization. In the same way, he challenged the prevailing judgments of Soviet air superiority. With care, he argued, the West could meet the Soviets on respectable terms.

At Athens he held his audience spellbound for an hour. "You could have heard a pin drop in that room," a minister reported. Yet the reaction was mixed. "It is the first time I have been lectured to in many years," remarked a German diplomat. "I do not particularly enjoy it."

The following month McNamara distilled his Athens lecture into the landmark commencement address at the University of Michigan at Ann Arbor. Beyond his direct prescription for

NATO, he set out his ideas on the conduct of nuclear war. As it turned out, he probably attempted too much in the speech.

For one thing, he muddled his thesis by arguing that primary nuclear targets for the United States should be the enemy's military forces. Politically, it was a difficult position for a nation which had renounced the first use of nuclear weapons. McNamara had to backpedal in the following weeks to a more general deterrent threat of retaliation. But even more important from the European standpoint were his thoughts on the management of the Western deterrent and how it should be organized.

"There must not be competing and conflicting strategies to meet the contingency of nuclear war," he said. "We are convinced that a general nuclear war target system is indivisible, and if, despite all our efforts, nuclear war should occur, our best hope lies in conducting a centrally controlled campaign against all of the enemy's vital nuclear capabilities."

As for small, independent nuclear forces, he argued that they might serve as a temptation rather than a deterrent. "Indeed," he said, "if a major antagonist came to believe there was a substantial likelihood of it being used independently, this force would be inviting a pre-emptive first strike against it."

In essence, McNamara assured the allies that the United States had "undertaken the nuclear defense of NATO on a global basis." The important thing for them was "to strengthen further their nonnuclear forces and to improve the quality and staying power of these forces." Washington wanted its allies to take part in nuclear planning, he said, but he left little real doubt where he believed final control should remain.

The response from London was prompt and anguished. Britain had made her start toward nuclear power in World War II cooperation with the United States. In recent weeks the United States more than once had helped her keep it going. A week after the speech McNamara issued what was described as a clarifying statement: "What I said at Ann Arbor was that limited nuclear capabilities operated independently were dangerous. But Britain's bomber command aircraft with their nuclear weapons have long been organized as part of a thoroughly coordinated Anglo-American striking force and are targeted as such, although of course political control remains with the British Government. I was, therefore, not referring to Britain, which was wholly clear to anyone reading the speech in its entirety. We in the U.S. appreciate the important part the British play in our coordinated strike plans."

Which left France, the only other Western nation on the costly road to nuclear power, as the ostensible target of McNamara's admonition. France had been excluded from American nuclear assistance, and now President de Gaulle was pursuing an increasingly independent political course in the alliance as well. In reality, however, McNamara had little more use for the British nuclear force than for the French. This was a background fact, well known to the British, of considerable importance in the political fiasco of the Skybolt affair a few months later.

The Skybolt was a political as well as military weapon from the beginning, though its early political implications stemmed from interservice rivalry in the United States. The Air Force had conceived of Skybolt as the answer to the Navy's Polaris. An air-to-ground missile with a range of a thousand miles, Skybolt would be launched from bombers outside enemy territory and thus, it was hoped, be relatively secure from attack.

Britain in 1960 had seized upon the weapon to extend the life of her Vulcan bomber force as an alternative to her own costly Bluestreak missile development. The United States would pay most of the costs of research and development; in exchange Britian would permit American Polaris submarines to use the naval base at Holy Loch in Scotland. Thus, with the British strategic role in the balance, the political stake of Prime Minister Harold Macmillan's government in the success of Skybolt was immense.

Yet the diplomacy between the two governments over Skybolt strangely took on the characteristics of a dialogue of the deaf. The missile was in technical trouble even before the Kennedy

Administration had settled in. Extremely complex and expensive, the missile was getting a hard look from McNamara by late 1961. The evidence was still conflicting, however, and for the time being he continued the program.

Each time an American official mentioned the possibility that Skybolt might not work, the British response was one of quiet agony. It seems clear in retrospect that the two governments had different conceptions of their agreement. London understandably emphasized what it regarded as the American obligation to the British deterrent. McNamara, to whom the primary political role in the affair appears to have flowed almost imperceptibly, was more interested in cost effectiveness from the U.S. domestic standpoint.

Beyond that, of course, were other obvious considerations. He had little sympathy for either bombers or small independent nuclear forces. In NATO he was interested in what he called a "single chain of command" for the nuclear deterrent. With the costs and the failures of Skybolt mounting, he finally threw up his hands in early November, 1962.

Cancellation, he told the President, was the only sensible course on Skybolt. Rusk, and then Kennedy, agreed. There was general appreciation for the problem this would cause the Macmillan government, and any doubt on that score was erased by the horrified reaction of David Ormsby-Gore, the British Ambassador. With hindsight, however, it appears that this was one of those cases in which everyone was saying the proper things, but without full comprehension of the forces at work on the other side.

More than a month passed before McNamara went to London for talks with Peter Thorneycroft, the Minister of Defense. During the entire period there was little communication between Washington and London. The State Department, bogged down internally over the future of United States–European relations, left the diplomacy to McNamara. He, in turn, was treating Skybolt primarily as a technical and management problem, with less regard for the political implications.

Each government, apparently, was waiting for the other to

propose alternatives. The British, knowing McNamara's views on nuclear control, were suspicious of him. Those who had thought it through agreed there were in fact few alternatives open. The United States might offer nothing to replace Skybolt. This would drive Britain politically further along the road into Europe, a course to which she already was committed in principle. This was the decision favored by some of the European specialists in State. Or the United States could drop Skybolt for itself, letting London pick up the costs of further development, then make up its own mind when to cancel the project—as it surely would. This was the approach favored by other Europeanists, including George W. Ball, the Under Secretary of State. Ball's reasoning may have been influenced by the belief that the end result would be the same as under the first alternative. Britain would be forced toward Europe, but there would be less strain in U.S.-British relations in the process. Or the United States could offer Britain the Polaris missile as a substitute, a frequently mentioned alternative. Polaris, with a potential lifespan longer than Skybolt's, was less in harmony with the strictures of the Ann Arbor speech, however. It might keep the British nuclear force alive longer than Skybolt.

But McNamara, when he finally arrived in London on December 11, stripped the American position of most of its flexibility with one stroke. Before leaving, he had called Ball and reported what he intended to tell the press at London Airport. Watch it, Ball warned, you'll exhaust our alternatives. Besides, he cautioned, it was bad form to talk to the press in such detail before the conversations with the British Government.

McNamara, possibly aiming to make certain Skybolt received the *coup de grâce,* made his statement anyway. "We are taking a hard look at all of our programs," he said. "This includes Skybolt, which is one of our bigger programs. It is a very expensive program and technically extremely complex. It is no secret that all five flight tests attempted thus far have failed, and program costs have climbed sharply.

"Nevertheless, we have continued to release funds fully supporting the project, and nearly $500 million have been released to date. During our meeting today Mr. Thorneycroft and I will review the current status of the Skybolt program and its prospects for the future. As I have said previously, no decision has been reached by our government on the program for fiscal year 1964."

That last was not quite accurate, for the decision in fact had been made. In any case the cumulative effect was to leave Skybolt a very dim future indeed. Moreover, the British Government that chose to adopt Skybolt on its own after that description would have to be most obtuse politically. Many in London believed McNamara was trying to drive Britain out of the nuclear business altogether.

Naturally enough the McNamara-Thorneycroft discussions that followed were hardly a model of camaraderie. Thorneycroft concentrated on the political implications, McNamara on the technical issues. When Thorneycroft finally brought up Polaris, McNamara wondered whether Britain would agree to commit any missiles it received to a NATO multilateral force. That, Thorneycroft said, would have to be held open as a matter of sovereign right.

By now the British press was baying at American heels out of an assumption of betrayal. "It's the greatest double cross since the Last Supper," muttered a British politician. Even those in Washington who had seen the political implications in the exercise had not anticipated the magnitude of the outcry. Some felt the British Government was feeding the fires in order to improve its bargaining position, making the Americans feel guilty, as it were. A week later, when Kennedy and Macmillan met for four days of talks at Nassau, the Skybolt affair had become the dominant item of an agenda on which it originally had not even appeared. On the American side, there had been almost no diplomatic preparation.

McNamara arrived in the warm sunlight of the Bahamas, carrying his bulging briefcase, unchallenged as the dominant American theorist at the conference. Kennedy himself had accepted fully the McNamara position. During a television interview shortly before leaving for Nassau, he commented that he saw no reason to spend $2.5 billion for Skybolt when it failed to offer "$2.5 billion worth of national security." It was a McNamara sort of argument—and the agreement that came out of Nassau was a McNamara sort of agreement.

On paper, it was a masterpiece of ambiguity. Britain would receive Polaris missiles from the United States, providing her own warheads and submarines. The missiles would be committed to the Western alliance "except where Her Majesty's Government may decide that supreme national interests are at stake." The communiqué vaguely contemplated "multilateral" nuclear forces in two separate passages. Only the initiated could know—as was actually the intent—that one referred to a NATO force composed of separate U.S. and British units, and the other to a force of mixed nationalities, including other NATO countries, with the United States retaining the finger on the nuclear trigger.

For the Europeanists in State, Nassau was a disaster, and it was a personal one for George Ball. Ball was State's man at Nassau, since Rusk had stayed behind as host for a diplomatic reception in Washington. The Under Secretary warned that the Nassau agreement would hand De Gaulle an issue, that it would set back European integration. He lost resoundingly.

Only a hint of it appeared in his joint press conference with McNamara after the conference, however. McNamara dominated the gathering, concentrating first on Skybolt and the reasons for junking it. Then he volunteered: "At this point I think it is important to recognize that President Kennedy and his advisers have had three major objectives toward which we have been working for some time. One is to gain clear recognition of the indivisibility of strategic nuclear war. The second is to prevent the further proliferation of nuclear weapons and the further development of independent national nuclear forces. The third is to gain recognition that the strategic nuclear forces are not universal nuclear deterrents, deterring all forms of political and military aggression." He then went on to make a strong case for greater nonnuclear forces.

Whereupon Ball broke in to note that a fourth objective, or "one that might be regarded as combining all of these, is the objective of trying to bring about institutional arrangements for greater cohesion in the Western world. Therefore any approach that was made to the problem of the development of a nuclear deterrent for the defense of the free world ought to be done within the framework of the kind of arrangements that we are making for the cohesion of the Western world on a political and economic basis."

"Exactly," McNamara said. None of the questioners noted that the objectives cited by the American leaders were not all necessarily compatible. Above all, the reaffirmation of the special relationship between Washington and London might destroy Britain's application to enter the European Common Market, which was what Ball was talking about.

Ball came away from the Skybolt affair convinced that McNamara, for all his managerial genius, lacked sensitivity to political issues. In a rare burst of bitterness, he made this plain in 1968, without mentioning the Secretary of Defense by name, in his book *The Discipline of Power:*

From the distance of more than five years, I can see two things quite wrong with the American position at Nassau. First, we had painted ourselves into a corner, for we had, even before the Nassau Conference, made clear to the world that we thought the Skybolt project was a failure, an announcement which the London press interpreted as an act of bad faith for which we had to make amends. Second, we did not recognize that the problem was ninety per cent political and only marginally military. In our anxiety not to sully the sacred principles of cost effectiveness we ended by extending the life of the British deterrent far longer than we would have done had Skybolt succeeded.

As for France, the Europeanists had sounded the alarm. But

apparently no one fully anticipated the role the Nassau agreement might play in French policy. Macmillan had even ventured the notion that De Gaulle seemed to have some understanding for the special relationship between the United States and Britain. Few, in turn, really expected De Gaulle to take up the humiliating afterthought offer of Polaris to France on the same terms as Britain. But De Gaulle managed to make Nassau sound large in the background three weeks later when he vetoed British entry into the European Common Market and questioned whether the United States really would use its nuclear weapons to save Europe.

Years later most of the diplomats who were involved still regard the Skybolt affair as an example of bumbling political execution, and some regard it as a disaster. "We were grossly remiss in State," a senior State Department official said from eight years of hindsight, "and McNamara did not really comprehend the broader implications. No one can argue that De Gaulle would not have kept the British out of Europe anyway, but we certainly helped him."

From McNamara's standpoint, it was a satisfactory enough solution under the circumstances. The United States, to be sure, once more had rescued British nuclear capability, and thus preserved a small national nuclear force. Still, it had forced a small step toward a more unified structure with the endorsement of the multilateral force and the British commitment of forces to NATO. That, to his mind, was progress.

For the record, he called the Nassau agreement "a major milestone in the long march to a truly interdependent Atlantic alliance." Yet it seems clear that his overriding concern had been with Skybolt and the military, not the political, consequences. From his own hindsight, he concluded that he still would have canceled Skybolt, but he would have made certain Britain kept abreast politically.

With the Skybolt experience behind him, his first ventures into personal diplomacy hardly could be described as great popular successes in Europe or with many American diplomats. As always, however, McNamara was more interested in results than popularity. The results he sought, in which political sensitivities were annoying diversions, had to do first of all with the structure of the NATO forces and the way they would be controlled.

These were not necessarily the first considerations of others in the foreign policy hierarchy. To the dedicated group of Europeanists in State, the overriding purpose of U.S. policy toward Europe ought to be the political unity of the continent. There was a strong case to be made, against the background of history. That unity might lead ultimately to a European nuclear force, under a central directorate free of a U.S. veto, was understood and accepted by many. To those who so believed, the prospect was far preferable to political fragmentation, and possible proliferation of nuclear weapons, among states acting independently.

The goal of European unity did not conflict with the general aims of other leaders in Washington—quite the contrary. But the Europeanists could see down the policy avenue with greater certainty and conviction than many others, including John Kennedy. And when the various policy lines crossed on the question of nuclear control, the conflict among the various positions became noisily apparent. As a result U.S. policy in Europe was highly motivated and elegantly phrased, but lacking in important specifics. The sharpest manifestation, following Nassau, was in the short, unhappy life of the multilateral force, or MLF.

Since the late years of the Eisenhower Administration, the idea of an MLF had been knocking about in several forms. Secretary of State Herter in 1960 first suggested a multilateral force of land-based medium-range missiles, then of Polarises. In May, 1961, President Kennedy committed five Polaris submarines to NATO command, though he, of course, would keep the U.S. finger on the trigger. Further, he looked to the "possibility" of a seaborne force "truly multilateral in ownership and control" if the allies wanted it—and after they had met NATO's nonnuclear goals. The common assumption behind all the proposals was that other European states—and most specifically, though seldom mentioned in isolation, Germany—either already wanted or eventually would demand national entry to the nuclear club unless they could be satisfied with a multilateral solution.

McNamara, of course, favored an approach that gathered nuclear ambitions into a single, integrated command channel. In early 1963 he even accepted publicly the idea of an independent European deterrent—a possibility raised by McGeorge Bundy the previous fall. After all, such a force presumably would embrace British weapons. If it did not also supersede General De Gaulle's *force de frappe,* it at least might give that force a community character, linked closely with U.S. weapons.

"If our European NATO partners wish to create a European strategic nuclear force," McNamara said, "we certainly should have no objections. But we should insist that that force be closely integrated with our own so that it could be jointly targeted, and directed in coordinated fashion. Furthermore, we are convinced that such a force could be successfully built only as a collective European undertaking, and not on the basis of separate national efforts."

In practical terms, however, this was a most unlikely prospect. Europe was of no mind for such cooperation, least of all France. But it was France that did give sudden, vigorous life to the MLF debate. Three weeks after Nassau, De Gaulle barred Britain from the Common Market. And a week after that, France and Germany signed a treaty of cooperation.

Washington reacted almost instinctively. Most officials recognized that the sequence of the two events was more symbolic than a chain reaction of cause and effect. When old Konrad Adenauer and Charles de Gaulle stood together before the altar in the massive cathedral at Reims, much could be said for the reconciliation of two nations that had warred twice in the century. To many Americans—and Europeans—the symbolism seemed broader: of exclusive alliances, of the sort of European pattern that had led to trouble in the past, especially with Britain excluded from a leavening role. The impression was sharpened as De Gaulle stepped up his attacks on U.S. policy, questioned U.S. commitment to Europe, and continued to diminish French participation in NATO.

With that the MLF movement, which never had been tightly organized, began to develop as a counter to European fragmentation. The various U.S. proposals were distilled into a plan for a fleet of surface ships, manned by crews of mixed nationalities, armed with Polaris missiles, with participants sharing the costs. An American mission took to the road to explain the plan and probe European reactions. Slowly, in some cases reluctantly, eight NATO governments agreed to take part in the MLF soundings. Whether the U.S. road show was selling the plan more than explaining it is a matter of considerable debate. What is certain is that the enthusiasm of the Europeanists from Washington caused other nations to believe the United States was selling. There is no doubt, in any case, that the MLF advocates—some skeptics called it the "multilateral farce"—had gotten out ahead of the President of the United States. John Kennedy never really made up his mind.

The MLF was thus too fragile politically to carry all the aspirations loaded aboard the demonstration vessel—a U.S. destroyer with a crew of seven nationalities—which put to sea in 1964. A mystique had settled over the project, by which the MLF appeared to symbolize Atlantic unity, European cooperation, and the preservation of an integrated nuclear deterrent, all in one highly problematical military experiment. Individually none of its most ardent supporters would have made such claims for it. But the mystique was there, fed by the implacable opposition of General De Gaulle, the long-distance rumblings from the Soviet Union, and the keen interest shown by the West Germans.

Whether the Germans actually wanted a nuclear voice at the outset, or whether the United States assumed and then awakened the interest, is not certain. President Johnson, with typical force, spurred the project forward in early 1964 without actually committing himself. The impression of Presidential support was greater than the fact.

The Germans became committed, in any case, partly because of needling from the MLF theologians in Washington. Chancellor Ludwig Erhard, who had succeeded Adenauer, and his Foreign Minister, Gerhard Schroeder, were told that Washington and Bonn had to assert leadership. Britain was wavering, Italy unresponsive. Thinking he had the signals clear, Erhard unwisely suggested at a Berlin press conference in October that the United States and the Federal Republic might proceed bilaterally if others delayed. By implication, Erhard was talking about German-American alliance, bypassing NATO. The reaction of the other members of the alliance was thoroughly predictable.

The reaction in the White House was one of astonishment and near horror. It promptly began to back away from the Erhard language. Lyndon Johnson came quickly to attention. A former policy adviser has described the President's reaction when confronted with a particularly involved paper on the MLF: "Does this keep our finger on the trigger? Then tear the damned thing up." Still, the political lines were crossed. Schroeder arrived at the NATO meeting in December to demand a concrete decision— on the very day the President pulled the plug on the MLF in Washington.

The United States would cooperate, Johnson said, but the Europeans, especially the British and the Germans, would have to agree on a solution. On the face of it, this had been the American position all along. But the question of intent was paramount, and now the United States was withdrawing the cutting edge of support. Bonn was left exposed. The NATO meeting ended with the MLF considerably diminished in stature, but Gerhard Schroeder, for one, felt he had been betrayed.

Through all this, McNamara continued to pursue his central theme. He wanted integration of the Western nuclear deterrent. At the same time, he urged other members of NATO to strengthen

their nonnuclear forces. The MLF seemed compatible with the
first goal. He favored it as long as it showed promise, and as
long as it was clear that the United States intended to retain final
control of its own nuclear weapons.

Here he differed slightly with the Secretary of State. Rusk,
though he agreed with McNamara in substance, was willing to
leave diplomatically murky, for political effect, the possibility
that the United States might someday contribute to an independent European nuclear deterrent. McNamara, in any case, was
not involved in the more intimate theology of the MLF itself.
Afterward he received passing marks from both sides of the U.S.
internal debate, which still could raise blood pressures at a mere
mention five years later.

Nevertheless, the MLF was important to McNamara's role in
foreign affairs. When Washington began to back away from it in
1964, he carefully underscored again the U.S. nuclear commitment to Europe. America could not distinguish between its own
security and that of its allies, he told the NATO Council in
December.

The entire U.S. arsenal was "at the service of NATO," he said.
"I do not foresee large-scale nuclear war in Europe with sanctuaries in the United States and the Soviet Union. The United
States has no plans for such a war. But alternative plans are
necessary for contingency planning. If we respond to an emergency, we must have the right forces. We must study the capabilities of both sides, and the intentions of the enemy within his
limitations."

His vehemence with the nuclear guarantee appeared to bear
fruit in a slight warming of French-U.S. relations. An early result
was French agreement to coordinate the targeting of the *force de
frappe* with the U.S. Strategic Air Command.

But his more important contribution, as the year-long process
of scuttling the MLF got under way, was his offer of what
amounted to a substitute. When the Defense Ministers of NATO
met in Paris on May 31, 1965, he proposed organization of a

select group in NATO to work out a greater allied role in the planning and use of strategic nuclear forces. Carefully he explained that he did not intend to exclude, but to complement, any more concrete organization that might evolve.

At first the idea was regarded by many as an essentially meaningless sop to the West Germans. By now Bonn stood vulnerable as the only ally firmly committed to MLF. And for a time its leaders showed little inclination to accept the compromise way out. Chancellor Erhard, whose sense of political timing frequently seemed to ignore reality, still insisted in the fall that he wanted to discuss with the Americans some form of more direct access to nuclear weapons.

To the surprise of many, however, McNamara's plan for a special committee began to gain momentum. As a substitute for the MLF it promised a number of potential benefits. It might silence the professed Soviet fears about German access to nuclear weapons, and thus make Moscow more receptive in the running debate over a treaty against the spread of nuclear weapons. The first French reaction, tolerant, though France would not participate, offered relief from some of the tensions in NATO. Finally, the special committee gave McNamara a chance to confront the allies with the harsh frustrations of nuclear strategy he had known for five years.

He did so—with perhaps unseemly relish—during a series of special planning meetings in 1966. "We are going to insist that the Germans stop talking about a finger on the trigger without a plan to use it," he told John McNaughton, head of International Security Affairs in the Pentagon, as they prepared for the sessions. "We are going to make them resolve the question of whose finger, and when it is to push."

The gatherings did not begin in the happiest atmosphere, for other reasons as well. McNamara had become increasingly impatient with German reluctance to improve conventional forces, with German nervousness about the steadfastness of American will, with German evasion of support for the U.S. position in

Vietnam. For its part, the government in Bonn felt it had been
left exposed by Washington on the issue of the MLF, and it was
exceedingly tired of hearing McNamara's lectures on the organization of NATO.

In May the news magazine *Der Spiegel,* published in Hamburg,
reported that McNamara "assessed very unfavorably" the German
Defense Minister, Kai Uwe Von Hassel, and regarded him as a
man of "moderate intelligence and narrow vision." Quickly Mc-
Namara sent off a message to Von Hassel: "Normally I would
not have to assure you of my high regard, but the assertion about
you in the May 23 issue of *Der Spiegel,* which is attributed to me,
is so outrageously untrue that I can't let it pass unchallenged. All
best wishes." Wherever accuracy lay, the episode illustrated the
acrimony in McNamara's relations with the Germans.

Not all Germans, however. It was no secret within the U.S.
Government that McNamara found many European statesmen
dull and excessively bound by tradition. He once remarked that
the only NATO defense minister who didn't bore him after an
hour's conversation was Franz Josef Strauss, Von Hassel's predecessor, a flamboyant Bavarian who frightened some—but certainly bored no one.

Therefore it was with some enthusiasm that McNamara fixed
the ground rules for the operation of what later evolved into the
NATO Nuclear Planning Group. He ordered small tables for the
participants, with room only for Defense Ministers and Chiefs of
Staff. He insisted there must be no reading of prepared positions:
documents had to be sent around in advance, so the meetings
could be used for freewheeling discussion.

Inspecting proposed agenda items, he noted the absence of
anything like "control of launch," which could be freely translated into "finger on the trigger." Why not? he wondered. A German official explained that Bonn did not want to embarrass
Washington, since American law forbade the transfer of nuclear
weapons. Don't worry about that for a minute, McNamara insisted, there are things we can do without changing the law. We

can put all fifteen fingers of NATO on the trigger if necessary. If you think we should change our law, say so, and we'll discuss it.

The upshot was that the German Government took over the task of working out plans for the management and use of static atomic demolition devices, or, more simply, mines. It proved to be a frustrating education. When McNamara left the Pentagon almost two years later, there still were no certain answers. McNamara had proved his point, and the Germans had been given their comeuppance.

But it was, after all, an education. As the Europeans learned more about the complexities of nuclear management, their enthusiasm for the Nuclear Planning Group grew. At the end of 1966 it was installed as a permanent arm of NATO, and its prestige developed steadily. It solved none of the broader political problems of European organization, for which some in Washington had looked to the MLF as a vehicle. It did help drain German interest away from a more active role in nuclear management. Thus it contributed to the easing of tensions within the alliance and, more broadly, to the eventual approval of the nonproliferation treaty. Finally, it would contribute later to the formal adoption of the McNamara strategy by the NATO Council.

In the meantime McNamara was pursuing his own style of personal diplomacy on another front as he somewhat gleefully conducted his first seminars in the Nuclear Planning Group. Once again the object of his attention was Germany.

By the fall of 1966 Bonn was far behind in its current commitment to spend about $700 million a year on American military equipment for the *Bundeswehr*. From the German standpoint, domestic political will had stopped well short of the 500,000-man force originally planned, and finding a use for that much hardware was becoming difficult. But the U.S. balance of payments deficit was pressing heavily on Washington. Since much of the deficit flowed from U.S. forces in Germany, and the U.S.-German agreement was designed specifically as an offset, the Administration decided to make Bonn shape up. The assignment fell primarily to McNamara.

The critical point was reached when Chancellor Erhard arrived in Washington in September for consultations with President Johnson. There had been little preparation on a specific position and negotiating tactics within the Administration. At one point the President had scheduled a conference to include State, Defense, and Treasury. But it had been canceled, and as officials converged on the White House to talk with Erhard, most of them had no notion how the German leader was to be handled. "What a hell of a way to run a government," sighed George C. McGhee, the Ambassador to Bonn.

What followed was a frontal attack on Erhard by McNamara, with the support of Henry H. Fowler, Secretary of the Treasury. West Germany had made an agreement, McNamara said in effect, and would have to live up to it. "Bob hit him high, Fowler hit him low," a witnessed recalled. "It was brutal." Erhard, a burly, gentle economist, was no match. Setting aside the political hazards at home, he agreed that Germany would fulfill its commitments, with the understanding that new arrangements would be made when the current agreement expired the following year.

When he returned home, the cries of *"Gummiloewe"*—"rubber lion"—from his critics were louder than ever. Indeed, Erhard's political acuity left a great deal to be desired. Here was no exception. Instead of emphasizing that he had obtained relief for Germany in subsequent agreements, he argued stoutly that he had proved his nation to be one that kept its bargains. It was hardly the mood of his Christian Democratic Party, or of his people, and a few weeks later he was forced to resign. Many German politicians and diplomats, and some Americans, placed the blame squarely on McNamara.

The Secretary himself felt it was "perfectly absurd" to suggest that he was forcing the Germans to buy unneeded hardware. "We don't expect them to buy anything from us they don't require or which they can get elsewhere at lower price, higher quality, or with better delivery terms," he insisted. "They haven't come anywhere near the standard of equipment that we have in our forces to meet NATO commitments. There are ample unfulfilled requirements."

The more important question, however, was whether the United States, by acting on short-term financial rather than long-term political considerations, had sabotaged its own self-interest. "It's hard to say," a senior diplomat intimately involved with European affairs remarked. "Erhard probably would not have survived anyway. But in execution it smelled too much like the Skybolt affair." It was ironic, in any case, that the responsibility for the fall of Erhard, staunchly pro-American, scornful of the Gaullist prescription for Europe, dedicated to European unity embracing Britain, should rest even partly on America's doorstep. The following year the offset agreement was rewritten, with others negotiating for the United States, to accommodate Erhard's successor.

What the episode demonstrated once again, at the very least, was that the Secretary of Defense operated with a very heavy hand. At the same time, his uncompromising technique began to show results elsewhere. When President De Gaulle ordered NATO out of France in 1966, the massive move that followed, under American guidance, was a marvel of speed and efficiency. More important, however, was the adoption of the strategic doctrine with which he had bludgeoned the alliance for almost seven years.

It had been a tortuous process. As early as 1962 McNamara had challenged the current estimates of overwhelming Soviet strength on the ground. Communist divisions were lean; many of them were undermanned. In practical terms, he argued, the West was able to confront the potential enemy on nearly equal footing. He fixed NATO goals more realistically at thirty divisions instead of the higher levels projected a decade earlier.

Even the reduced goal was too much for the alliance. The

maximum it ever produced in Europe was twenty-six divisions. The withdrawal of the two committed by France left the target even more remote. But McNamara's argument against primary reliance on nuclear weapons had taken hold. By the time NATO defense ministers gathered in May, 1967, they had in hand a new set of ground rules from the Council of Ministers.

In effect, the Council said, NATO should begin to look more to the political intentions of the Warsaw Pact as well as to its military strength. By now, it appeared, the Russians had begun to learn that unlimited attack would bring terrible retribution, and were likely to probe with greater circumspection. NATO should begin planning for the longer term, on a five-year projection based on what its members were willing to provide. More important, from McNamara's standpoint, NATO would try to prolong the nonnuclear phase of any conflict as long as possible, providing time for diplomacy to work and for rational consideration whether to "go nuclear."

The change was not quite as far-reaching as it seemed. In 1963 the Military Committee of NATO had approved language setting forth the doctrine of flexible response. France, however, backed away. Not until General De Gaulle severed his military ties with NATO was the way clear for formal adoption. McNamara, jubilant, was not one to underestimate the value of getting it down on paper as official NATO strategy at last.

"Now we're getting somewhere," he said happily on the plane back to Washington from the spring meeting in 1967. Though he was under heavy pressure in the domestic debates over the war in Vietnam and the deployment of an antimissile system, he was in remarkably good spirits. He seemed to be savoring what he regarded as a real victory for the United States, aides reported, as he chatted lightly about books, current events, and the art galleries he had visited with his wife during a brief recess in Paris.

But it quickly became apparent that several allied governments —and important members of the U.S. Congress—had conceptions of what was significantly different from McNamara's.

Indeed, the United States helped set the pattern. The new offset agreement with Germany contemplated the "redeployment" of 35,000 American troops back to the United States. Britain, retrenching around the world, would return home more than 10 percent of her troops in Germany. Then the Germany that once almost panicked at the thought of American cutbacks suddenly announced heavy cuts in its defense projections for later years. In Washington leading members of Congress began to press harder for a truly major reduction in American troops on the continent. NATO allies remained profoundly skeptical at assurances that these troops, once withdrawn, would be replaced quickly. To them, American troops committed to NATO in the United States, however mobile, and those in Europe were not quite the same.

The contradictory influences continued to grow. NATO now was accepting McNamara's strategic doctrines. It now was prepared to agree formally that nuclear weapons were not the quick answer to nonnuclear aggression. On that point the McNamara educational campaign had taken root, partly through the work of the Nuclear Planning Group. NATO still was not ready, however, to provide the forces he felt were necessary to enforce the strategy at the lower levels of conflict.

The aspect of the new thinking that bothered him most was the turn to Soviet "intentions" rather than capability as a guide for NATO force levels. In the Council meeting at Paris the previous December he had been almost contemptuous of British proposals to reduce war stocks and force levels.

"It would be perfectly absurd to assume lesser intentions and ignore the power implications of capability," he told staff members grimly. "It is a great fallacy and absolutely irrational to write off Soviet intentions as small or nonaggressive. Intentions are a function of capabilities." Bitterly he recalled that NATO allies had once argued against higher troop levels because Soviet power was overwhelming; now they justified holding back with a reduced assessment of Soviet plans. "What we must have," he said, "are balanced forces."

Against that background, his triumph at the end of 1967 was considerably diluted. On December 14 the NATO Council announced a strategy "based upon a flexible and balanced range of appropriate responses, conventional and nuclear, to all levels of aggression or threats of aggression." It represented the first fundamental strategic change since 1956. There could be no doubt that McNamara had been the single key figure in bringing it about.

There remained a nagging doubt, however, whether McNamara's nuclear teaching or a more relaxed stance toward the East played the deciding psychological role. The Soviet Union had abandoned direct confrontation in Europe and turned to asserting its influence in more subtle ways. NATO was becoming more of a political clearing house, with less emphasis on military power as individual members searched for their own paths to detente. And always in the background stood the American nuclear arsenal, as it had for twenty years, should deterrence fail and the ground forces prove inadequate. The European allies continued to take far more comfort than McNamara from the 7,000 tactical nuclear warheads the United States had stationed on the continent.

McNamara, in any case, saw substantial progress in the changing strategy. "The essential first step has been taken," he said in his final message to the Council. Ground forces had been much improved in quality. It remained now to refine them: to provide better training, equipment, and logistics, and the mobilization base that would keep pace with the Warsaw Pact in a crisis. America, he said, would continue to play its part.

What had developed, whether or not with deliberation, was a trade-off. Unable to obtain the level of conventional forces he wanted, McNamara had to settle for a fresh concept of how and when they, and their nuclear counterparts, would be used. Whether or not it would make a difference in practice if crisis came could not be forecast with certainty. This had been the unanswered question for twenty years, formal guidelines aside. What had unquestionably changed was the perception of nuclear weapons in NATO. To McNamara, this was adequate.

In one of the mild ironies of history, he was not on hand to witness its ratification. His final message to NATO was delivered by Paul H. Nitze, his Deputy Secretary, one of those who had planted the seeds of flexible response in the State Department two decades earlier.

His influence was strongly felt despite his absence. The new weapons and the politics of weaponry had blurred the historic lines between military strategy and diplomacy. While McNamara did not set out to wrest a diplomatic role from the Department of State, neither did he hesitate to assume it when he felt the circumstances demanded. In the end, he created for himself a political function unprecedented for a Secretary of Defense.

It proved to be one of the most instructive of McNamara's experiences in government. For in his diplomatic role he saw most clearly the vastly different perceptions of national interest by closely allied nations in the same set of events. Despite their acquiescence in McNamara strategy, he could not be certain that they would provide the means to fulfill it.

He also was forced to leave unresolved the question that had assumed steadily increasing prominence in his last two years in office. Would America, now beginning to turn inward, maintain abroad the power necessary to sustain the West unless the allies moved more quickly to share the burden? McNamara could see the dangers unless a balance was found. "The plain truth," he said, "is that the day is coming when no single nation, however powerful, can undertake by itself to keep the peace outside its own borders."

8

Vietnam: Years of Illusion

At Honolulu on January 14, 1962, Lieutenant General Lionel C. McGarr, commander of the American military in Vietnam, described eagerly his plans for the Viet Cong in War Zone D, a jungle sanctuary. He would take two divisions from the Army of the Republic of Vietnam (ARVN), he said, and "clean them out."

In the audience of military men and civilians from Washington, an aide passed McNamara a note: "This man is insane." McNamara nodded and whispered back, "Burn that." "Splithead" McGarr—another of those nicknames unkindly bestowed by subordinates who may or may not be motivated by affection—was completing his tour, anyway, and would soon be replaced.

The exchange stemmed from several facets of the Vietnam quandary. McGarr's thinking was conventional, typical of the tactics pursued while the military situation deteriorated earlier. Washington's collective ignorance on Vietnam was still monumental. But the new Administration thought it had learned something about the weaknesses of ARVN. It also was seized with fresh awareness that the problem in Vietnam was not conventional, or at least that its elimination was more complex than sending conventionally trained soldiers into the field to fight setpiece battles.

193

Already several steps had been taken which deepened the American involvement. The January, 1962, meeting at Pacific Command headquarters, in Honolulu was the second of several such monthly sessions. Together they represented McNamara's own effort to grasp realities which had eluded so many before him. For the time being, his course had been set by the stopgap actions taken by the Administration during that first year.

Kennedy himself had considerable knowledge of Vietnam. He had visited Indochina in 1951, and he had continued a close interest in the area through the collapse in 1954 of the French campaign to preserve empire. Above all, the young politician on the rise had concluded that a colonial government, lacking the support of the population against a nationalist movement, Communist or not, was doomed. He applauded when the Eisenhower Administration, after wavering, decided in 1954 against direct intervention to save the French at Dienbienphu.

Kennedy was unprepared for the situation he inherited in January, 1961, however. The period between 1954 and 1961 had covered a convulsive shift of fortunes. With the formal partition of Indochina and the separation of Vietnam into northern and southern sectors, the United States had quickly provided aid to the fragile government of Ngo Dinh Diem. For a time Diem did well. He consolidated his power, put the economy back on its feet, and, with quiet American advice and training, began reorganizing the shattered army.

Diem unquestionably was a patriot. For a time he generated something approaching popularity. But by late 1957 the rising despotism of his regime increasingly alienated even the strongly anti-Communist elements of the population. Resentment at the power of Diem's relatives grew steadily. By far the most influential was his brother Ngo Dinh Nhu, arrogant and contemptuous of Westerners, who ruthlessly gathered to himself almost unlimited authority. Beside Nhu stood his wife, a coldly beautiful woman who openly hungered for power.

By most assessments there was no direct cause-and-effect rela-

tionship between the rising popular discontent with the regime
and the resurgence of Communist terrorism in 1957. Ho Chi
Minh, the President of North Vietnam, apparently ordered terror
in the south in 1957 both because he feared Diem might succeed
and because Diem had canceled the elections—which Ho expected
to win easily—decreed in the 1954 Geneva Accords. By 1958,
southerners who had moved north in 1954 had been retrained for
guerrilla war and were returning to the fight in the south. The
death toll of local officials and government loyalists rose steadily
in the countryside. Yet in the areas they controlled, the Viet
Cong, successors to the dominant Communists in the Viet Minh
who had defeated the French, frequently managed to offer a
persuasive carrot with the stick.

Neither the Diem government nor the Americans on the scene
seemed to appreciate fully the scope of deterioration. In 1960
alone, 3,000 local government officials were killed, some of them
in particularly grisly fashion for psychological effect. Guerrillas
opened attacks on regular army units, almost invariably with
success. In grim reprise of the early 1950s, armored units trained
by Americans for another kind of war thundered fruitlessly to the
rescue of men already dead, their weapons added to the Viet Cong
arsenal. In November three paratroop battalions rebelled briefly
in Saigon out of frustration at the regime's management of the
conflict.

The Kennedy Administration thus inherited growing crises on
two fronts in Vietnam. In the case of the Viet Cong, Communist
inspired, with strong nationalist appeal, crisis was well advanced.
In the popular resentment against the regime, Communism aside,
it waited for a spark.

Even before Laos was shunted off into a face-saving cease-fire
and negotiations, Kennedy had approved short-term plans to increase military and economic aid to Saigon. Vice President Lyndon Johnson returned from a survey of the area with a firm
recommendation for a greater U.S. commitment, linked to reforms by the Diem government. The introduction of combat

troops, Johnson said, was neither necessary nor desirable, at least for the time being. In October Kennedy asked for another look. General Maxwell Taylor, then the President's military adviser, and Walt W. Rostow, deputy to McGeorge Bundy, Kennedy's national security adviser, flew to Vietnam for their now historic survey. Reinforcing the course already set, their reports proposed reforms by the Diem government, a parallel U.S.-sponsored counterguerrilla campaign, a heavy infusion of retraining and equipment—including helicopters and the men to operate them—to put ARVN back in the war.

Taylor and Rostow went even further. Taylor recommended preparations to send as many as 10,000 American troops to defend installations and for possible emergency relief of ARVN. As the general saw it, this would serve both as a demonstration of American will and as a morale booster for Saigon. Rostow urged contingency planning for retaliatory air strikes against the north. Within the basic policy position that the Vietnamese themselves would have to win the conflict, Taylor and Rostow argued in effect that the Americans must show them how, in detail, and go further if necessary.

Up to a point the President agreed. The United States was committed in Vietnam. He knew that the commitment was related not only to Laos and the rest of Asia but to the recurrent crises in Europe as well. How far he would have carried it in a changing climate will be debated for years. But his immediate decision was to increase substantially the flow of money, matériel, and advisers to the Diem regime, without ruling finally on the introduction of American combat troops. The momentum was established: the exuberant new theories of limited war led toward, not away from, such tests as Vietnam. Kennedy had chosen to make in Vietnam the stand he had avoided in Laos.

Both McNamara and Rusk tried to make certain the President knew the possible consequences. Apart from the merits, they pressed hard the point that even the limited increase might prove to be self-feeding. That Kennedy wanted to avoid the nightmare vision of military and civilian leaders alike, a land war in Asia, was certain. He spoke to aides of the danger. Still, one remarked later, "I am not sure he fully understood. He had a lot of company."

For the Secretary of Defense, this had been up to now a period of vigorous action in the organization and management of the Department. He was shaping his tools of flexible response. He had surfaced less visibly in the policy decisions. His me-too role in the Bay of Pigs debacle would haunt him. When Berlin heated up, he began to come into his own with both the development and execution of policy. His voice was being heard, but it was not yet a dominant one.

There was no doubt, however, where McNamara stood on policy as the helicopters flowed into Vietnam, as the number of U.S. military men rose from 600 to 6,000 in six months, as Americans began to die. Like Kennedy, McNamara had been brought to attention by Khrushchev's promise on January 6, 1961, of support for "liberation wars or popular uprisings."

It was a challenge he was prepared to accept in political terms. In military terms it appeared to be a direct test for the doctrine of flexible response at the lower end of the spectrum. Like Kennedy also, McNamara regarded the survival of a non-Communist government in South Vietnam to be important not only for its own sake, but also for its possible influence on the probing by the Soviet Union of the United States position elsewhere.

The Secretary of Defense felt he had failed to seize his responsibility for Vietnam in the early months. The critical appraisals had been made by the White House through the Johnson and the Taylor-Rostow missions. McNamara began to make up for lost time with intense concentration in late 1961 and early 1962. For better or worse—and in the end to his own anguish—he became the dominant public figure on Vietnam policy beneath the two Presidents he served.

For one reason, it was a role seemingly conceded to him by the Secretary of State. Some former members of the Kennedy Administration have argued that this was a conscious decision by Dean Rusk, that he regarded Vietnam as more a military than a political-diplomatic problem. In any case, Robert McNamara detected a leadership gap on Vietnam, and when he was faced with a vacuum, his instincts were to fill it. Beyond that, the military side of the complex military-political problem was far more visible.

McNamara was certain he recognized both sides of the equation. "In these conflicts," he said, "the force of world Communism operates in the twilight zone between political subversion and quasi-military action. Their military tactics are those of the sniper, the ambush, and the raid. Their political tactics are terror, extortion, and assassination. . . . We have been used to developing big weapons and mounting large forces. Here we must work with companies and squads, and individual soldiers, rather than with battle groups and divisions. . . . We must learn to simplify our tactical weapons, so that they can be used and maintained by men who have never seen a machine more complicated than a well sweep."

Thus he knew the test was not military alone. The United States, he said, "must help these people to provide a more desirable alternative to Communism, and to do so will require all the means at our disposal—political, ideological, technical, scientific, and economic, as well as military." The multiple requirements— political, economic, and military—of counterinsurgency warfare were fully acknowledged. With time, however, it was clear that neither McNamara nor anyone else at the highest level fully comprehended those requirements or knew how to fill them.

The political goals were sound and the military goals apparently modest. The stakes appeared high in a test that reached far beyond Vietnam. Yet performance of the next several years developed almost as if the leading participants on the Saigon-Washington side had set out to avoid what they proclaimed to be the route to success.

These were days of innocence. The American public had only the faintest conception of what was happening in Vietnam. In

February, 1962, when an alarmed journalist asked about a report that a U.S. helicopter had been shot down, McNamara replied blandly, "I suspect that it was an Army helicopter functioning in a training role with the South Vietnamese. They have asked that we train their helicopter pilots, not only train them in the technique of operating the helicopter but also train them in the relationship of helicopter operations to ground operations."

A month later the reporters were back, this time wondering about word that American pilots were flying combat missions against guerrillas. "We should be very clear as to the role of the United States in South Vietnam," McNamara said. "We are there at the request of the South Vietnamese Government. President Diem has asked that we supply training and logistical equipment to the South Vietnamese. That we are doing. . . . The transition training of the Vietnamese pilots in multiplace aircraft is being carried on by U.S. pilots. To obtain the full range of such training, it occasionally takes place under combat conditions."

There were degrees of innocence as well. McNamara set out to erase his own with his customary intensity. In four consecutive months he flew to Honolulu to talk with Admiral Harry D. Felt, the Commander in Chief, Pacific, and others responsible for the effort in Vietnam. For the March meeting he ordered in General Lyman L. Lemnitzer, the Chairman of the Joint Chiefs of Staff, and General George Decker, the Army Chief of Staff. From Saigon came Ambassador Frederick E. Nolting and General Paul D. Harkins, McGarr's successor and commander of the Military Assistance Command there.

When it was over, the reporters were once again waiting. "My discussions today with Admiral Felt, General Harkins, and Ambassador Nolting on the situation in South Vietnam have been the most encouraging we have held so far," McNamara announced as he headed for his waiting plane. "I am pleased to learn that the armed forces of Vietnam are taking the offensive throughout the country, carrying the war to the Viet Cong, inflicting higher casualty rates, and capturing Viet Cong weapons and supplies in greater numbers." He added a note of caution: "We must not, of course, expect miracles overnight—a war of this kind takes time. However, there is every sign that the government and people of South Vietnam have the will and the capacity, with our support, to win."

With that he boarded a "McNamara Special," a huge transport plane converted for passengers, and returned homeward. The unreality of all this unfortunately would not be established until much later. Other passengers reported that on the return trip McNamara worked for a while, then relaxed with a book of philosophy.

Even uncommitted witnesses in South Vietnam at the time were divided on the state of the war. ARVN added its own peculiarities to the standard tactics which were proving to be so inadequate. Many units—critics insisted most—observed a dawn-to-dusk war, interrupted by a long break for lunch. The night was left to the busily recruiting—and terrorizing—Viet Cong. New American advisers, dedicated, capable men, fumed as Vietnamese officers ignored their efforts to adjust tactics, seek out the enemy, and seize back the night with ambushes and patrols. They could only advise, of course; they could not order the sensitive Vietnamese.

In the political war McNamara was enthusiastic about plans to expand Saigon's control. The primary vehicle was to be a network of strategic hamlets, well protected, from which, in theory, government control would spread. By late 1962, however, as the system grew, it was operated more and more by Ngo Dinh Nhu as a means of oppressive control and weakened by haphazard expansion. In Saigon the government made only faint gestures toward the popular reforms demanded by the United States.

Still, there was some military progress with the American commitment of 1962. For a time the helicopter both demoralized the guerrillas and inspired ARVN to greater aggressiveness. On occasion the Viet Cong broke and ran when faced with a helicopter assault. But at the same time, the U.S. military leadership in Saigon simply was not following the public guidelines stated in Washington. With some exceptions, it too treated the conflict in

standard textbook terms, without much regard for its guerrilla
nature.

Where official American analysts differed chiefly over the
record of this period was the point at which the decline was re-
sumed. Without question the Saigon reports of the time were
grossly overoptimistic. The Viet Cong had doubled its strength
from some 12,000 to 25,000 hard-core combatants. Its active
support in the countryside was in the tens of thousands at the end
of 1962. The government of the United States was trapped in a
web of self-deception. Among these most deceived was the Secretary of Defense, a critical link in the policy-making chain.

In McNamara's case this was more noticeable in retrospect
because he was highly visible and because his public image was
that of a man who, above all, revered facts.

"Every quantitative measurement we have shows we are winning this war," he said after he returned from his first trip to
Saigon in April, 1962. At that point the quantitative measure-
ments may have pointed in the right direction, however inaccu-
rate they were on specifics. If so, it was only for a brief period.

On most occasions McNamara's public stance was one of careful optimism balanced against forecasts of a "long, hard struggle
extending over a period of years." In January, 1963, he announced, as did the President, that the enemy drive in South
Vietnam had been "blunted." Even as late as June, he still felt
free to give a relatively optimistic outlook: "Although the conflict will continue for some time to come, I believe we are making
significant gains, particularly in the carrying through of the vital
strategic hamlet program, in the gradual extension of government
control, and in the key indices of comparative defection and the
growth in spontaneous intelligence reflecting the growing loyalty
and confidence of the people of Vietnam in their government."

In retrospect the remarks seem nonsensical. Yet in context,
they reflected the reporting from Saigon. The optimism in the
Embassy was being questioned only by a handful of State Department and White House aides.

In McNamara's case, as a close friend put it later, "He was

trying to quantify the unquantifiable. Someone in Saigon might say, 'Mr. Secretary, I don't really have much idea how many VC there are in that province.' Bob would demand the best figure available, the guy would pull one out of the hat, and the error would be compounded right down the line." An aide shook his head over McNamara's effort to come to grips with Vietnam. "He kept saying, 'If we can learn how to analyze this thing, we'll solve it.' "

McNamara himself never came to accept the argument of some, that the Viet Cong in fact sustained their momentum without interruption until after the arrival of American combat forces in 1965. He still believed with hindsight, in fact, that there was a relative improvement in the military situation from 1961 through May, 1963.

He would acknowledge, however, that the United States Government, including himself, was guilty of an excessively optimistic appraisal of the situation through this period. He concluded finally that the reasons could only be near-total ignorance of Vietnam and the Vietnamese, and the absence of reliable factors by which to measure progress. As he saw it, the nation suffered from lack of specialists in this area corresponding to Charles Bohlen or Llewellyn Thompson, career diplomats who could draw upon decades of experience to interpret with sure insight any gesture or word from Moscow.

Then with the summer came the Buddhist crisis, an event that reshaped the Vietnam undertaking of the United States as it gained momentum. What began as a movement against discrimination turned into an effort to bring down the government. The series of Buddhist self-immolations that began on June 10 focused world outrage on government repression. With mandarin disdain, the regime refused to take the promised minimum steps of reform which American officials were convinced would still the disturbances. Madame Nhu gleefully applauded in public the "barbecues" by the Buddhists.

In the early morning hours of August 21, Nhu's police and

elite Special Forces assaulted Buddhist pagodas, killing some priests, wounding others, and arresting thousands. Nhu had done more than attempt to suppress the Buddhists with a single brutal stroke. He had underscored his contempt for the American Government. Only a few days earlier the regime had promised Ambassador Nolting, who was leaving, that it would not undertake this kind of repression: its policy was to be one of conciliation. Saigon was waiting for the arrival of Henry Cabot Lodge, the new Ambassador, the next day. The attacks had been timed to present Lodge with a *fait accompli.*

He had hardly hit the ground when he began getting feelers from leading generals about U.S. reaction to a coup. Talk of coups and countercoups had been an ingredient of Saigon life for weeks, as plentiful as reports on military progress, and in most cases about as accurate. Frustration in Washington at inability to sway the government in Saigon was nearly complete by now. This was a firm, if indirect, approach, and Lodge asked Washington for instructions.

What followed is still sufficiently controversial to stir bitterness in some of the principals at a mere mention. On Saturday, August 24, Kennedy was on Cape Cod. McNamara was taking a rare vacation. John A. McCone, the Director of Central Intelligence, also was away. Dean Rusk was in New York.

In the State Department a response to the Lodge cable was undertaken by those who remained, with Roger Hilsman, the Assistant Secretary for Far Eastern Affairs, one determined to see the United States prevail, bearing the immediate responsibility. As it happened, all those involved had severe doubts about the reported progress in Vietnam and were dismayed with the Saigon government. Hilsman was so unpopular with the American military that others had to be assigned as the State Department representative to accompany McNamara on his trips to the area.

The text of the reply to Lodge has not been made public. Hilsman's summary in his book *To Move a Nation* is the most detailed yet published. The generals in Saigon could be told, it said, something like the following: The United States disapproved of the action against the Buddhists and could not tolerate Nhu. Diem should have every opportunity to get rid of him and make reforms. If this failed, the United States would have no part in a coup, but if one occurred, Washington would support an anti-Communist military government.

According to Hilsman, the text was cleared with Rusk in New York and the President at Hyannis Port. This hardly describes their conversations, however. Actually they discussed the cable in vague terms over open telephone lines, and the implications were glossed over. Roswell Gilpatric signed off for the civilian side of the Defense Department. Gilpatric, in turn, reached Taylor some time after the cable had been dispatched. Given the dispersal of key decision-makers, it was a disorderly departure from the crisis management honed during the Soviet-American confrontation over Cuba the year before.

When he returned to town on Monday, McNamara was furious. He weighed in with vigorous objections, as did Rusk, Taylor, and McCone. Kennedy was dismayed at both the collapse of the decision-making process and the cable itself. He had assumed that the departmental clearances meant McNamara and Rusk had approved fully. Both McNamara and Taylor argued that the overthrow of Diem without a clear alternative would leave the future alarmingly uncertain. The opposite view, of course, was that almost anything would be better than the current chaos. To McNamara the cable seemed an appallingly callous death warrant, at least a license to kill. In subsequent messages the Administration tried to dilute its effect.

Out of the confusion came a sweeping review of U.S. policy in Vietnam. Kennedy himself acknowledged the quandary publicly.

The Saigon government might gain popular support with "changes in policy and perhaps personnel," he said, and "in the final analysis, it's their war. They are the ones who have to win it or lose it." He agreed that a reduction in U.S. aid might have some influence on the government, but "on the other hand, you might have a situation which could bring about a collapse."

Like every President faced with critical decisions on Vietnam, Kennedy was trapped with visible American strategic interests at stake and a weak client to preserve them. He specifically had adopted earlier the so-called domino theory, which held that if South Vietnam fell to the Communists, the rest of Southeast Asia would follow: "I believe it. I believe it. I think that the struggle is close enough. China is so large, looms so high just beyond the frontiers, that if South Vietnam went, it would not only give them an improved geographic position for a guerrilla assault on Malaya, but would also give the impression that the wave of the future in Southeast Asia was China and the Communists."

McNamara, like most officials in Washington, interpreted the President's remarks about personnel "changes" as an invitation to Diem to separate himself from his brother. Whether this distinction, as opposed to getting rid of Diem himself, was clear to the plotting generals is unknown. In any case, they had subsided temporarily, to consolidate their support among their colleagues. Washington meanwhile was searching furiously for a policy course. There still was some hope that Diem without Nhu would adopt a more moderate stance. But there also was an awareness that this possibility might no longer be open.

In the White House, Defense Department and State Department reports became fixed ever more solidly in opposing positions. The war, Defense said, is going well and the government is at worst tolerable. We are losing, the spokesmen for State said, the government is tottering, and Nhu has to go. The debate began to focus on the specific actions the United States might take to force changes by the regime; McNamara, at first, resisted the more stringent proposals.

But finally, troubled by the deadlock in the debate at home, now nagged by growing doubt about what his own reports were telling him, he set out again for Vietnam himself. Accompanied by General Taylor, he was gone nine days. This time the results were strikingly different. General Harkins was still winning the war on paper. But dissenting voices at lower levels were becoming louder and more numerous. Lodge had taken a hard look at Saigon, disliked what he saw in both military and political terms, and set out to turn McNamara around. He succeeded partially. McNamara conceded a need for active pressure to force the Diem government to change course.

It was a breakthrough of sorts, and it was the most important development at a meeting of the National Security Council on October 2. The McNamara-Taylor report held firmly that the war was continuing to progress favorably, but conceded that further political disaffection could change that trend. McNamara did not reverse course easily.

On the military side, plans would be drafted to clean up the major Viet Cong threats by the end of 1965. At the same time Vietnamese would be trained to take over the roles being performed by Americans. Politically, the United States would begin to withhold aid funds gradually and thus force the government to make reforms. Lodge, whose cool arrogance already was beginning to make the Diem regime nervous, would let Vietnamese officials come to him. When they did, he would tell them what had to be done.

The public statement that followed the NSC meeting seemed so remarkably optimistic that its deeper implications were generally overlooked. It had been drafted and redrafted by McNamara, with a dissent from William H. Sullivan, the State Department officer who had accompanied him to Saigon. It came out of the NSC over the objection of McGeorge Bundy.

According to the most pertinent paragraph:

Major U.S. assistance in support of this military effort is needed only until the insurgency has been suppressed, or until the national security forces of the Government of South Vietnam are capable of suppressing it. Secretary McNamara and General Taylor reported their judgment that the major part of the U.S. military task can be completed by the end of 1965, although there may be a continuing requirement for a limited number of U.S. training personnel. They reported that by the end of this year, the U.S. program for training Vietnamese should have progressed to the point where 1,000 U.S. military personnel assigned to South Vietnam can be withdrawn.

Against the background of turmoil in Saigon, Washington's commentators peered at the statement with the fascination they would accord a strange bug. Some saw it as a gesture to calm a restive Congress, which was beginning to demand cuts in aid unless Saigon improved. Others suggested McNamara was warning Diem that American patience was not without limit. Both groups were partly correct. Apparently few carried the analysis one step further.

For McNamara, according to officials familiar with his thinking, contemplated a deadline to the Vietnam commitment, win or lose. The Secretary of Defense believed the United States would have to wind up its direct involvement in Vietnam by the end of 1965. If the effort had failed, then the departure would have to be glazed over with the assertion that the U.S. role, which after all was advisory, had been honorably fulfilled.

This, of course, was not the common interpretation of the McNamara-Taylor report, which from hindsight was simply that the two had made a gross miscalculation. Nor is it provable today. Even if McNamara now should step forward with a retrospective explanation, which is most unlikely, allowance would have to be made for the influence of time and intervening events.

Taylor, whose report it was also, certainly did not intend that the United States should get out at any cost. The language, indeed, left open what would happen if the assumptions proved wrong. By endorsing it, Taylor presumably was being tolerant of McNamara, confident that common sense as he saw it would prevail as events demanded. But the statement, written and rewritten, was first of all McNamara's. Taylor's interpretation of it was less important than that of McNamara. What McNamara wanted was language that suited his policy purpose, as vaguely put as necessary to secure Taylor's approval. McNamara conceived Taylor's support to be essential.

The principals who claim certainty that McNamara meant to lay a base for liquidation of the commitment insist also that he believed this to reflect the conviction of the President. Needless to say, particularly in the light of later events, others intimately involved reject this belief. In any case, the effect of McNamara's indulgence in a bit of naïve and clumsy duplicity soon would be neutralized by events.

For the moment, however, the package approach that came out of the NSC meeting assumed the survival of Diem. For most of October there was no change in the attitude of the Saigon government as the first economic restrictions were applied. Then on the last day of the month Diem asked Lodge to accompany him on a brief trip out of Saigon. Along the way he asked the Ambassador what the Americans wanted of him. Lodge told him—including the exile of Nhu. Diem made no commitments. But neither did he rule out reform.

Whether or not he was approaching compromise will never be known. For the next day the generals launched their coup, and both Diem and Nhu were murdered.

Their deaths closed a sadly bungled episode of the exercise of military policy for political ends. There were so many might-have-beens, as there always are in the political genesis of armed conflict. If ARVN had been trained differently, if the political nature of the undertaking had been better understood, if the assessments of progress had not been so grossly incorrect, if the United States had acted sooner to take Diem in hand, if the August 24 cable had been drafted differently . . . or perhaps McNamara was right, and the central weakness was the failure to comprehend the Vietnamese, and all that this failure implied.

McNamara never believed, even long afterward, that Diem had served U.S. purposes badly until the Buddhist crisis. As a strong leader, however far from ideal, and as a patriot, Diem appeared to him far preferable to the totally unknown. But the deed was done, and it was time to pick up the pieces.

On the day of the coup, just before it erupted, General Harkins had proclaimed that "victory, in the sense it would apply to this kind of war," was only months away. The chief of the American advisory group announced that ARVN had been trained to the point that it was "as professional as you can get."

Yet even as the planned withdrawal of 1,000 Americans began, it was depressingly clear that the Viet Cong were gaining rapidly. Whether or not enemy progress had been constant became irrelevant. What was certain was that the Viet Cong had stepped up their pace by September and from the day of the coup were running wild. Weaknesses in the strategic hamlet program completed the bleak picture.

It was a period of depression for McNamara. The death of Diem was a failure of both policy and performance. He was shattered by the assassination of John Kennedy three weeks later. Aides reported he was driving himself with greater fury. As a military junta led by General Duong Van Minh struggled to establish control in Saigon, his hopes for liquidating the American presence, with some remnants of national prestige intact, began to look less and less realistic.

This was a period of reassessment for the new President of the United States as well, of course, and McNamara set out in mid-December to spend two days with NATO ministers in Paris and two days on the scene in Saigon. As he left Orly Airport in Paris for Saigon, the tires blew on the "McNamara Special" when his pilot made an emergency stop in the fog to avoid a commercial airliner. No one was injured, but it had been close enough.

Under all circumstances, he was in remarkably good spirits when he arrived back in Washington on December 21. He betrayed not a trace of disorientation from his travels. He was still the perfect performer who could leap hemispheres and immediately absorb and translate incredibly complex data without a pause to adjust his internal clock. (General Westmoreland once remarked with awe, "He has an unbelievable constitution.") Hatless, freshly shaved, he was the faithful executor of his new President's policy.

The rate of Viet Cong attacks had increased greatly after the overthrow of Diem, he said, and this was to be expected. He had reviewed with the new government its "plans for bringing the war to the Communists in 1964 and prosecuting it successfully." He remained "optimistic that the plans when carried out will blunt the Communist drive for subversion against the people of Vietnam." It was an ironic choice of words, for he had reported the drive blunted a year before.

Had he been frightened when the tires blew at Orly? "I didn't know enough to be afraid," he grinned.

The new President made his basic policy decision quickly, and surprised no one. On New Year's Day Lyndon Johnson restated the U.S. guarantee to the junta. The United States would "maintain in Vietnam American personnel and material as needed to assist you in achieving victory," he said. He also ruled out neutralization as a sop to aggression, for that "would be another name for a Communist takeover."

Yet McNamara was still hopeful in late January, when he told the House Armed Services Committee that perhaps he could withdraw a majority of the 16,500 U.S. troops then in Vietnam by the end of 1965. He persisted in thinking of liquidation, and was beginning to counter the background rumble of sentiment for the introduction of American combat forces.

A few days later, in a revealing passage, he testified that, "Last fall I was not as optimistic perhaps about the course of the war as I was about being able to bring back our personnel in certain numbers by the end of last year and also by increments. I still am hopeful of doing that. . . . I say this because I personally believe that this is a war the Vietnamese must fight. I don't believe we can take on that combat task for them. . . . But after all, the training, by the very nature of the work, comes to an end at a certain point."

It became steadily more apparent, however, that if the United States should withdraw, it would do so against a background of South Vietnamese collapse. Fragile political ties between Saigon and the hamlets crumbled. The government of General Minh lasted less than three months. Then Major General Nguyen Khanh, commander of the Army's First Corps, took over in a bloodless coup, claiming that members of the junta had been plotting neutralization. It was the beginning of the revolving-door changes of government that shattered both the political and military efforts for critical months.

McNamara adjusted to Johnson's restatement of policy. He had been asked to stay in the government, and he agreed. The despondence that followed the death of John Kennedy began to lift. Told by the President in March to go to Saigon and prop up the Khanh government, he did so with vigor.

Suddenly the world was treated to the astonishing sight of a grinning Robert McNamara, the computerized man, standing shirt-sleeved beside the General and waving to enthusiastic crowds. He patted babies. He made speeches that approached the florid. Back in Washington, he offered analyses that conceded the extent of deterioration, but also emphasized short-term gains. Thus he became known once again in the yet small circle of war critics as a Pollyanna, or a warmonger, or both. Slowly he came to understand more fully the pressures on the President: out of his own nature, and the peculiar inheritance he had received from Kennedy, Lyndon Johnson was unlikely to yield, perhaps could not, except under the most dire circumstances.

Once again, during his next trip to Saigon, another flicker of danger broke through the antiseptic barrier of formal briefings and inspections of secure areas. After the Viet Cong mined a bridge along the route he would take, he endured the humiliation of wearing a protective vest as he rode through the streets.

The personal deadline of 1965 now had evaporated. McNamara's sense of purpose again stabilized on the original goals: "Our role in Vietnam," he said, "is to assist the Vietnamese civilian and military forces until they are able to destroy the Communist insurgency, keep internal order, and provide a stable, independent government."

When Senator Wayne Morse labeled it "McNamara's War," the Secretary of Defense snapped back: "I must say I don't object to its being called McNamara's War. I think it is a very important war and I am pleased to be identified with it and do whatever I can to win it."

Divisions persisted among various levels of the decision-making and operating machinery, however. Three overlapping schools of thought on the nature of the war were established during the Kennedy years. For the most part, the military treated Vietnam in straightforward military terms. Before Diem's death General Earle G. Wheeler, who had succeeded Taylor as Chairman of the Joint Chiefs of Staff, specifically rejected the idea that Vietnam was primarily a political or economic problem: "The essence of the problem in Vietnam is military." A second group, largest among the civilians, understood that this was first of all a guerrilla challenge, but it placed military treatment above the political. The third group was that small contingent that argued for overwhelming concentration on the political and development fronts. From all he said, McNamara belonged in spirit to the third group, but in execution he belonged to the second. His execution was that of the total administrator, dealing not only with grand design but also with minute detail, to the point that his military critics would say that he had sacrificed design for detail.

As successive governments passed through the revolving door in Saigon, McNamara's frustration became more pronounced. "The problem in South Vietnam is very clearly a political-economic-military problem," he remarked. "It is a problem that requires the support of the people if it is to be solved." But his alternatives were shrinking visibly. Saigon was impotent with intrigue, leaving the countryside supine before the Viet Cong.

Washington was unwavering in its fundamental support, but the signals as to its specific course were contradictory. In the spring McNamara left open in a speech the possibility of a direct attack on the north. Word leaked out of a Dean Rusk background briefing that China and North Vietnam risked war with the United

States. Yet when Premier Khanh in July demanded an invasion
of the north, he was reprimanded by Maxwell Taylor, who had
left the Joint Chiefs to become Ambassador to Saigon. Most
senior military men were doubtful or opposed outright to direct
U.S. troop involvement. Later, when the decision to go ahead was
reached, they reacted in the military way: they wanted to win it.

Though McNamara had made his basic decision to go with
Lyndon Johnson, he found it more and more difficult, as the
summer and fall progressed, to confront the President with the
situation in Vietnam. The realities, even then, included evidence
of North Vietnamese regular troops in the south.

Johnson had set out to overwhelm, not just defeat, the Republican candidate for President, Senator Barry Goldwater, and the
Senator's unrestrained saber-rattling propelled Johnson in the
opposite direction. "We are not about to send American boys
nine or ten thousand miles away from home to do what Asian
boys ought to be doing for themselves," he said, with variations,
in October.

Along the way he had gained an important tactical weapon,
though it would prove to be highly controversial itself, in the
rising domestic clamor over the war. No one seriously questioned
the reality of an attack by North Vietnamese torpedo boats and
gunboats against the U.S. destroyer *Maddox* in the Tonkin Gulf
on August 2. Evidence of a second attack on the *Maddox* and its
mate, the *Turner Joy,* two days later, was less convincing, and
later even McNamara would confess doubt that it occurred. Yet it
was the second incident that caused Johnson to free the Navy,
with McNamara's full endorsement, for retaliatory air strikes
against the boats at four bases in North Vietnam. The door now
was ajar.

Carefully and convincingly, McNamara marshaled the evidence
that caused Congress to approve overwhelmingly what became
known as the Tonkin Gulf Resolution. In a critical passage, it
authorized the President to "take all necessary steps, including
the use of armed force, to repel any armed attack against the

forces of the United States and to prevent further aggression."
Many members later regretted the blank check in that last passage, especially as they came to doubt that the second North
Vietnamese attack actually occurred, and even that the first attack
justified the reaction.

The United States did not respond, however, when the Viet
Cong carried out their first direct assault on an American installation. They killed five Americans and destroyed six B-57 bombers
at Bien Hoa two days before the Presidential election.

But Johnson was listening more closely to his advisers than
most outsiders appreciated in the final weeks of the political
campaign. He later told *Newsweek* correspondent Charles W.
Roberts that he decided in October he would have to bomb North
Vietnam. It was a revealing admission, weighed against the spirit
of his campaign oratory. There was no mystery about the reasons,
in any case. The Viet Cong, operating on a grander scale, were
shattering South Vietnamese battalions. Their arms were new and
more powerful.

With the election out of the way, the President turned back to
Vietnam. On November 28 he was handed a summary of the
options open to him, ranging from massive attack on the north to
abandonment of the undertaking. Its primary authors were William P. Bundy from the State Department and John T. McNaughton from Defense. Ultimately Mr. Johnson chose option "C"—
which called for "measured response with air attacks on the DRV
[Democratic Republic of Vietnam] with a clear determination to
prevent Hanoi from conquering the South." The document did
underscore one of the beliefs that prevailed among most policy-
makers of the period: that the reaction of the North Vietnamese
to such a course would be essentially "defensive." It was a judgment which, in retrospect, had overtones of McNamara's complaint a year earlier: the Americans simply did not understand
the Vietnamese.

Yet the time was not yet ripe. The United States still did not
retaliate when the Viet Cong used explosives against the Brinks

Hotel billet for American troops in Saigon on Christmas Eve. Ambassador Taylor, an advocate of direct retaliatory "tit-for-tat" bombing of the north, was appalled. By now it was certain that troops of the regular North Vietnamese Army were in the field.

In a strange way 1964 had become the lost year of the war. Much of it had been spent propping up tottering leaders in Saigon. Politics in America had discouraged sharper military action. With a few critical deeds—as in the Tonkin Gulf—but more with words, the U.S. commitment had become fixed. To Robert McNamara it was the last year in which America could have disengaged within the terms of its original mission and, with hindsight, should have.

A precise chronology of the decisions made in the following weeks is not yet available, though the general outline is clear. McNamara and McGeorge Bundy laid the shrunken alternatives before the President on January 25, five days after his inauguration. Their analysis, which quickly became known as the "Fork in the Y Memo," warned of disaster ahead in the present course. Their options fell under two broad headings: political compromise leading to withdrawal of the 24,000 Americans then in Vietnam, or escalation by introducing combat troops and air strikes against North Vietnam. They believed the consequences of defeat were too great. Now, they suggested, was the time for the United States to apply its power. They needed answers.

For the moment the President left it open. There was little real doubt in the White House circle, however, how he would rule. Though the formal decision was still open, the real question became one of timing. Mr. Johnson, aware he was at the crossroads, sent McGeorge Bundy to Vietnam for a fresh appraisal.

McNamara was at home on Tracy Place recovering from a mild case of pneumonia when the call came from the Pentagon on February 6. It was just after 1:30 in the afternoon, twelve hours behind Vietnam. The Viet Cong had assaulted the American airfield and billeting area at Pleiku in the Central Highlands. Eight Americans were dead, more than 100 wounded; a score of aircraft had been destroyed or damaged. McNamara remained in touch by telephone for the rest of the afternoon, and at 7:30 P.M. joined the National Security Council in the White House.

By a process of almost silent elimination, the alternatives of withdrawal or doing nothing had dropped away. There were complications beyond those inherent in the military situation, however. Soviet Premier Aleksei Kosygin had arrived in Hanoi only hours before the Pleiku raid. Any American attack in the north would be linked politically to his presence. In the White House meetings the voices of George W. Ball, the Under Secretary of State, and Vice President Hubert Humphrey were raised with questions. Ball forecast requirements reaching beyond any rational judgment of American interest, but he, too, ultimately supported retaliation. Humphrey rushed back from Florida to caution that escalation, once started, would be hard to stop, but then he, too, adopted the dominant view.

From Saigon, Bundy, backed by the military and civilians alike there, approved retaliatory strikes. The plans had been ready for weeks. The National Security Council pored over McNamara's target lists, marked carefully on photographic maps of North Vietnam. For the next two days American and South Vietnamese planes struck training and staging areas in the north. On February 10 the Viet Cong blew up a U.S. Army barracks at Qui Nhon, and another retaliatory raid followed. The door was now open.

Within three weeks raids were being carried out without reference to retaliation. Elsewhere, too, the pace was rising. American planes already were attacking enemy supply routes in Laos. Aircraft manned solely by American crews began attacking the Viet Cong in South Vietnam, abandoning the fiction of combat training for South Vietnamese crews.

There was no doubt of McNamara's advocacy for the retaliatory steps. Privately he told friends that "this is exactly what I would do and I fully support it." He saw the enemy attacks on Pleiku and Qui Nhon as deliberate tests of U.S. resolve, timed to coincide with the Kosygin trip. Nor had he weakened in his sense of the strategic importance of Vietnam.

"The stakes in South Vietnam are far greater than the loss of one small country to Communism," he told the House Armed Services Committee in February. "The choice is not simply whether to continue our efforts to keep South Vietnam free and independent, but, rather, whether to continue our struggle to halt Communist expansion in Asia."

In his mind there was a distinction between the initial retaliatory raids and the sustained bombing of the north that followed. "Nobody thought of the first raids as being more than a political response," one participant in White House meetings recalled. "The question of military value arose as justification for continuing." That judgment appears too narrowly focused, since both civilian and military leaders had been thinking of the military value of bombing for a long time. Political considerations may have been dominant, however, in the specific decisions to launch the first attacks.

With the transition to systematic bombing, McNamara's role changed. He soon imposed restrictions, limiting bombing to military targets away from populated areas. Navy and Air Force commanders fumed. The risks and losses in the pursuit of minor targets seemed to them unwarranted. In broader terms, air strategists held that a heavy attack for maximum damage to North Vietnamese war-making capability would achieve American objectives faster, at acceptable risk. The issue was joined gently at first, but eventually would become one of the fundamental points of difference between the military and the Secretary of Defense.

McNamara held firmly to the strategic argument that unrestrained bombing might provoke the Soviet Union and China into direct intervention in South Vietnam or diversionary action elsewhere. More personally, he was revolted by the vision of the world's most powerful nation pounding a relatively primitive country into oblivion. Instead, he adopted Maxwell Taylor's concept for gradual application of force and shaped it for himself.

Overall the U.S. effort went slowly, under the circumstances almost softly, up the scale. Johnson sought an appearance of continuity, of unchanging policy. In March 3,500 Marines were debarked at Da Nang to defend the U.S. base there. Two months later, 9,000 Marines, airborne troops, and Seabees landed, their role still ostensibly limited. Then the State Department announced that American forces would be available for combat assistance to South Vietnamese forces, which by this time were being shattered at the rate of a battalion a week.

Still, the White House persisted in denial that the primary military mission had changed. On June 16 McNamara announced that U.S. military strength would be increased to more than 70,000, including 21,000 ground combat troops. Next the B-52 strategic bombers based on Guam dumped heavy loads of explosives on War Zone D, which General McGarr had wanted to "clean out" with two ARVN divisions more than three years earlier.

McNamara soon recognized that it still was not enough. North Vietnamese forces were cutting aggressively into the waist of South Vietnam, threatening to divide the country. On July 14 he flew to Saigon to confer again with General William C. Westmoreland, who had replaced Harkins as head of the U.S. Military Assistance Command, Vietnam (MACV), a year earlier. Westmoreland's report was grim, and it was supported by Maxwell Taylor, who in 1961 had foreseen the day when American combat troops would be required in Vietnam. McNamara was convinced. In or out, he told the President back in Washington, we must send in combat troops in force or face defeat.

For his part McNamara saw no acceptable alternative to the commitment of enough troops to stem the tide. In his mind the nation had come up to another of those critical periods, more critical than December, 1961, August, 1963, or the broad vacuum of 1964 when indecision became a decision. Only now more than the treasure and the prestige of the United States was directly engaged. With the interim steps of 1965, its commitment had been stamped unambiguously in blood.

If the nation was to commit major forces, McNamara felt, it should realize it was at war. He proposed the commitment of more

men to Vietnam, 185,000 by the end of the year, with a total of
380,000 to be ready by mid-1966. To obtain the additional manpower, he advocated the summoning of Reserves. Equally important, he recommended that the President ask Congress for direct
political support and the money—"several billion dollars," one
official put it—to fund the war.

Behind McNamara's position was more than the desire to alert
the nation to what it was undertaking and, he hoped, to unite it.
He wanted to demonstrate to the enemy the will the nation had
shown in the Berlin and Cuba crises. Already protest rallies
against the bombing were growing at home and abroad, along
with the disapproval of several friendly governments. Senator
Morse was describing the American role in Vietnam as "im-
moral and Godless"—and illegal as well. But the greater clamor
was for expansion of the war, to strike harder and get it over with.

Partly for that reason, McNamara's recommendations were too
much for the President, and apparently the Secretary of Defense
did not press his case strongly. One of the Administration's concerns had been to avoid generating a war psychosis, for fear it
would get out of hand and lead to great power confrontation.
Besides, the Great Society programs were making their way
through Congress, and Johnson feared the kind of sacrifices Mc-
Namara proposed would endanger them.

Instead, he ordered McNamara to revise his plans. Finally, on
July 28, Johnson announced the results: troop strength in Vietnam would be raised to 125,000, he said, and the monthly draft
quota would be increased from 17,000 to 35,000. The draft was
the substitute for a sharp, unambiguous activation of Reserves. In
August he asked for $1.7 billion to help finance the war, as
McNamara testified, "through January." Both the President and
McNamara made it clear the requirements for men and money
would go higher.

As it worked out, the compromise would become one of the
burdens on the Administration's credibility, which already had
been damaged by creeping escalation. The prospect of greater

public cleavage, of reduced support on the one hand and increased pressure to escalate on the other, besides the cost of mobilizing Reserves, had seemed an unbearable political burden. Despite the warning that more would be required, the decisions came to symbolize what many interpreted as sneaking into a major war. The critics could see confirmation in the massive requests later for money to pay for the July decisions.

McNamara had been overruled on domestic policy regarding the war. But apparently he still did not see the decisions as Americanization of the conflict. The United States had the commitment, it had the planes and men on the ground, and as he remarked to aides, "We are getting the hell kicked out of us."

No one in authority, one Administration official recalled, "really believed that we were taking more than temporary measures which could soon be reversed; the war would be over." To the Secretary of Defense, the basic decision was not to win the war with American troops, but to prevent catastrophe and convince the enemy America meant business.

It was reached in a tight White House circle, and even some of McNamara's closest associates in the Pentagon did not know the details of the debate. "I thought it would go the other way," one confessed.

Looking back, McNamara could see the failures: the failure to provide security in the countryside earlier, the failure to achieve a stable government that could command popular support, the failure to meet the guerrilla in his own shadow world.

"We still haven't learned how to fight guerrilla war," he told his staff fretfully.

But more important to the adventure in Vietnam, the first half of 1965 showed McNamara the rational man at work. The failures were past. With the great power of the United States coming gradually to bear, the enemy ultimately must understand the futility of his undertaking and abandon aggression. McNamara now knew America faced an unbelievably tenacious opponent, one whose determination promised, as he warned publicly, "a long war." Still, with faultless logic as he saw the balance of forces, he concluded that U.S. power would convince the Communists "they can't win in the south." Once that hurdle was past, he said, "we presume that they will move to a settlement."

He had become the principal architect of the American intervention. McNamara's war had entered a new phase, and innocence was not quite dead.

9

Vietnam: Years of

Reckoning

SOMETIME in 1962, before Maxwell Taylor became Chairman of the Joint Chiefs of Staff, he summoned several officials concerned with Vietnam to conduct war games in which direct American intervention was assumed. Taylor took the role of Ho Chi Minh. John A. McCone, the Director of Central Intelligence, played John F. Kennedy. With careful regard for military and political factors, the grim scenario was pushed through with what seemed to be logical escalation. Eventually William H. Sullivan, the State Department officer who performed as Vo Nguyen Giap, North Vietnam's Defense Minister, overran most of the Indochina peninsula. McCone finally threw up his hands. "We have one-third of our military establishment tied up here," he said, and retired from the field. So much for lessons learned.

Three years later Robert McNamara began to orchestrate an American presence that rose steadily through the fall and winter of 1965. Taylor remarked to staff members that the Secretary of Defense seemed remarkably cautious at a time of ever more intensive war-making. This was specifically not the case with some other Presidential advisers. The business of rating the executive team on relative aggressiveness is treacherous, however. Hardly anyone, except George Ball in State, was on record with fundamental reservations.

222

McNamara stood in any case as an efficient warrior. Dean
Rusk, like McNamara, was certain that success was essential to
the world-wide U.S. bulwark against Communism, though he appreciated the risks. Walt Rostow, who soon returned from State
to succeed McGeorge Bundy on the White House staff, developed
as one of the firmest and most optimistic of the hard-liners. Military leaders, once the decisions to go in had been made, predictably and understandably stood for victory. Distinctions among
them would become clearer later.

Mr. Johnson's every instinct was to win, as victory had been
defined in this strange war. But he awoke in the middle of the
night to check on the safety of the pilots sent over North Vietnam
to strike the targets McNamara had carefully limited. In private,
the President rated McNamara behind Rusk, McGeorge Bundy—
and later Rostow, of course—and himself in relative militance.
Still, McNamara betrayed no doubt about the efficacy of American power or the need to use it.

Despite the rising domestic dissent, most members of Congress
still had only a foggy notion of the kind of war under way in
Vietnam. Some understood the tactical hazards, a point illustrated
in a murky lecture McNamara absorbed from A. Willis Robertson, the aging Senator from Virginia, during testimony in
August, 1965:

ROBERTSON: Three Presidents have committed us to stand against
    aggression. A nation with a population the size of the city of New
    York and an area the size of Pennsylvania, that has no modern
    weapons, is a threat to our security, and the Chinese want to make
    a test there. Do they have Johnson grass in Vietnam that grows
    higher than a man's head?
MCNAMARA: I am sorry, I could not hear you, sir.
ROBERTSON: Do they have Johnson grass in Vietnam that is growing
    higher than a man's head?
MCNAMARA: They certainly have some kind of grass. I am not sure
    it is Johnson grass.
ROBERTSON: That is the point of it. I read that it is Johnson grass

and that it grows higher than a man's head. Senator Stennis and I
hunt quail with bird dogs. In a stubblefield we can find quail in
a short time, but in India, where one hunts one tiger in the high
grass, it takes a hundred men to find the tiger. We had a great
general from Lexington named Stonewall Jackson. He developed
vital tactics, which was interior penetration. Do you know what
that means?

McNamara: Yes, sir, I believe so.

Robertson: It was exemplified against Banks at Cross Keys and
Port Republic. Banks had 50,000 men. Jackson had 27,000. Banks
divided his forces to the interior penetration. Stonewall Jackson
concentrated first on one divided force and then the other, and
whipped them both. They didn't quit running until they crossed the
Potomac. . . . How can you make an interior penetration or a turning movement in Johnson grass higher than your head? They have
not found that out, have they? Did you know about the Johnson
grass when you told the President on March 26, 1964, about making war in South Vietnam? Did you know about the Johnson
grass?

McNamara: Yes, sir, I knew of the grass. As I say, I'm not sure it
was Johnson grass, but I knew there were difficult terrains in
which to fight in Southeast Asia and particularly in South Vietnam.

Tens of thousands of American troops were learning about the
high grass and the difficult terrain in the second half of 1965. In
any previous war, what happened during those months would
have been nationally acclaimed as a triumph of American courage
and adaptability. Fought in oppressive jungle heat during the
day, wet, penetrating chill at night, the battles of the Ia Drang
Valley marked the point at which the U.S. side stopped losing the
war—the military war. The 1st Cavalry Division lost 240 men
but took ten lives for each one it gave.

Yet this already was a poor war for heroes. In mid-October
anti-war demonstrations brought marchers into the streets in forty
American cities. A few days later General Curtis E. LeMay, the
retired Air Force Chief of Staff, complained that the United
States was doing too little, too late in Vietnam. He particularly

wanted heavier bombing of the north. On the other hand, Senator
J. William Fulbright, chairman of the Foreign Relations Committee, urged suspension of bombing as an encouragement to
peace negotiations. In November there were more demonstrations. Two pacifists burned themselves to death, one of them
within view of McNamara's Pentagon office. The national torment
had begun.

So, in a chronic, nagging way, had that of Robert McNamara.
There is no suggestion that the Secretary of Defense already was
making a pacifist nuisance of himself with a bellicose President.
Their conclusions were in general harmony. McNamara was
troubled at putting to use the tools he had created, yet confident
they would produce the programmed results.

"Bob was never comfortable as a hawk," a senior U.S. general
has since observed. "He supported the early bombing for the
immediate political purpose of causing the North Vietnamese to
negotiate. He favored the introduction of ground forces first
to prevent defeat, second to convince the North Vietnamese of
American will. To him, it was inconceivable they would continue
to fight. They would recognize reality." McNamara had a great
deal of company in Washington.

There was an immediate and fundamental cleavage between
McNamara and his military advisers over the conduct of bombing
operations, however. The Joint Chiefs of Staff had charted a
short, savage campaign to destroy airfields, ports, petroleum
depots, and transportation systems in North Vietnam. In military
terms it would be a maximum effort to eliminate the enemy's
means to wage war short of attacking his population directly.
The political results, as the advocates saw it, would follow naturally.

McNamara's orientation was first of all political. The bombing
was intended to put pressure on Hanoi. That pressure would be
gradual and strictly controlled. The sort of campaign favored by
the Joint Chiefs, he feared, would force direct reaction by China
and the Soviet Union, in Vietnam or at some other vulnerable

point. At the very least, the bickering Communist rivals would be encouraged to reunite.

Early in the bombing, it dawned upon some close witnesses that McNamara, rather than managing a positive process of escalation, was instead, as one put it, "actually holding the campaign to the minimum consistent with keeping control of it himself." It was a distinction that would become more and more important.

McNamara's explanations of the aerial campaign were the most articulate to come from the Administration, though for a time there was some confusion over the public policy behind the raids. In the early months McNamara put it most simply: "To get North Vietnam to cease its support of Viet Cong aggression."

As time went on he was more elaborate: "That air effort in the north is—as it should be—mainly an effort to interdict the lines of communication and military traffic. Anything beyond that, short of destruction of the North Vietnamese nation, is not likely to make a significant military difference so long as Hanoi believes that in South Vietnam the war can be won."

Gradually a more complete justification evolved: the bombing was designed to raise South Vietnamese morale, to reduce the flow of men and matériel to the south, to put a price on aggression for Hanoi. But the basic reason remained what it had been at the beginning: pressure on Hanoi to desist. McNamara and the Joint Chiefs of Staff remained sorely divided on execution.

The wonder is that the differences, though they were understood by some outsiders, failed for so long to burst explosively to the surface. The fact that they did not was testimony in part to the control McNamara had clamped over the Pentagon, in part to his influence with Lyndon Johnson. Essential in this was his avowed dedication to total loyalty upward. He demanded it, and he gave it to the President. "This is absolutely fundamental," he said once. "Neither I nor any other Cabinet member was elected: the President was." Thus he was capable of reasoned and articulate defense, with conscience undisturbed, of decisions he opposed once they had been made. He expected the same performance from subordinates. The alternative was to resign.

Yet the strain began to show with the deepening of the American involvement. McNamara had regarded a five-day suspension of bombing in May, 1965, as insufficient to draw from Hanoi a signal of readiness to talk. In November he proposed to the President a longer, unambiguous pause. That initiative evolved the following month into a thirty-seven-day suspension. It was accompanied by a sweeping, semipublic peace offensive in which American diplomats swarmed through the capitals of the world probing for signs of North Vietnamese willingness to negotiate.

It finally dissolved with rejection from Hanoi and domestic criticism of what some commentators later called "fandangle diplomacy." At the end of January sentiment in the National Security Council was overwhelmingly in favor of renewed bombing. But one of the nation's leading diplomats noted in his diary, "The Secretary of Defense is more interested in a political solution than others at his level." McNamara tried quietly to get the pause extended. But on January 31 Air Force and Navy planes again attacked, and now the bombs began to come closer to the economic-population complex of Hanoi, the capital, and Haiphong, the principal port of North Vietnam.

On the ground, U.S. strength was rising steadily. The President had said the previous July that he would supply troops as needed by his commanders. The import of that open-ended commitment had been recognized by only a few. Among them was Henry Cabot Lodge, who exclaimed privately, "My God, the Commander in Chief has just given up the only real power he has over the conduct of the war."

Westmoreland had surprised even McNamara to some extent with his early tactics. There was a general assumption in Washington that the field commander, who had greater freedom of decision on the ground than most Americans realized, would establish his forces on the coast first and move inland gradually.

Instead, Westmoreland attacked, leaping with his helicopters into the enemy's lairs. Although his so-called spoiling actions succeeded, the leaders in Hanoi simply raised the ante. They had ample grounds for doing so, for the political pattern of early 1966 in Washington and Saigon could only have been encouraging.

Dissent was growing in America. In Vietnam the government still could not find the key to popular support. The Political Action Teams deployed in 1965 had failed, as the pacification specialists put it, to "win the hearts and minds" of Vietnamese peasants largely because the military was unable to provide the protection the teams were supposed to exploit.

McNamara outwardly was calm as he continued to chart and defend forcefully the Administration's prosecution of the war. But he was growing edgier in the inner Pentagon circles. One associate noted that he became "damned near desperate" in searching for a formula that would produce popular support for a Saigon government.

Others watched curiously for McNamara's reaction as Senator Robert F. Kennedy, brother of the late President and a close friend of the Secretary, began publicly to detach himself from the Administration. In February, 1966, the Senator spoke out for a policy that would open a "share of power and responsibility" to the National Liberation Front, the political parent of the Viet Cong. Administration policy ostensibly included this possibility, in that former Viet Cong would be free to compete in elections once peace was established. There was no doubt, however, that the Administration intended to put down the military challenge first.

McNamara was publicly silent on Kennedy's behavior. Yet he realized its implications for his own position. It had started out as a bad year for him in several other respects as well. Congress was beginning to challenge him across the board, from management to relations with the military to strategic concepts. Then Hanson Baldwin of the *New York Times* put many of the funda-

mental criticisms into the context of the war in Vietnam. In his
analysis Baldwin reported shortages in personnel and equipment,
lack of readiness in military units, weaknesses in McNamara's
system. In sum it was a bill of particulars against McNamara's
performance where it counted most, in the crucible of war.

He responded quickly, summoning a now famous press conference to rebut the charges: most of the allegations, he said, were
false, others misleading. A flood of defensive statistics poured
over the accusations of shortages and lack of readiness. In approach it was a typical McNamara performance. His defense was
uncompromising, to the extent that his acknowledgment of scattered "inventory shortages," that "with large supply systems . . .
somewhere, sometime, something will be lacking," was diluted.
Above all, it was not a *mea culpa*.

"It is clear," he said, "that far from overextending ourselves
we have actually strengthened our military position. Our active-
duty forces are being expanded. Our reserve forces are being
strengthened and made more combat-ready. Our production and
logistics base is being vastly increased. And all of this is being
done without calling up the Reserves, without generally extending
tours of duty, without imposing the economic controls over wages
and prices, profits, materials, which is typical of emergency
conditions."

Many observers, including some of McNamara's admirers, felt
he was guilty of overkill in his defense. Better, they argued, for
him simply to make the point that the nation had performed mag-
nificently without formal mobilization, though with inevitable
difficulties, and then rest on his performance. McNamara was
in no mood for humility. He believed deeply that the buildup in
Vietnam had demonstrated the new capability of conventional
forces in the spectrum of flexible response.

His running exchange at the same time with the Senate Preparedness Subcommittee, under Senator John Stennis of Mississippi, underscored the point. The subcommittee staff had studied
four divisions in the strategic reserve at home and discovered

they were being used for training recruits. Thus they were not combat-ready. It was typical of McNamara, and the Pentagon beneath him, that extracting this information and making it public was hardly an easy process. It was also essential McNamara that he did not tell Stennis he had recommended summoning Reserves the year before to forestall this kind of problem.

Many of these pressures came to a head in the March press conference. Clark Mollenhoff, of the Des Moines *Register and Tribune,* a persistent critic of McNamara, knew of the Stennis report and smelled blood. He bombarded McNamara until the Secretary lost his composure: "Look, if you are not going to maintain order, will you please leave?"

"No," said Mollenhoff, and he persisted.

Then a German reporter asked a logical question: "Mr. Secretary, is it not true that despite the buildup of large reserves, the best-trained, best-equipped, and most mobile American units have been now absorbed by the Vietnam crisis so that the strategic mobility of the United States forces has been diminished?"

"Let me answer your question," McNamara snapped. "Where are you from?"

"From Germany."

"It is absolutely not true, and you are the first that ought to know it. I am sick and tired of having implications made that we have drawn down the forces in Western Europe when we haven't. The Seventh Army has been, is today, and in the future will be the most combat-ready Army in the world. It will not be affected in that respect by our operations in Southeast Asia. The first people that ought to know that are the Germans."

McNamara later apologized for the outburst. But his performance that day bore upon several aspects of his administration of the Pentagon. His sensitivity became a part of what was already being identified as the Administration's credibility gap— that unmeasurable and baneful distance between what the Administration said and what the public would believe. It was dramatized in a war that continued to grow to an extent for which the public was unprepared.

Within the military, troopers knew they did not always have the arms and the ammunition and the air support they wanted. They knew of the adjustments made in the Seventh Army, no matter how much McNamara discounted their importance, to accommodate Vietnam. Their officers, resentful at McNamara's assertion of control, were not displeased at evidence to support their prejudices. In Congress the customary supporters of the military view were in much the same mood. Whether or not the Secretary's statements were literally correct became in a sense irrelevant.

He was under tremendous strain and showing it more frequently. With some sympathy a McNamara critic, Representative Melvin Laird of Michigan, remarked that "Bob appears tired. He's been working seventeen hours a day for more than five years and he's getting a little testy. He should take off and get some rest." Shortly after the press conference outburst, McNamara left with his family for a week of skiing in Switzerland—friends said under direct orders from the President.

Few appreciated the cumulative pressures. One who did was Lloyd Norman, the military correspondent of *Newsweek* magazine. Norman reported with keen insight:

McNamara continues to present the façade of the ice-blooded, tireless, unemotional executive who doesn't waver in a crisis or under sniping from Congress and the press. But underneath this façade is a sensitive perfectionist who reads his press clippings eagerly for a kind word, who loses his temper when a Clark Mollenhoff torments him, and who bangs on desks and swears when the Germans, the British, the French don't accept his strategic concepts for NATO. His face greyer, his hair thinner, his voice tending to go hoarse when he is emotionally upset, McNamara reveals the erosion of more than five hard years in the Pentagon.

Above all, it was Vietnam that tested the Secretary and exacted its toll. When he returned refreshed from the week in Switzerland, there was once again political turmoil in Vietnam, and once again it erupted from relations between the government and the Buddhists. The outburst turned violently anti-American with the sacking of the U.S. Consulate and library at Hué in May. Once

more Buddhists began burning themselves to death in Saigon—
five in a three-day period. The disturbances coincided with
hearings on Vietnam by the increasingly hostile Senate Foreign
Relations Committee, and McNamara's appearance before the
committee was a masterful performance.

He dominated the old Senate caucus room from the moment he
strode on scene, well aware of the television cameras, and slapped
his worn yellow briefcase onto the witness table. Forcefully,
sometimes with passion, he made the Administration's case: We
were in Vietnam because South Vietnam had asked for help and
we had accepted obligations there; this was not a civil war, but
aggression from the north; China, despite her internal problems,
unquestionably had designs on Southeast Asia; South Vietnam
manifestly did not want Viet Cong rule. Not a single leader had
defected or urged surrender, despite the current turmoil.

Even Senator Wayne Morse saluted him for "your brilliant and
masterful support of an unsound policy."

By now the war had developed its own momentum. It was a
year marked by sweeping military escalation. At midyear the
United States had committed 285,000 men. South Vietnam had
total forces of 645,000, and other allies, principally Korea, had
contributed 30,000. Westmoreland's men were winning their
battles, exacting a terrible toll. But McNamara estimated total
enemy strength at 282,000, an increase of 50,000 in eight months
despite 32,000 killed. Infiltration from the north for that period
was put at 40,000. All together, McNamara's statistics revealed
a great deal about the enemy's tenacity—as well as his ability to
continue recruiting in South Vietnam.

The pace of bombardment in the north matched that of the war
in the south. At the end of June, Air Force and Navy planes
struck by daylight the petroleum supplies at Hanoi, Haiphong,
and Do Son. Civilian casualties inevitably rose as bombs thundered into populated areas. With the nonmilitary damage mounting, Hanoi gave maximum effort to reap the obvious propaganda
harvest.

So it went into the fall and winter. Incongruous as it may seem, several close associates of McNamara agree that he did not understand the extent of casualties among the innocent in Vietnam, south and north, until late 1966. He was frustrated additionally because military measures several times conflicted with political efforts to generate negotiations.

These were critical months in his evolution as administrator of the war. He had shackled the military from the beginning in its aerial campaign against the north. He had joined eagerly in the search for a path to negotiations, and he had looked particularly for reasons to extend the bombing pauses with which the Administration tried to coax Hanoi into negotiations. Nevertheless, he had engineered the bombing, however restricted; he had poured in the troops, and he remained the trusted adviser of a President committed, semantics aside, to military victory in South Vietnam. None of it was showing the results so confidently foreseen in 1965.

The public record is almost, though not quite, silent as to McNamara's thoughts during these months to the extent that they varied from the established policy. What was unquestionable was his bitter disappointment at the pace of the schemes to bring about social and economic reform in the countryside.

Civilian casualties would have made it difficult enough under the most favorable political circumstances. Too often the bombers struck where their only political effect was to drive hearts and minds to the Viet Cong. It was too often difficult for troopers understandably worried about their own casualties to distinguish between the pajama-clad uncommitted peasant and the pajama-clad Viet Cong. Too often, they yielded to frustration and fired without discrimination.

The political circumstances, in any case, were not the most favorable. Time and again the United States by choice or necessity had focused on the top of the Vietnamese political spectrum rather than on the broad base of the population. The Ky government had committed itself to a massive development program. Political turmoil and different conceptions of what constituted development emasculated the effort. The Americans were thinking of social and economic reforms. The Vietnamese largely ignored the concept and thought in terms of rural construction. South Vietnam wallowed in a sea of corruption.

Nevertheless, when McNamara visited Vietnam in October for the eighth time, he could report that military progress "has exceeded our expectations." The Saigon government had acted "very courageously, very wisely, and very foresightedly" with measures against inflation. The "concept" of the pacification program had proved its soundness, and General Thang, who was in charge, was "one of the most aggressive, one of the ablest, administrators that I have ever been associated with."

However, "one must also recognize that the progress has been very slow indeed," and the pace would have to be stepped up. Hanoi remained undaunted by its terrible losses on the battlefield, he said, and continued to replace them at a rate estimated at 4,000 to 7,000 a month. Translated realistically, it was a lean report.

The thread of veiled frustration that ran through his careful phrases was reinforced by word from associates that he looked to a ceiling of something like 400,000 men. Privately he expressed hope that artillery and aircraft would round out the military requirement, permitting greater concentration on development. But that hope, too, was quickly dashed, and the number of men continued to rise.

By now another powerful force was at work on the Secretary of Defense, and it proved to be the critical one: the cumulative effect of domestic dissent against the war. Most of it came from students and teachers, from intellectuals whose credentials the Secretary of Defense respected.

Some of it was imbedded deeply within McNamara's own circle of friends. Senator Robert Kennedy became steadily more critical of Administration policy. So the man most directly responsible for the execution of the war during long and trying days was in moments of relaxation a comrade of one of its determined critics.

As early as the spring of 1966, he had begun to put himself on
record, in a series of speeches, with his convictions on world
order. Speaking before newspaper editors in Montreal, he argued
eloquently that the essence of security lay beyond military power.
Instead, he said, it was to be found in economic, social, and
political development, through which rich nations must acknowledge their interest in the security and well-being of the poor.
There was a hint of Vietnam in one passage: "Certainly we have
no charter to rescue floundering regimes, who have brought violence on themselves by deliberately refusing to meet the legiti-
mate expectations of their citizenry."

But in August a Marine Corps report asserted that North Vietnam could continue the war indefinitely at its current rate of
casualties. And in October a *Congressional Quarterly* survey indicated that of 454 Senators and Representatives, all but 81 favored
the present U.S. course in Vietnam or even stronger military
action.

The whipsawing effect of attitudes on the war, like those on
strategic weapons during the same period, was increasing in
tempo. McNamara was shocked when he was elbowed and shoved
by student anti-war demonstrators at Harvard after a seminar in
November.

Challenged to debate, he then was shouted down. "I might
add," he cried above the din, after recalling his own Harvard
years, "that I was a lot tougher and a lot more courteous than
you." More jeers, and he added, "I was tougher than you and I
am tougher today."

Toughness was a quality he saw in himself and admired in
others. "Ho Chi Minh is a tough old S.O.B.," he mused at a staff
meeting. "And he won't quit no matter how much bombing we
do. I'm as tough as he is and I know I wouldn't quit no matter
how painful the bombing."

He was now unwilling to meet fully the requests for more troops
in Vietnam. Rather than continue weighing the country down
with Americans, McNamara wanted to sharpen up the pacifica-

tion program with Vietnamese personnel, who ultimately would have to do the job anyway. He no longer bothered to praise the current Vietnamese pacification or military efforts, but he still had hope that, with retraining, ARVN units would improve the situation.

Whether or not his frustrations and doubts had solidified into a fundamental conviction against further escalation by the end of 1966 remains unclear. Several close associates were convinced this was the case, and the evidence is impressive. Moreover, he had begun to shift the primary judgment on "need" for American forces on the ground from the military to civilian authorities. His doubts about the bombing of North Vietnam were growing even as he began to lose the struggle to keep targeting restricted.

The campaign had been "successful" or "effective," he said. He did not use the word "necessary," and more and more his reservations popped to the surface.

Here at least the evidence was clear. In January, 1967, he told the Senate Armed Services Committee firmly, "I don't believe the bombing that I could contemplate in the future would significantly reduce the actual flow of men and matériel to the south." Indirectly he disclosed that he had been doubtful about attacks on petroleum supplies the year before. He had argued that North Vietnam still would be able to meet its limited needs—as it did, when the supplies were bombed later.

Now he was being overruled, one by one, on some of the targets he had excluded from the approved list. In January he publicly opposed bombing in heavily populated areas. Soon the bombers struck at power plants inside the population complexes of Hanoi and Haiphong. In April he made a strong case at a press conference against bombing North Vietnamese airfields. Three weeks later the fields at Kep and Hoa Lac were attacked. McNamara then defended the decisions staunchly—the fields were hit, he said, because North Vietnamese planes had become more active against U.S. bombers.

More important for U.S. public opinion, a record 274 Amer-

icans were killed in the last week of the month, bringing the total
for the war to 8,560.

"Now as to whether our nation can afford this," McNamara
told Congress. "Are we running out of money? The answer is no.
The only thing we are running out of in this country is will. I
want to emphasize this, we are not running out of economic resources, we are not running out of money, we are just running
out of patience and will."

In April the biggest anti-war demonstration yet brought
125,000 into the streets of New York.

There no longer was any doubt in the minds of close McNamara associates that the Secretary was deeply troubled. He was
falling more and more out of step with the course he himself had
developed.

The basic policy remained, as it had been from the beginning,
a variation of his own concept of flexible response. If he overstated his dissent, he would lose his effectiveness in the White
House. If he resigned, he would unleash the war, as he saw it,
besides abandoning a task in which he was still the dominant
figure in the public mind. Moreover, he still appreciated the possible long-range consequences of undisguised defeat in Vietnam.

His state of mind crept to the surface in unusual ways. On one
occasion he authorized direct quotation from a background interview: "I never discuss my personal views on matters which are
in the President's province. I don't believe the government of a
complicated state can operate effectively if those in charge of the
departments of the government express disagreement with decisions of the established head of that government.

"I never discuss any recommendations I might have made to
the President before the policy decision was made. To do so
might strengthen my position but would weaken the President's
at the cost of the nation. I don't believe the public would gain
by such discussion. Our responsibility as Cabinet Officers is
to the nation, through the President. If we express our disagree-
ments in public we would weaken the President and the govern-

ment, and in turn that would weaken the nation." The remarks had the ring of dissent crying for release.

Privately he told associates the bombing of the north made no positive contribution to the war. Reports from the Central Intelligence Agency, consistently less optimistic than military estimates, more and more supported his position.

As a close friend saw it, "I don't think I overstate it to say Bob was in torment by the spring of 1967." One of the nation's prominent military figures described McNamara's anguish in less personal terms: "Bob had come to doubt the application of military power for political ends, whether he recognized it or not."

In April came the first direct hope of relief, in a tentative offer of the Presidency of the World Bank. One who reacted quickly, who had shared the sleepless nights of recent months, was Margaret McNamara. At a dinner party a few days later she spoke quietly to a friend. Her husband was torn inside, she said, and felt he had to get out. They had been up until four that morning talking about it, she said, and he would like the World Bank. Later that night the friend spoke to McNamara for confirmation. He was loyal and would remain so, the Secretary said, but he felt the time was coming for him to leave. The bank indeed would be a challenge. But meanwhile the war continued.

In the weeks of the spring and early summer, McNamara tried to put order into the fragmented political development effort by placing it all under Westmoreland's MACV. The various agencies involved, including AID, the CIA, the U.S. Information Agency, and the Department of State, were supposed to coordinate under Robert W. Komer, who had been assigned as Westmoreland's deputy for civil development. Many officers at sensitive places in the program simply continued to follow the popular axiom: "Grab 'em by the balls and the hearts and minds will follow."

This weakness weighed heavily upon McNamara as he made his ninth trip to Vietnam in early July. He had moved the civilian pacification effort under MACV in near desperation against the advice of some close associates. Now he detected only faint signs of progress. When he returned to Washington five days later, he could report a few definite gains in other areas. Saigon was moving rapidly toward elections under the new Constitution. Inflation had been reduced to comprehensible levels, partly by breaking the shipping bottleneck in the port of Saigon. Where it counted most, on the state of the war and the winning of the hearts and minds, even McNamara's public assessment was notably cautious.

Talking with reporters after reporting to the President, he noted carefully that "the military commanders stated" that reports of stalemate were ridiculous. "In their view," military progress had occurred and was continuing. Pressed for his own assessment, he conceded that "I was quite persuaded of the reasonableness of their view and the correctness of their appraisal." Still, he added, "I know the danger of accepting at face value all that is reported to me."

Into that single remark he compressed his bitterness at six years of overoptimism based in great measure on faulty statistics and analysis. His own guidelines had failed him, in part because others did not operate by the same standards. The Vietnamese, for example, were ready to present the Americans with any figures Washington seemed to want to hear.

More troops would be required beyond the 480,000 then authorized, he admitted. But he emphasized, without revealing figures, that he hoped to get by with fewer than Westmoreland was asking for.

"I am certain of one thing," he said, "that we must use more effectively the personnel that are presently there." He particularly wanted to increase the ratio of combat to support troops. This, in effect, was what Westmoreland wanted to do by adding more men—but the gap between their estimates of need was in the tens of thousands. McNamara later regretted his implied criticism of Westmoreland, for his deeper criticism on effectiveness of forces applied to the Vietnamese.

By now his own effectiveness was slipping. The precise moment when his star began to wane in the White House may never be clear. His perception that his usefulness was over obviously was nagging him as early as the spring. He was affected profoundly by the death of John T. McNaughton, the young Assistant Secretary for International Security Affairs, in a domestic air crash. McNaughton had helped chart the course of gradualism in Vietnam with McNamara, and their disillusionment with the undertaking coincided.

One of their final joint efforts, along with Paul Nitze and Cyrus Vance, had been a proposal in April to draw bombing back to the 20th parallel, thus limiting it to North Vietnam's southern panhandle. It was rejected, for the time being, in the absence of enemy willingness to reciprocate.

McNamara's mood naturally affected those closest to him. During his July trip to Vietnam, his wife had to enter the Johns Hopkins Hospital in Baltimore for treatment of serious ulcers. He told other officials that those ulcers more equitably should have been his own. The hospital staff reported that after his return from Vietnam the Secretary of Defense, gray-faced behind a day's growth of heavy beard, raced in at odd hours almost every night for at least a few minutes with his wife.

Through it all, the bombing remained the catalyst for his disaffection. Despite his careful public support of policy, he had left only a faint case for the campaign in the north during his testimony the previous January. In August, before Senator John Stennis' Preparedness Subcommittee, he gave it even less credence.

The presentation was carefully prepared and exquisitely balanced. McNamara set out, with the help of key aides, to accomplish contradictory goals: to destroy any objective argument for increased bombing, while claiming that its limited purposes had been served; to make clear his own views, without obviously running ahead of the President.

The sources and lines of supply for North Vietnam's needs at home and in South Vietnam, he said, were such that Hanoi could overcome anything short of "the virtual annihilation of North

Vietnam and its people." No one, McNamara said, had proposed the population slaughter necessary to do more than make this logistics process more difficult and costly.

He acknowledged his differences with the Joint Chiefs of Staff, the extent of which he had so carefully obscured before. Of the 427 targets on the current JCS list, he said, all but 57 had been authorized. In his judgment, of the 57, 7 were of little value, 9 were minor petroleum dumps, 25 were lesser targets in "populated, heavily defended areas," 4 were more important targets in such areas, 3 were ports, 4 were airfields, and 5 were in the buffer zone near the Chinese border. His blanket objection covered most of these: "I am Secretary of Defense and I am responsible for lives and I am not about to recommend the loss of American lives in relation to these targets."

A few of the total had greater importance, airfields and ports especially, and the most important of all was the Port of Haiphong. Apart from its strategic value, military leaders regarded mining or bombing Haiphong as a matter of great psychological importance. McNamara conceded that the United States could close Haiphong—at considerable cost. But he stood firmly on the argument that nothing the United States could do would prevent North Vietnam from finding other routes of supply and maintaining the flow of men and matériel south.

Even now, he did not draw the obvious conclusions for the record from his own testimony. "I would like to restate my view," he said, "that the present objectives of our bombing in the north were soundly conceived and are being effectively pursued. They are consistent with our overall purposes in Vietnam and with our efforts to confine the conflict." But bombing would not win the war, he declared. There was no easy way out.

On the face of it, his argument was primarily a defense of current policy, and a case against escalation. There was more to it than that, however. For any who accepted his analysis in full, the objective case for continuation went out the window. Logically, McNamara would have had to recommend an unconditional end to bombing unless it was to be justified solely in terms of its psychological effect, north and south.

Still he could not openly challenge policy. He had stretched his own standards for official discretion to the outer limits. At the very least, he had disavowed publicly some of the options open to the President. If Mr. Johnson now chose to increase the bombing, it would have to be over the public opposition of his Secretary of Defense—or without him entirely.

Members of the Stennis subcommittee were unimpressed, to put it mildly. They also were keenly aware that McNamara already was losing, while the military—and they—were winning the internal struggle over bombing restrictions. McNamara testified on August 25. In the preceding weeks Admiral U. S. G. Sharp, the Pacific commander, General Wheeler, and the Chiefs of Staff had extolled the bombing and urged its expansion. All this time, the President was clearing more of the disputed targets for attack. At the end of the month the subcommittee weighed in with a report that adopted, without qualification, the military judgment and demanded "the force that is required to see the job through."

"The simple fact is that President Johnson was more impressed by what he was hearing from the Joint Chiefs of Staff than from the Secretary of Defense," remarked a participant in the White House debate. The President, with obvious symbolism, in the later stages began to put Westmoreland up in the White House during his trips to Washington.

McNamara, however, was still striving for effectiveness, rather than victory on every issue. He advanced and retreated. But he was losing one of his great advantages, of being able to shape the military dissent he reported to the President in terms that left him the greatest effectiveness. Lyndon Johnson now was getting the military view directly from the military.

McNamara still had one major contribution to make to the Administration's public position that summer. It surfaced in the President's speech at San Antonio on September 29, in which

Johnson significantly changed the U.S. terms for negotiation with North Vietnam. Until then, Hanoi had demanded an unconditional end to the bombing, with the half-promise that then there could be talks. The United States had offered to end bombing if North Vietnam stopped sending men south.

In the so-called San Antonio formula, which had been handed privately to the North Vietnamese in August, Johnson said: "The United States is willing immediately to stop all aerial and naval bombardment of North Vietnam when this will lead promptly to productive discussions. We would, of course, assume that, while the discussions proceed, North Vietnam would not take advantage of the bombing cessation or limitation."

The changes were apparent. The United States now asked for nothing more than a promise of "productive discussions" in exchange for ending the bombing. No longer was there a demand for specific enemy de-escalation. By implication, Hanoi could continue its normal flow of men and supplies. The only caveat: the United States obviously would decide for itself if the enemy was taking advantage of its restraint.

McNamara was one of the principal authors of the San Antonio formula. Working with him were Paul Nitze, by then Deputy Secretary, and Paul C. Warnke, who had succeeded John McNaughton as Assistant Secretary for International Security Affairs, Nicholas deB. Katzenbach, the Under Secretary of State, who was becoming more and more active in the search for a peace formula, and Henry A. Kissinger, the Harvard professor who later would become the chief strategist of the Nixon Administration.

For the time being, it appeared their effort was wasted. Hanoi took the position that even the San Antonio language fixed unacceptable conditions. Not until months later would its effect be seen in the terms under which talks actually began. And McNamara, from that point forward, was on his way out.

At the end of September Hanson Baldwin of the *New York Times* reported that the President had called for a member of the

Joint Chiefs of Staff to attend all future White House discussions on the bombing of North Vietnam. It was not believed to be a reflection on McNamara, Baldwin wrote, but rather a device by which the President could say he always sought military advice before making military decisions.

Baldwin was being unwontedly kind to McNamara. Time now was running short. In mid-October the President let McNamara know the Presidency of the World Bank was in the cards. When he had talked briefly with Johnson about the bank months earlier, McNamara had emphasized his readiness to stay in the Pentagon as long as he was needed. Now he had his answer.

Now, indeed, he had little to lose. In the next two weeks the Secretary of Defense, as an associate described it, "finally bit the bullet." On November 1 he turned in a memorandum to the President, distilling on paper the results of a year of soul-searching and doubt. His argument was for nothing less than the reversal of the American course, meeting the terms of most moderate critics of current policy.

The American public would not tolerate the escalation necessary to bring the war to an unambiguous military victory, he said, nor would it tolerate a simple continuation of present policy. Therefore the United States should (1) stop the bombing of North Vietnam unconditionally in an effort to generate negotiations; (2) fix a ceiling at the currently authorized level of U.S. personnel, and (3) begin to turn the war over to South Vietnam as rapidly as possible. Bombing of the north was worthless except as a negotiating card, he argued; therefore the United States would be giving up nothing substantial by stopping it.

It is fair to say that from that day Vietnam was no longer "McNamara's war." But these were not easy decisions for the President to take. For the time being he held fast.

Not until November 29 were the arrangements complete for the announcement of McNamara's appointment to the World Bank. The last few days were particularly trying, for the word leaked out in advance. The speculation that McNamara was being eased out was inevitable, and mostly accurate.

When the announcement finally came, General Westmoreland, just back in Saigon after conferences in Washington, was unreserved in his praise for McNamara. "I don't believe anybody in the history of the United States has performed with greater distinction," he said.

General Wheeler, who had maintained a careful liaison between military and civilian viewpoints, had a concise reply to reports that some of the Chiefs had threatened to quit unless McNamara left: "Bullshit."

But Hanson Baldwin reported a few days later that many military men were relieved. He was, of course, correct.

McNamara agreed to remain long enough to prepare the next budget. Otherwise, he was impotent for all practical purposes as the war approached a critical point. For even as Westmoreland spoke confidently of turning more to nation building and the development of ARVN, Hanoi was preparing what it hoped would be a decisive stroke.

The enemy called it the Winter-Spring Campaign, and it was focused on Tet, the Vietnamese lunar New Year holiday. While major American forces were occupied on the periphery of South Vietnam, and half of ARVN was on leave, enemy forces surged into province and district capitals, most major cities, airfields—targets of prime military and political importance. It resulted in a bloody military defeat for the Communists, with as many as 50,000 killed. It was, on the other hand, a psychological disaster for the United States.

As one commentator wrote: "The victory was over the hearts and minds of the people of the United States, and ultimately over the President himself."

McNamara was no longer in a position to influence the inevitable military backlash from Tet in the United States. Westmoreland, invited by the Joint Chiefs to state his maximum needs, responded quickly. His report was translated into a request from the Chiefs for 206,000 men over the next ten months.

McNamara knew the request would add $10 billion to a defense budget already projected near $80 billion, and finally break through the barrier against the mobilization of Reserves. But by then he had only a few days to go, and it was far too late for him to bring his will and power of persuasion and compromise to bear.

In his final posture statement to Congress he methodically set out the scope of what gradually had become one of the major wars in the short, violent history of the nation. Total allied forces in South Vietnam had reached 1.3 million, with 1.4 million—including 525,000 Americans—scheduled by June. There were 3,100 helicopters, 1,000 fighter-bombers. B-52s out of Guam and Thailand were flying more than 800 sorties a month.

On the enemy side were something like a quarter of a million men, with the precious advantage of the guerrilla and the even more important quality of motivation, lacking in the forces of South Vietnam. The enemy had lost 188,000 men to all causes in 1967, by McNamara's rough estimate, and still more came. Most important to the U.S. role, 9,350 Americans had died in 1967 alone, for a total of 16,000 since 1960.

Despite his own disaffection, McNamara still honored the strategic factors that had drawn two Democratic Administrations even deeper into the war.

"Southeast Asia remains for the United States a test of the viability of our collective defense policy," he said, and, he might have added, a test of flexible response as he decreed its practice. Small, independent nations must have the opportunity to develop free of aggression. "Our role in this process will be particularly important," he said. "We must see the Vietnam conflict through to a conclusion that permits the growth and maturing of regional cooperation."

It was a muted cry. There was no trumpet sounding the charge here. His own stake in Vietnam, from his strategic concepts to his personal management, was greater than that of any other individual except the President himself. Once again, in private conversations, he recognized errors, two of them fundamental: support of a weak government lacking popular appeal, and intervention without the public, unequivocal request of other friendly governments in the area. What he was saying, perhaps without fully realizing it, was that the Vietnam intervention, under the circumstances in which it developed, was a mistake.

The mistakes he identified were essentially political. Long ago he had seen and defined the ingredients of success in Vietnam, economic, military, and political. They had failed to blend. When he reflected on Vietnam privately later, he was unrelenting on his military formula. If he had it all to do over again, he still would not apply the sudden, massive power the military had demanded. He still would apply the pressure gradually.

But under the conditions that prevailed, it had to become an American war. And an American war it became, to the point that even leaders in Saigon seemed to expect the country to be handed over to them, tidily wrapped in the Star-Spangled Banner. The U.S. military was prepared to fight it on those terms.

Westmoreland had faith in his own forces. In the early stages he had little understanding of the need to build a nation, and little use for ARVN. Only when it was too late, and the price too high, did he focus on what came to be known as Vietnamization. Only with American exhaustion did Washington, and Saigon by necessity, return to original premises. The Vietnamese would have to win it or lose it themselves, after all.

Not even McNamara, who had stated the premises six years before, had been able to fit all the factors together. Nor could he turn it around when his chosen course failed. What he had done was lay a foundation for others who might succeed.

By February he was marching to a beat far different from that which guided the still-dominant hawks in Congress, the military—and the White House. The House Armed Services Committee, where Chairman Mendel Rivers shared an abiding mutual dislike with McNamara, did not bother to invite him for delivery of his

final posture statement. Yet publicly he was out of step also with
the students and the liberals to whom his spirit cried for harmony.

"I am learning more and more about Vietnam every day," he
said in a farewell television appearance. "There is no question I
see better today than I did three years ago or five years ago what
might have been done there. . . . I think the actions that this government has followed, the objectives it has had in Vietnam, are
wise. I do not by any means suggest that we have not made mistakes over the many years that we have been pursuing those
objectives."

On February 27, two days before his departure, he made a final
official plea against escalation. He and Dean Rusk and Clark
Clifford, who would succeed him, had gathered with senior advisers in the State Department to survey the alternatives once
again for an Administration groping for a new policy. When
Clifford suggested the introduction of more men, the passion of
McNamara's opposing argument, already made to the President
four months earlier, startled his listeners. But he had long since
lost the controlling voice.

Was he fired? The short answer is a subjective yes. The longer
answer is that the short answer is unprovable. Mr. Johnson chose
this time, and these circumstances, to relieve his Secretary of
Defense.

The best evidence for individual judgment, in any case, is to
be found in the complex relationship between Robert McNamara,
the intellectual technocrat, and that most complex of men, the
second President he served.

10

Two Masters:

The Rise and Fall

ONE day during the Cuba missile crisis, while Robert McNamara and John Kennedy were deep in discussion, along came Caroline Kennedy, almost five. When she saw her father, she hastily stuffed something in her mouth. "Caroline, are you eating just before supper?" the President asked.

Without answering, Caroline moved quickly in the opposite direction. "Caroline," Kennedy called. Still no answer. "Caroline," the President called again, raising his voice, "what's the answer to my question—'yes,' 'no,' or 'maybe'?" Kennedy's amused distraction as the world hung at the edge of nuclear war impressed McNamara greatly. This, he said later, telling the anecdote and paraphrasing Hemingway, was "grace under stress."

From their first meeting in the Kennedy house on N Street, Kennedy and McNamara admired each other. "The President-elect is most impressed by you, Mr. McNamara," a Kennedy aide remarked as they left the house. McNamara looked surprised. "Senator Kennedy is an impressive man," he said.

Slowly a lasting warmth developed between Kennedy and his Secretary of Defense. In many ways they were different. The President was born to wealth. He accepted fame easily, and he enjoyed people. A wry wit, never far beneath the surface, was directed often at himself.

McNamara had taken the road to wealth out of necessity, to recoup from the cost of his wife's treatments for polio, though it was always the challenge of business, rather than the money, that mattered to him. His official relationships with subordinates were often efficiently impersonal and abrupt. His amusing, gracious aspect was suppressed except in a small circle in Washington, and even within that circle most agreed that the Secretary of Defense was sometimes peculiarly shy.

Kennedy and McNamara met at crucial points of personality, however: in their zest for challenge, their respect for performance, their sense of dignity, their demand for rational action. McNamara quickly crossed the Kennedy line between official and personal relationships.

McNamara found an intellectual haven in the Hickory Hill Seminars. These were the disputations, stimulating gatherings of a dozen or so New Frontiersmen and their wives, with a leavening of outside voices on whatever subject intrigued the participants. Robert Kennedy organized them to offset the grind of day-to-day problems. The meeting place changed often, and at least two were held in the White House. The President amused one gathering by close questioning of the senior Arthur Schlesinger's criteria for rating of Presidents. Already he seemed to be trying unconsciously to fit his own embryonic Administration into history.

The Secretary of Defense was a vigorous participant. He could make, moreover, compelling arguments for notably thin causes. "I hope he is never seriously wrong," remarked an impressed witness to such a performance. "Just think what happens when Bob comes up against someone else in a gray area of discussion. The other guy hasn't a chance."

President Kennedy came to rely on him more and more. If he had failed to sound an alarm before the Bay of Pigs fiasco, that could be attributed to inexperience; he had plenty of company in

those who should have known better. He learned quickly in the
areas outside his experience. He soon brought the military under
unambiguous control, to cries of anguish from military supporters
in Congress. His execution of response to the Berlin crisis, however ponderous, made the political point. It did so, moreover, by
signaling U.S. intention without provocative waving of nuclear
rockets.

Through it all, he had the unwavering support of the President.
"It is absolutely essential," McNamara said firmly, referring to
this support. "I wouldn't stay here a minute without it."

Kennedy was at first surprised and then gratified at the range
of McNamara's interests. McNamara vigorously attacked problems in civil defense, space, intelligence, paramilitary operations,
foreign aid, and foreign policy generally. He became what Theodore Sorensen has called the star and strong man among the
newcomers to the Kennedy team.

When Big Steel challenged Kennedy's attempt to hold a wage-
price-productivity balance in April, 1962, he and his domestic
advisers turned quickly to McNamara. Defense was by far the biggest single steel customer in government. McNamara proclaimed
his shock at the price increase of $6 a ton. He foresaw a $1 billion
increase in the cost of defense, he said, and unhappy consequences for the balance of trade. Whereupon he began switching
purchases to companies that had kept prices unchanged pending
the government's reaction. It was an important aspect of the Administration's overall pressure, and steel capitulated. Some who
remembered when McNamara had arbitrarily raised Ford prices
to the GM level a few years earlier were quietly amused: he was
learning the whimsicalities of power.

His tenacity showed in his personal relationships as well. Washington's tight intellectual elite at first could not quite bring itself
to believe that this strange titan of business, so reserved on first
meeting, actually could be stimulating, humane, even kind. When
Philip L. Graham, the brilliant publisher of the Washington *Post,*
was struck by the illness that eventually led him to self-destruc-

tion, McNamara asked to visit him. Graham, who was seeing no one, refused. Others, less determined, had made similar polite gestures. But it was McNamara who persisted. Finally Graham agreed, and the result was a rousing discussion of current issues that restored fire to the eye of the patient.

Kennedy found in McNamara an intense supporter of initiatives for arms control and disarmament. Like the President, McNamara felt that the nation must be able to negotiate from strength. This he was determined to provide. Regretfully, he came to recommend resumption of American nuclear tests in the atmosphere, on both political and military grounds, after the Soviets in 1961 broke a three-year moratorium on testing.

Two years later, however, when the limited test-ban treaty was proposed, McNamara's campaign in support of it was decisive. Against those who argued that a successful antimissile system required continued testing of warheads on the rockets, he insisted that it was the testing of the rockets themselves and more laboratory work that were essential. The warheads could be tested underground. His position finessed important points of the debate, but it proved to be effective.

Critical to Senate approval of the treaty was the support of the Joint Chiefs of Staff. The Chiefs, behaving normally, as McNamara saw it, had little use for the treaty. Aside from the purely military implications, some of them were worried that such measures would induce a euphoria in which Western deterrence would erode. Above all, they feared the Soviets would cheat undetected, and thereby gain a technological lead which the United States might never overcome. McNamara delivered the Joint Chiefs for Kennedy by simply wearing down their arguments. He brought them together with a team from his own staff and specialists on technical questions, sat them down together in a room, and told them to talk it out. "If you insist on opposing this treaty, well and good," he said, "but I am not going to let anyone oppose it out of emotion or ignorance." His premise was the obvious one, that the acknowledged risks in the treaty were outweighed by the long-range gains.

The meetings lasted for almost two weeks. One by one, the doubts were resolved. To such arguments as the possibility of undetected Soviet testing of superweapons underground, the experts demonstrated that a hole of unimaginable magnitude would be required. The Administration had to pay a price for the Chiefs' support, however. It promised to remain ready for atmospheric tests on short notice, to improve its methods to detect cheating, and, of course, to continue underground testing. The compromise worked out well for everyone, including, as the great powers suspended nuclear air pollution, the world public.

With each such performance, McNamara raised himself further in John Kennedy's eyes. His total loyalty, his willingness to go to the mat, his refusal to accord holiness to tradition, commended him to the President. From the White House, apart from more formal praise, came the word that the President regarded him as the most valuable member of the Cabinet other than his brother Robert. There were strong suggestions that McNamara would become Secretary of State in the second Kennedy Administration.

Kennedy liked Rusk. But he also was frustrated by the Department of State's caution and seemingly glacial pace, and by Rusk's impassivity. He muttered once that he could predict without fail State's position on any issue, that it would be slow in coming, and that it would be totally unimaginative. McNamara, he said approvingly, had made things move in Defense. Rusk, a dignified Georgian, was not helped by his reserved attitude toward the Eastern liberal circle around Kennedy, and the attitude was reciprocated.

It is a subject on which McNamara has remained publicly silent. His relations with Rusk were good, and remained so for seven years. He did not hesitate to range ahead of State on foreign policy when that Department, in his opinion, was too slow. He was always careful to touch base with Rusk first, however. From all accounts, Rusk seldom if ever objected as McNamara charged off with an initiative that custom would have left to State.

In at least one unguarded moment McNamara has acknowledged that he knew he was supposed to succeed Rusk. The word had been passed to him by Robert Kennedy. The President himself had said as much to his friend Charles Bartlett, the Washington columnist. Some of McNamara's own trusted staff let him know, in turn, that they wanted to move with him if the transfer came to pass.

He thought like the President on most issues: on Southeast Asia, on Europe, on strategy. They shared a disdain for the predictability of the military. In his own area McNamara was caught up in an Administration that promised high standards of security while working to reduce world tension. More generally, he was inspired by policies that recognized social and economic injustice as root causes of much of that tension.

Vietnam baffled both, as it baffled many others then and later. By most accounts, Kennedy was far more skeptical than his Secretary of Defense of the reports of progress there during the turbulent days in 1963. With his own disillusionment in the fall of that year, McNamara turned abruptly. He proposed to give Saigon a fighting chance, but then to get out without further increasing the American commitment. The death of Ngo Dinh Diem reinforced his conviction. He believed, moreover, that this was the path the President would choose.

This was perhaps wishful interpretation. More than once Kennedy gloomily forecast failure if the United States bored deeper into Vietnam. He frequently underscored the primary responsibility of the South Vietnamese for their own security. Yet he also said firmly that "we cannot desist in Vietnam." Like McNamara, some other members of the Kennedy Administration believe Kennedy would not have introduced combat forces. Some held that he would have sent men to hold strategic points, but no more. What then, when those points were attacked? Kennedy started the process of escalation; where he would have turned it around or limited it can only be speculated. And there are others, in the Administration at the time, who are certain Kennedy would have entered Vietnam at an even faster pace than his successor. One of the late President's closest advisers put this view bluntly, after a guarantee of anonymity: "We would have been in up to our ears, sooner, if Kennedy had lived."

McNamara was in his office, deep in a discussion of the budget with McGeorge Bundy, Jerome Wiesner, the President's science adviser, and Kermit Gordon of the Budget Bureau, when Kennedy was shot. Quickly he and the Joint Chiefs alerted forces throughout the world; no one knew whether the assassination in Dallas was keyed to a larger plot. Despite his own grief, he was a figure of monumental stability in the tortured hours and days that followed. For hours he sat in the crowded VIP suite at Bethesda Naval Hospital and listened as Jacqueline Kennedy talked out her grief. From time to time he issued the orders that had to be issued. As both official and friend, he insisted that Kennedy must be buried at Arlington rather than near the family home in Massachusetts. As official, he exercised his strong sense of duty and loyalty to the Presidency itself while Lyndon Johnson gathered the threads of power.

McNamara himself was not sure he could or should stay with the new Administration for the long term. In the bleak dawn after Kennedy's death and after Johnson had asked him to stay, Arthur Schlesinger, Jr., noted McNamara's uncertainty "whether the relationship would work." Where their official paths had crossed, as in the Aeronautics and Space Council, which Johnson had headed as Vice President, their relations had been more guarded than warm. But when a columnist speculated that McNamara would not fit into the new team to be gathered around Johnson, the new President immediately called and told McNamara to pay no attention. The first few weeks went well. McNamara himself was dedicated to an orderly transition. Besides, Johnson simply refused to accept immediate resignations from close Kennedy associates.

Two men less alike than McNamara and Johnson would be hard
to imagine. McNamara had cultivated a taste for music ranging
from Beethoven to Bartok to Lester Lanin, for art from the old
masters to the avant-garde. On his night table at home (beside a
white telephone for the White House, gray for the Pentagon
command center) over the past months had been *Karakoran* by
Fosco Maraini, *Emerging Nations* by Max Millikan and Donald
Blackmer, *The Bridge on the Drina* by Iva Andric, *Britain in
World Affairs* by Lord William Strang, and *The Guns of August*
by Barbara Tuchman. These were not the idle-hour staples of
Lyndon Johnson.

Johnson's world was more narrowly focused on constant intense politics and official tasks to be performed, and he mixed
them with instinctive and total pragmatism. His earthy imagery
and bawdy stories were notorious. McNamara's language, however,
never strayed beyond an exasperated "God damn it." His sense of
political possibility, academically acquired, was sometimes naïve.
The distance between Southwest Texas State Teachers College
and Harvard University never could be entirely bridged.

At the time of the transition, much of the bloom had worn off
McNamara's reception in official Washington outside the executive circle. Congress had recovered its breath following the initial
McNamara storm. Now some of its more influential members were
making known their irritation at being lectured like unruly fresh-
men. They discovered that the Secretary not only had taken the
Pentagon in hand, he was ready to take them on as well. They
ran up against an iron will in such matters as closing of unneeded
bases and selection of weapons. Cost effectiveness, to their minds,
was producing peculiar results when, for example, it dictated
against nuclear power for Navy ships.

The muzzled military, outwardly silent, complained privately
to friends in Congress and the press that the Secretary was paying
it dangerously little attention on critical decisions. Under the circumstances, it might have seemed like a good time for McNamara to move on.

For some men, yes; for McNamara, no. First of all, there was the sense of duty and challenges still unmet. The overhaul of military power, strategy, and management was not yet complete, in fact was just beginning. Vietnam had refused to yield to a rational plan.

Thus there was, after all, a community of interests between the new President and the Secretary of Defense. It was to be found chiefly in respect for tenacity and accomplishment, and in the broader goals both saw for the nation. But perhaps an equally important reason McNamara stayed was the early evidence that in many areas he would be even more powerful, with freer movement, under Johnson than under Kennedy. The new President, it turned out, like Kennedy, had long since identified McNamara as the ablest of the new men in Washington. At the start of his deliberately restrained Vice Presidency, Johnson had surveyed the newcomers at the first Cabinet meeting. Leaving, he remarked to a reporter, "That man with the Stacomb in his hair is the best of the lot." At the end of 1963 that appraisal still held.

Within two months of the assassination, observant outsiders had identified McNamara as the strong man of the Johnson Cabinet. Any doubt about his role as primary executor of policy in Southeast Asia soon vanished. When Johnson made a considerable public production of cost-cutting, he sent a letter to McNamara urging savings wherever possible. McNamara happily obliged by restating his formula for "buying only what is needed, buying at the lowest sound price, and reducing operating costs."

With full support from Lyndon Johnson—sometimes when it hurt politically—McNamara intensified his cost-reduction program. Ultimately he would claim savings of well over $15 billion during his tenure, much of it documented by audit. His program of closing unneeded bases, even more sensitive, also continued without letup, eventually shutting down 967 installations, freeing 1.818 million acres of land, and eliminating 207,000 jobs. He developed elaborate measures to ease the economic impact of base closures on local areas and find jobs for those displaced. Yet, inevitably, there was much unhappiness. "Phase out McNamara," demanded a bumper sticker popular in the hard-hit San Diego area in 1964.

The cost-reduction program did not escape without criticism of another kind. Some of the savings looked to outsiders like the sort of cuts that would have been made by any competent management. One reporter was so exercised at some of McNamara's claims that he pilfered a stack of the Defense Department's public relations release forms. Soon the Pentagon was inundated with announcements of fictional awards for money-saving actions: to General Custer, for cutting $18.51 from maintenance costs by leaving behind his Gatling guns; to the planners who saved $20 million by not fortifying Guam before World War II; to the designer who permanently sealed parachutes to avoid the costs of repacking. Indignant, McNamara threatened to hold weekly seminars for the Pentagon press corps, asserting that a good program could be killed by ridicule.

A Congressional study led by Representative Porter Hardy of Virginia cast serious doubt on some of the claims of savings. But the fact remained that McNamara, even after the critics had done their worst, had saved a great deal of money.

"Bob McNamara is the smartest man I ever saw," Lyndon Johnson said, and in many areas he gave the Secretary of Defense his head. McNamara responded with the kind of loyalty that concealed his own views when he was overruled. One area in which he refused to help the President in 1964, however, was in solving the problem of Robert Kennedy.

The pressures on Johnson to accept Kennedy as his candidate for Vice President were formidable. They were inherent in the situation, in the passing of the Kennedy mantle from the assassinated President to his younger brother. They grew in popular sentiment and they were actively encouraged by Kennedy allies within the Democratic Party. Kennedy wanted the nomination. Johnson feared he would lose votes unless he neutralized the pressure, yet he knew his Administration would never be his own with a Kennedy looking over his shoulder. As one possible solution, he turned in the spring to his Secretary of Defense.

In his admiration for McNamara, Johnson could envision him as a sort of administrative sub-President, unleashing his awesome talents on the social and economic problems targeted by the Great Society concept. The Kennedy problem would be solved, though the immediate political liabilities could be considerable. McNamara was, after all, a nominal Republican. Party advisers greeted the idea with something less than boundless enthusiasm. Johnson still went so far as to talk it over with McNamara and, in effect, indicate that he could have the nomination if he would take it.

It is not clear whether the President fully understood at the time the relationship between McNamara and Robert Kennedy. From the days of the Cuban missile crisis their friendship had developed a closeness never even approached by that between John Kennedy and McNamara. In any case, McNamara gently but firmly rejected the overture. He thought Robert Kennedy should have the nomination.

Johnson eventually solved the Kennedy problem by ruling out as running mate all Cabinet members and those who sat with the Cabinet regularly. It was a clumsy, transparent device, all the more so since he had approached McNamara. Some friends of the Secretary of Defense, however, suggested that Johnson never could have chosen a Republican, even if McNamara had been receptive. Their assessment was that the President, first of all, was groping for a solution, and, second, nailing down the loyalty of McNamara against the inevitable rejection of Robert Kennedy. McNamara hardly could have failed to appreciate the President's testimonial of confidence. If the more Machiavellian motives inspired the President, they almost certainly were superfluous at that point, however. By then McNamara was committed.

McNamara, in any case, was drawn quickly into the developing political campaign even before Hubert H. Humphrey was nominated to run with Johnson. For months Senator Barry Goldwater

of Arizona had made McNamara a particular target as he sought
the Republican nomination. Candidate of the Republican right
wing, Goldwater was also a major general in the Air Force Reserve. As early as January he charged that American missiles
were undependable as a replacement for the manned bomber.
McNamara reacted with a private outburst—Goldwater, he said,
was a "damned fool"—that startled associates: publicly, he
labeled the charges "reckless and irresponsible," and, of course,
untrue.

In March Goldwater invaded Detroit, the site of McNamara's
industrial triumphs, and zeroed in on the Secretary of Defense
personally. McNamara was a loser, he said: "A one-time loser
with the Edsel right here in Michigan, a four-time loser in terms
of trips to Vietnam, and an all-time loser if his policies and the
policies of the Administration that supports and applauds him are
not changed in 1964." Even more provocatively, Goldwater
claimed that McNamara's policies were reducing U.S. military
choices to "withdrawal or nuclear holocaust"—the opposite of
the intention of the strategy of flexible response. About the kindest charge he made was that McNamara was pursuing "unilateral
disarmament."

By August, after the Republican right wing had seized the
party and nominated Goldwater, there was little visible of McNamara's own Republicanism. When he went before the Democratic
Platform Committee, his statement was a rousing partisan declaration of what the Kennedy-Johnson Administrations had accomplished—from increased ground forces to Presidential control of
nuclear weapons. As for the old days: "The defense establishment we found in 1961 was based on a strategy of massive nuclear retaliation . . . which even the American people did not
believe . . . in which each military service made its own independent plans . . . the stepchild of a predetermined budget. The
strategic nuclear force we found in the Defense Department was
vulnerable to surprise missile attack."

When Goldwater returned to the attack with the forecast that

U.S. nuclear power would decline by 90 percent over the next decade, McNamara was waiting for him. The assessment was "totally without foundation in fact," he said. "It is false, and if the Senator would trouble to inform himself, he would learn that it is false."

Whereupon he, Mrs. McNamara, and their son Craig flew off to Switzerland, and father and son joined a party of seven in an assault on the Matterhorn. Rock slides caused by bad weather killed climbers in parties above and below them. McNamara finally was forced to turn back at the 13,200-foot level.

McNamara's remarks before the Democratic Platform Committee had caused a squall in Northeast Harbor, Maine, to rival any bad weather on the Matterhorn. Thomas Gates, Jr., McNamara's predecessor, in Maine at the time, had judged that the McNamara testimony could only be interpreted as an attack on him. Gates remained silent publicly, but he was seething, a friend told McNamara. McNamara sent a long telegram to Gates, recalling all the good things he had said about the Gates period in the Pentagon and casting his own offending testimony in the context of reply to the Goldwater assaults. "As you know," he concluded, "I have the highest regard for the contribution you made to the Defense Department and for the assistance you gave me when I became Secretary."

In his reply Gates broke a four-year public silence and mercilessly reviewed the speech McNamara had given before the committee. "I submit that these statements are not a true representation of the Department of Defense of which you assumed charge in 1961," Gates wrote. ". . . I cannot believe that you agree with these statements yourself. I am totally unable to reconcile what you told the platform committee with the tone and content of your dispatch to me." McNamara had come close, but not quite, to an apology. Gates had come close, but not quite, to an accusation that McNamara was playing politics with the national defense. Apparently both were satisfied.

The Secretary of Defense was meeting every test imposed by

a President whose demands were total. Johnson's gratitude, like his demands, was massive. In December, decorating Army Captain Roger H. C. Donlon with the Medal of Honor for heroism in Vietnam, the President abruptly digressed to draw a moral in civilian service to country. "This man," he said, turning to McNamara, "represents to me in our civilian life what Captain Donlon represents in the military life, the very best in America." McNamara's eyes filled behind his old-fashioned glasses. "Thank you, Mr. President," he managed in a husky whisper.

Critics in Congress, even as they challenged McNamara's specific decisions, still voiced admiration for his managerial prowess. In one of its last reports under Carl Vinson, the House Armed Services Committee conceded that "There are few men with the capability of grasping the complexities of the Department of Defense with such completeness as to permit the leadership which Mr. McNamara has so fully demonstrated; and to make the changes that he has made without the chaos which is the almost inevitable consequence of radical reform."

Johnson's confidence in his Secretary of Defense grew steadily in 1965. "The phone rang constantly," a member of the inner circle said. "The President called Bob six times a day and three at night, frequently on things he knew very little about." Usually McNamara presented options and probable consequences, sometimes with his own recommendation, sometimes without. Frequently delicate suggestions were made privately in a "draft memorandum," the word "draft" serving to reduce its official standing pending a Presidential decision.

This method, perfectly in keeping with the President's style, also reflected the evolution of the decision-making process over four Administrations. James Forrestal had conceived the National Security Council as a funnel for the integration of military and political policy. Its first years were its best. During the Eisenhower Administration its procedures became fixed and largely sterile, particularly since foreign policy across the board was so dominated by John Foster Dulles. John Kennedy was primarily his own foreign minister, and the importance of the NSC faded. Kennedy obviously would not be limited by a formal structure such as the NSC in seeking advice on, for example, the Cuban missile crisis. He reached out for the talent he trusted, and what became known as the Executive Committee, or Ex Comm, was the result. More generally, the NSC went into decline: even its advisory authority on foreign policy withered to impotence. Under Lyndon Johnson, less oriented to foreign affairs and infinitely more secretive, the influential policy circle became even smaller and the estate of the NSC remained low.

McNamara's rules in dealing with the President were similar to those employed by Vice President Humphrey, who early in the Administration cautioned the President that the National Security Council and the Cabinet were leaky with gossip. I'm going to be rather quiet in these meetings, Humphrey told Johnson. If I make a recommendation and you accept it, everyone's going to talk about my influence prevailing. If you turn me down, the gossip will say you disregard my advice. I'm going to give you my ideas on really sensitive issues in private. Johnson agreed, though he sometimes badgered Humphrey into expressing himself. As Humphrey predicted, the word usually got around.

McNamara refused to let this happen to him. "I'm not going to have everybody in government keeping score on my standing with the President," he told senior staff members. In most cases, of course, his personal position on important issues was clear from the deliberations within the larger circle of advisers in the Pentagon. Usually it was equally obvious that the decisions from the White House concurred with his recommendations.

At times, however, the evidence was ambiguous. Few were certain what he had told the President when, in fact, he recommended sending U.S. ground troops to rescue the Vietnam commitment at mid-1965 (Accepted). Nor did many know that he wanted to reinforce the decision with revenue measures and the summoning of Reserves (Rejected). The rejection, later resulting in large budget supplements, contributed substantially to what became known as the Administration's credibility gap the following year. But win or lose, it was no surprise to anyone that McNamara adopted each decision, once made, as his own.

Despite the uncertainties of Vietnam, early 1965 was a time of vigorous and exciting, if frequently eccentric, government. Therein lay the key to McNamara's admiration for Lyndon Johnson. Seldom did McNamara drift, even in private, into an appraisal of the men he served, but at least once that summer he mused at length on the personality and power and style of the thirty-sixth President. Lyndon Johnson, he said, *governed*. Johnson wanted to move ahead. For that he needed maximum support by the public and in Congress. Twenty hours a day, every day, he tried to avoid the fragmentation of power. When it fragmented, he set out to recreate it. The President might not read Toynbee, but he read the American mood, and tried both to shape it and to act upon it. John Kennedy had style and grace and intellect; Johnson was action-oriented. Kennedy therefore had greater facility generally in the intellectual exercises of foreign affairs, the attempts to anticipate problems and prevent them from surfacing. Foreign relations usually were more subtle than domestic issues, McNamara believed, and the solutions were never so obvious as in domestic affairs. The solution in Vietnam, for example, was not obvious at all. But McNamara was sure Johnson would do nothing in Vietnam to cost him critical support at home.

Even into the late fall, it still seemed possible to balance the complex of foreign and domestic issues and retain the Johnsonian consensus. There was continuing talk that McNamara would be assigned responsibility even broader than those of defense, perhaps as a czar over domestic programs. His advice across the spectrum of government had never been more eagerly sought. November was some sort of high-water mark for McNamara's influence, and it was the month in which he emerged most clearly in public as something other than the human calculator of the popular image.

On Tuesday, November 9, when a power failure blacked out

the Northeastern States, the President's first call for reassurance was to his Secretary of Defense. The next day McNamara accepted the sword of the aluminum industry, which abandoned a price increase when he threatened to dump the government's 1.4 million tons on the market (an act of "industrial statesmanship," he called the capitulation). And the day after that he flew to the President's ranch in Texas for a major foreign policy review.

The following week he was still at it as man-of-all-work for Lyndon Johnson. This time he announced plans to open up the copper stockpile, control exports, and ask Congress to permit suspension of import duties in order to bring that market back into line. The circumstances were quite different from those in aluminum—for one thing the domestic copper industry did not dominate the world market, and some businessmen were not dismayed to see the government step in—but Lyndon Johnson's reliance on McNamara showed where the threads of power ran.

That same week the McNamaras attended two glittering parties for Princess Margaret of England. To the first, at the Cleveland Park home of Attorney General Nicholas deB. Katzenbach, McNamara drove his 1960 Ford Galaxie. A house guest of the McNamaras reckoned it memorable to watch the Secretary of Defense search for a parking place while other guests debarked from chauffeured limousines. McNamara simply refused to use official cars except for official business.

He achieved minor social notoriety the following evening at a White House party. As Maxine Cheshire reported it in the Washington *Post*: "The ravishing Christina Ford, who has been described as a 'tiger kitten of a woman,' was the sensation of the evening as she danced and danced and danced with Defense Secretary Robert McNamara." The new wife of McNamara's former boss, Mrs. Cheshire said, "displayed a magnificent figure in a strapless white crepe dress which required her to stop periodically and tug it back into place. At one point, she didn't quite react fast enough."

Margaret McNamara was unperturbed. She knew where M

Namara, as a junior Pentagon officer put it, "gets his transistors replaced." It was in the comfortable home on Tracy Place, with its enclosed garden and large patio, opening off a living room usually decorated with fresh flowers. Only Mrs. McNamara knew that her husband now sometimes awakened at 3 A.M. out of worry about Vietnam. Besides, the hints of incipient swinging could have little effect on the image of a subject who occasionally stole away alone in the evening, entered a Washington theater after the house lights went down, and to avoid attention ducked out as they went up again.

That November may have been the last of the truly good months. McNamara showed up at a costume party for Averell Harriman with his head wrapped in aluminum foil. No one, needless to say, had any difficulty guessing his identity. A minor official in the Pentagon reported with some surprise and unlimited gratitude that both the Secretary of Defense and his wife had called him to chat while he was in the hospital. An enterprising reporter learned that McNamara, who is left-handed, inserted the wrong leg in his trousers first, thus destroying forever the Pentagon myth that "he puts his pants on just like I do." An astonished aide discovered that his boss, who could recall the smallest fact about the Sparrow missile, sometimes forgot his home telephone number.

The word got out that a 14th Street shopkeeper had refused to take a check in payment for a camera from somebody named Mac something or other whose best identification was a Michigan driver's license. McNamara had wanted to take the camera with him to East Asia. In Saigon a dealer sold him a porcelain piece supposedly from the Ming Dynasty. On his next trip the Secretary carried the fake back for a refund.

With the turn of the year, Vietnam began to spoil everything. A $12.1 billion budget supplement, however inevitable and expected, helped to sharpen internal differences over the war. The pressures on the Great Society program mounted. Still, Washington was nearly breathless at what was surely one of the great administrative teams of all time: Lyndon Johnson, with intimate knowledge of his massive machinery, wielding the levers of power from his own desk; Robert McNamara in firm control in his own massive department, rising victorious from countless battles, with time left over for extra assignments. Tom Wicker brought it together in the *New York Times:* "Probably it can all be said in a sentence: Lyndon B. Johnson and Robert S. McNamara have confidence in each other."

That, too, would soon change in a subtle way. McNamara's continuing close association with Hickory Hill may have had something to do with it. In February he knew in advance that Robert Kennedy would propose a political role for the National Liberation Front in South Vietnam, thus running ahead of the current operating policy. No one has reported Johnson's private views on the McNamara-Kennedy friendship. But popular speculation had it that the President, whose own concept of loyalty was personal as well as official, was too proud to be unaffected by it and too proud to make that known to McNamara. Slowly their senses of direction and purpose on the war began to diverge.

The President was taken aback by the first in a series of public addresses given by McNamara that spring and summer. Speaking to the American Society of Newspaper Editors in Montreal on May 18, McNamara delivered what was in broad outline a rejection of military power as the essence of security. Unchallengeable military power was, of course, necessary, he said. But for an adequately armed nation the decisive elements of foreign policy were to be found in the character of its differing relations with developing nations, its wealthy friends, and with those that might be hostile. America must actively seek better understanding with the last group and acceptance of greater responsibility for peacekeeping by the second.

The true essence of security was to be found, however, in the orderly development of that first group, those nations of the nonindustrial southern hemisphere seeking to break out of ignorance and poverty. The planet, McNamara said, is becoming a more dangerous place to live on—not merely because of a potential nuclear holocaust, but also because of the large number of *de facto* conflicts and because the trend of such conflicts is growing rather than diminishing. At the beginning of 1958 there were 23 prolonged insurgencies going on about the world. As of February 1, 1966, there were 40. Further, the total number of outbreaks of violence has increased each year: in 1958, there were 34; in 1965, there were 58.

But what is most significant of all is that there is a direct and constant relationship between the incidence of violence and the economic status of the countries afflicted. . . . Among the 38 very poor nations—those with a per capita income of under $100 a year—no less than 32 have suffered significant conflicts. Indeed, they have suffered an average of two major outbreaks of violence per country in the eight-year period. That is a great deal of conflict.

Given that relationship between violence and poverty, McNamara argued, the role of the wealthy nations in effecting the remedy was clear. The

irreducible fact remains that our security is related directly to the security of the newly developing world. And our role must be precisely this: to help provide security to those developing nations which genuinely need and request our help and which demonstrably are willing and able to help themselves. . . . Military force can help provide law and order, but only to the degree that a basis for law and order already exists in the developing society, a basic willingness on the part of the people to cooperate. Law and order is the shield behind which development, the central fact of security, can be achieved.

There is no absolute evidence that McNamara was speaking other than in the meditative general sense, marking a desirable blueprint for the future. Yet the speech created a sensation, both for its presentation of the Secretary of Defense as philosopher and humanitarian and for its inescapable implication that Vietnam was an unsound investment.

As for the reaction of Lyndon Johnson, "I caught hell for that one," McNamara confided to a friend later. At the White House, a staff member explained privately that the President believed the speech diffused the sense of purpose and resolution he was trying to project at that time of trial.

The address attracted attention in yet another respect. To many classical geopoliticians and power traditionalists, it was simplistic to the point of naïveté. McNamara did not ignore the risks of great-power rivalries by any means. Nonetheless his critics detected an unwarranted shift of focus from the relationships which historically had been held to cause great wars. In any case, the speech identified this Secretary of Defense as one with interests unlike those that had occupied his predecessors.

In the months that followed, McNamara pursued the parallel themes of development and social change. He offered tolerance for much of the growing protest by the young, but challenged youth to conquer its environment, not retreat from it. "It is not really the computer that is in question," he told students in his daughter's graduating class at Chatham College. "It is whether or not Dr. Strangelove is sitting at the computer's console."

Increasingly he underscored his Department's own activities beyond normal military concerns. Over considerable opposition in Congress, he started a plan to draft 100,000 men per year who otherwise would be rejected for military service (McNamara's "Fizz Kids," a Pentagon skeptic called them) and then, once they were in uniform, bring them up to physical and mental standards; the intent was to use the military as a means of rehabilitation. He was shamed to learn how little had been done to overcome racial discrimination in offbase housing. The turnabout in the Washington area was dramatic after he placed property owned by balky landlords off limits to all military personnel. Project Transition was developed to provide counseling, training, and job placement for men leaving the military.

His desire to make his Department become an immediate constructive force in society grew along with his increasing disillusionment with the war. Yet these unwarlike pursuits had the

unqualified support of Lyndon Johnson. McNamara's parting
with the White House developed with more of a drift than a rush.
But his inner turmoil over the war was apparent to close associates
by the spring of 1967. He and his wife, who wanted her husband
relieved of his burdens, had talked of his need to leave.

On April 18 McNamara had lunch with George D. Woods,
whose five-year term as President of the World Bank was to end
the following December, in Woods' private dining room at the
bank. It is not clear whether third persons had spoken to Woods
of McNamara's distress or whether Woods, an old friend, had
simply done the obvious in approaching McNamara. In any case,
Woods said he wanted to recommend McNamara to succeed him.
Would McNamara be interested?

As McNamara recalled it, he told Woods he hadn't thought of
it, but the bank obviously was a challenge in a field of primary
interest to him. Its principal function—guiding development with
loans to poor nations—was in perfect keeping with the theme of
the Montreal speech. In short, of course he was interested. However, he told Woods, his first obligation was to the President, and
"I could not do anything unless the President released me."

A few weeks later, as McNamara reconstructed it, "I reported
my conversation with Woods to the President. I remember it was
after a Cabinet meeting, and I lingered to talk with him. I said,
'Mr. President, I have to report this to you. I've told you before
and I tell you again, I will stay as long as you think necessary.' I
repeated what Woods had said. The President did not say anything at the time."

Thus began a long summer. It was the summer of Margaret
McNamara's illness, of occasional defeats by the military in White
House councils, of his own increasingly open stance against the
bombing of North Vietnam. Lyndon Johnson complained to a
visiting Senator that "McNamara's gone dovish on me"—though
he had long rated McNamara as the least militant of those in his
inner circle.

Throughout the year the growing unworkability of the relationship must have been apparent to both McNamara and the President. "I was always amazed at Bob's technique with his Presidents," an official who watched him with both Kennedy and Johnson remarked. "He worked hard to draw them along with him, but he always retreated when he got out too far ahead. He knew he could be no more effective than his support from the White House." Thus by early 1967 Johnson was moving past him on war-making policy, or, perhaps more accurately, McNamara was backing up.

In private conversations McNamara had been openly envious of McGeorge Bundy, who had left the White House the previous year for the Ford Foundation. He, too, had been offered the prestigious foundation assignment and he turned it down because the President asked him to stay. His own plan had included four or five years of service. But his commitment in the final analysis, as he saw it, was to the President, and thus there was no option of simple resignation, especially against the backdrop of Vietnam, so long as Lyndon Johnson wanted him to stay.

George Woods, meanwhile, was busy. He talked to the President but, still lacking a commitment on McNamara, scouted around for other possible successors. Reluctantly he agreed to stay on another year if necessary.

It turned out to be unnecessary. For that was the summer the telephone stopped ringing. The direct lines from the White House, which used to ring "six times a day and three at night," were silent. "That was important to Bob," a former official said. "I think he read too much into it. Perhaps not."

The concern ran both ways. At one point during the summer, when Mrs. McNamara was in the hospital with ulcers, Johnson called the Secretary of Defense to inquire about her. "A fine man," the President said quietly, according to witnesses, as he put down the telephone. "A fine woman. We mustn't have another Forrestal." Others close to McNamara later reported that the Forrestal analogy flashed across their minds also still later in 1967. They dismissed it angrily.

The President must have known that some of McNamara's friends outside the executive circle that summer were insisting strongly, almost publicly, that he had turned away from the war. Some even argued that he never had really approved the intervention. However correct the first judgment may have been, the second was neither accurate nor a service to him.

In any case, the differences within the Administration were becoming steadily greater. Two factors were at work. McNamara, first of all, was beginning to argue actively for scaling down the war. His proposals in the spring to draw the bombing of North Vietnam back to the 20th parallel demonstrated that conclusively. Perhaps equally important was the consideration indicated by hindsight, that the President did not comprehend how early McNamara had become disillusioned with the prolonged bloodshed. Johnson long had rated his Secretary of Defense as a less than ferocious hawk, and he had remarked on the less than militant tone of some of the 1966 speeches. Still, the precisely written reports and recommendations from the Department of Defense had conveyed none of the personal dismay detected by those close to McNamara. The McNamara of Hickory Hill still was not the McNamara of the Pentagon. Thus an element of surprise may have contributed to Johnson's own dismay with his Secretary of Defense.

The divergence became even greater when McNamara resolved to give his August testimony against escalation—and, by implication, continuation—of the bombing in North Vietnam. He discussed the pending testimony with the President personally, although only in general terms.

"It was quite a scene," a former White House aide recalled. "They were both pretty hot." In the end, the President told McNamara, in effect: You are on your own. I won't pull the rug out from under you. But I am not accepting the argument, in just that way, right now.

At this point Johnson was walking a high wire. He neither could accept McNamara's views in full nor was he ready to assault

North Vietnam as the Joint Chiefs and their supporters in Congress recommended. Apart from Vietnam, he was beleaguered on other issues, including pressure for deployment of the Nike-X antimissile system, even as he was trying to find a way to slow down the arms race.

There were some pluses for McNamara in those weeks. He made his contribution to the San Antonio negotiations formula. The massive escalation he feared did not occur in Vietnam. "Bob was determined that not a single additional soldier would be sent to Vietnam," a former aide said, the bombing issue aside. But in September he had to make his tortured compromise on the ABM. And finally the President exercised his option on McNamara.

In mid-October the World Bank came up again, for the first time since the spring, in a conversation between McNamara and Johnson. "On October 16," McNamara recalled later, "I was talking with the President in the inner office outside the Oval Room. His wife was out and so was mine, and we sat and talked about a wide range of subjects until nine-thirty. We had no dinner, just talked.

"In passing, the President brought up the question: 'Are you still interested in the World Bank?' 'Of course I'm interested,' I said. He used to kid me about the Montreal speech, its very broad interpretation of security, that it's far more than the strength of armies and far more than military hardware. I felt that security is a function of economic strength and stable regimes.

"The President said, 'I want to help you get that post.' I said, 'Mr. President, I know enough about the constitutional process and government that your obligation is up, not down, that you have absolutely no obligation to me. I deeply appreciate your affection. I don't ask for anything and all I expect is the opportunity to serve you, to whatever degree necessary.' He did not say any more."

Two weeks later, when McNamara submitted his private proposals to stop the bombing of the north, freeze troop levels, and begin shifting the burden of fighting to the South Vietnamese,

the President was still exploring the alternatives open to him. He
removed McNamara's name from the twenty-three-page memorandum and sent it to a handful of his principal advisers for
comment. When their reactions came back, all opposed a complete cessation of the bombing. The risk to beleaguered American
forces at Khe Sanh, then under siege, and in the northern areas
of South Vietnam in general appeared too great. Only two, Secretary of State Rusk and Under Secretary Nicholas deB. Katzenbach, supported a cutback to the 20th parallel above the North
Vietnamese border. Ironically, the reaction of Clark Clifford, who
later would reverse his field as he succeeded McNamara, was one
of the most uncompromising of all.

Clifford's response reached the White House on November 7.
Ironically as well, that also was the day McNamara reaffirmed
publicly his faith in the national purpose at a time when American
self-confidence was eroding.

"We appear to believe that we cannot simultaneously wage war
against aggression abroad, and a war against poverty, urban
decay, and social injustice here at home," he said in a speech
before the National Association of Educational Broadcasters on
November 7. "That we cannot afford it is a myth. . . . What we
may lack is the will power. If we do lack it, so be it. But let that
be our conscious choice. Let us face the issues honestly and
admit to ourselves that we simply do not want to make the
effort." It was his last formal address as Secretary of Defense.
This one, too, had the ring of self-examination.

Johnson meanwhile went to work on the World Bank appointment with a secrecy and speed that surprised even some of the
principals. The President, moreover, flatly refused to submit to
the Bank's Board of Directors a choice of names: he was for
McNamara, he said, "first, second, and third."

That the secret held as long as it did was surprising. The
nomination went to the Bank on November 22. For several days
there was silence as the ponderous process of ratification, includ-

ing notification of 106 nations, got under way. When the word
leaked out, speculation ran wild for two days.

Finally, on November 29, an hour and a half after the unanimous confirmation vote by World Bank directors, McNamara
burst into the Pentagon's second-floor television studio with the
familiar long stride, carrying a two-page statement. The assem-
bled reporters, who had been waiting for hours and who had
pretty much taken the iron-man Secretary of Defense for granted,
were shocked at his appearance. Some noted for the first time his
haggard face, the loose hang of the dark medium-weight suit.

His statement was a brief recitation of the public circumstances
surrounding his move. "I have greatly valued the opportunity to
serve my country as Secretary of Defense," he said, his voice
catching. "And I am profoundly grateful to the President for his
unfailing support and friendship. I have worked with him in
complete harmony and with the highest regard." He would stay
into 1968, long enough to complete his work on the next budget,
he announced. Then he left as quickly as he came, leaving reporters with pencils poised over notebooks and questions unanswered.

In the White House the President also traced the developments
of the past months. "The nation as well as its President owes him
a debt of gratitude and the highest honors which can be bestowed," he said. "I shall miss him greatly as a member of my
Cabinet, as one of my closest colleagues, and as my valued
friend. . . . But I could not justify asking Secretary McNamara
indefinitely to continue to bear the enormous burdens of his position, nor could I in justice to him and to this nation's obligations
to the World Bank, refrain from recommending that he be selected
as President of the Bank."

Washington was thunderstruck. Part of the astonishment
stemmed from ignorance betrayed. During all the activity since
the spring there had been only one public hint—in a September
issue of *Newsweek* magazine—that McNamara might move to

the Bank. More important, few in Washington understood the depth of the differences, along with the paradoxically continuing respect, between the President and his Secretary of Defense. What many did understand, especially those who had experienced it, was the difficulty of separating gracefully from Lyndon Johnson.

There was speculation that Johnson felt he had been made victim of a political end run in the early moves by McNamara, Woods, and others; that McNamara had become a net liability, and that the President regretted having accepted his advice on the war and on nuclear strategy. McNamara's August testimony discounting bombing, some felt, was the key. From White House sources came the semiofficial explanation that Mr. Johnson simply had to act, quickly, in order to secure a choice, challenging post for a deserving servant who had requested it: one, moreover, who was near exhaustion. Most students of the eccentric President were perfectly prepared to accept a blend of all these reasons.

One element of the speculation achieved near certainty. If the President intended to run again the next year, as was generally assumed, he could not retain a Secretary of Defense who had become highly controversial in his own right and who was more and more assertive with his personal views. That speculation may or may not have been justified at the time. For Johnson had indicated to McNamara, Rusk, and Westmoreland, well before the announcement of McNamara's move to the World Bank, that he would not run for re-election. They simply did not know whether or not to accept his words at face value.

There was still work to be done, preparing the budget and the posture statement. On January 23 the North Koreans seized the spy ship *Pueblo* in international waters off their coast. Just what the United States might have done to prevent the capture of the ship and crew was far from clear, but the public impact of the episode was to make America once again look humiliatingly impotent.

McNamara spent a grueling day on February 20, as the Senate

Foreign Relations Committee challenged in a public hearing the Administration's account of events in the Tonkin Gulf three and a half years before. Once again McNamara staunchly insisted that North Vietnam, indeed, had launched a second attack against U.S. destroyers in the gulf, leading to retaliatory air strikes and the resolution by Congress that authorized the Administration to make war. But McNamara, too, recognized privately that the evidence was less than compelling.

Senator J. William Fulbright, the committee chairman, and Senator Albert Gore of Tennessee left no doubt at all that they disbelieved the Administration's case. "I do not in any sense question your patriotism or your sincerity," Gore said. "On the other hand, I feel that I have been misled, and that the American people have been misled. . . . From all the testimony you have submitted here today, the Administration stands revealed as having acted very hastily and out of proportion to the provocation."

Finally, on February 28, it was all over. The President filled the East Room of the White House with friends and official foes of McNamara (Mendel Rivers was there) to honor him in the flood of television lights. Present, too, was the man who would succeed him, Clark Clifford, who had helped draft the National Security Act, and whose talent search in 1960 had come up with the name of Robert McNamara.

Johnson awarded McNamara the Medal of Freedom, the highest decoration for a civilian. The Secretary, the President said, was "one of America's most valuable public properties." He had "helped to give America the strongest, most efficient military power in history," and "now he is going to try to build the kind of world that alone can justify that strength. . . . America is grateful for what he has done."

McNamara at first was unable to answer. He struggled for a moment, breathed deeply, and managed, "Mr. President, I cannot find words to express what lies in my heart today. I think I had better respond on another occasion."

One more ceremony lay ahead, a final military review the next day on the small parade ground below the River Entrance to the Pentagon. The President was late. Then the Pentagon's executive elevator, overloaded with high officialdom, stuck between floors and held the President and Secretary of Defense captive for twenty minutes. Once outside, they were soaked by a cold, steady rain which already had paralyzed those waiting.

McNamara stood, hatless and coatless, rain streaming down his face, as Deputy Secretary Paul Nitze read the Presidential citation accompanying the Distinguished Service Medal. During his service, it said, "he has built our Nation's forces to a pinnacle of new strength and efficiency. . . . He has not only created strength which is flexible and adaptable to the dangers threatening the Nation, but he has been a wise counselor of restraint in its use."

"Bob McNamara's career is just about the textbook example of the modern public servant," the President said. ". . . Your country is grateful to this good man."

The Secretary of Defense left his office for the last time that day at 4:55 P.M.—for him, a preposterously early hour. He and his wife were on their way to catch a plane for a month of skiing and rest. Five minutes after he left, his suite was the scene of what one staff member described as "the damnedest party you ever saw. It was a wake."

11

Reprise

Since his youth, he had turned to the mountains and snow in times of stress. Now, after the final break with the Pentagon, McNamara flew to the comfortable lodge he and his wife had built near Aspen. The hard skiing across the meadows and the slopes was both pleasure and rejuvenating challenge. "Come on out," he shouted to a caller from Washington after two weeks. "It's just wonderful."

While he prepared for the World Bank, Washington was still recovering from the surprise of his departure. Some of those outside or on the fringes of power finally concluded that, in some not quite comprehensible way, he had been fired. It had something to do with the complexities of Lyndon Johnson and the faint signs of McNamara's turn from the war. But most of them simply threw up their hands. Soon the cocktail and dinner gossip circuit had other preoccupations as President Johnson began his own slow and painful turn toward limiting the bombing in North Vietnam and his own withdrawal from public life.

In the circumstances, it perhaps was not surprising that much of Washington returned to the comfortable myths about Robert McNamara, the human computer, "Supermac," the machinelike man. His own contribution to the mythology had been substantial.

279

In the cavernous Pentagon office, he had sought quantification and coldly objective analysis. Indeed, he had relied heavily upon computers. Still, he disliked intensely the computer analogy often applied to himself. "The computer is a tool," he said once. "It is no better than what goes into it and what is done with what comes out." He would allow for intuition in this process, he explained, "but not emotion." This, too, was the rational man at work.

Never was there any doubt in the early years who was in charge. It was this assertion of control, more than innovation, that characterized his official performance. Too often men forget, when a titan appears, how little new there may be as his raw force sweeps away the doubts that have confounded his fellows. The McNamara Monarchy was not founded on ideas freshly generated from suite 3E880 or even the broader reaches of the Pentagon. The concept of graduated, flexible military response, tuned to every occasion, had fermented for more than a decade both inside and outside the government. Multiple amendments to the National Security Act had strengthened steadily the foundation for strong central management of the Pentagon. All the basic weapons which would sustain the McNamara strategy were well on their way by 1961. Even the specific management techniques of orderly long-range planning and costing had filtered out of the think tanks into the Eisenhower Pentagon well before the end of 1960.

What McNamara and his civilian team did was take all these ingredients and shape them into an identifiable whole. The Secretary himself was the principal architect, and the relentless defender, of what became the illusion of the perfect pyramid. "I am responsible for the operations of this Department," McNamara said. "And I am responsible for the actions of all the personnel in the Department. Any errors, therefore, are my errors. They are not to be charged to others."

This was the required stance. The executive branch of the United States Government will not work otherwise. But it was more than that. McNamara deliberately stamped his own signature on the Pentagon in unprecedented fashion. The mistakes must be his, apart from the roles of those who had gone before and those who influenced him in office. And so must the triumphs.

When he finished, the record showed both, along with a great number of decisions on which only years of testing could provide final judgment.

In the national concern with more public issues, the internal changes in the distinctively McNamara Pentagon received little public attention after he left. For many, however, the internal changes were a critical measure of his administration. Would they be overturned, or allowed to die slowly, or would they survive?

The most important criterion grew from his initial assertion of absolute civilian control at the top. He had taken the military out of the business of domestic political propaganda and softened its voice in foreign policy. More than any of his predecessors, he had reduced debilitating service rivalries. Many military men would question fiercely whether these were positive steps, to the extent that they stifled initiative and discarded professional military judgment. Nonetheless they bowed.

McNamara actually had lost much of his control in the internal struggle over Vietnam before 1968. Military advice had gained currency as his declined. Both the war and the ABM debate diluted his fiscal authority, and high officials of the Budget Bureau would concede that they—accustomed to his iron rule— had let him down by not intervening. But there were principles at issue as well as specifics. On balance, the principles of civilian administration still were more firmly implanted than when he arrived. What was certain was that the armed services were more of a unified institution in 1968 than they were in 1961.

No final judgment could be made even three years later whether this condition was permanent. For one reason, the Nixon Administration restored the National Security Council as a clearinghouse for policy, and this absorbed and diffused many of the military frustrations that McNamara had confronted personally with great relish. Nor did his successors concern themselves with the minute details to which McNamara had devoted so much time.

More reliable guidelines would appear as the war in Vietnam continued to fade and the war budget was recast to provide permanent forces for the long haul. Other situations that had plagued McNamara's relations with pressure groups were changing at the same time. Military supporters in Congress, responding to the mood of the country, were less vocal. Secretary Melvin Laird, who succeeded Clifford, drew expertly upon his years in Congress both to soothe his former colleagues and to give the military its innings. But the great schisms of the past always had occurred when money was shortest, and that test would come again sooner or later. At the beginning of 1971, some aspects of the competition for the forthcoming budget sounded faintly like a revival of the interservice struggles. For the time being, what was important was that the military rivalries for the ears of Congress and the President had not yet developed with their former intensity.

Even the more controversial management concepts were retained. His successors found the complex programming system he adopted from Charles Hitch to be a valuable tool, and its basic focus on total needs in contrast to parochial service considerations had gained general acceptance. The evolution of systems analysis, which once could make McNamara's critics froth at the mere mention, is instructive. McNamara had used systems analysis to originate ideas, and it had become an instrument of his control over the military. "It was remarkable," according to a former Presidential aide, "how often systems analysis would justify the things Bob wanted to do anyway." When Laird took over, he turned the systems analysts into evaluators of military ideas rather than originators, a deft distinction which converted the military more often into allies instead of frustrated opponents.

Laird was working nonetheless with the tools McNamara left. McNamara had entered the same place at another time, when the tools were still scarce. Had he been more modest in creating them, the Pentagon might well have defeated him totally, as it had others.

In any case he would have been incapable of an administration of comfortable compromise and tentative decisions, as the years at Ford had demonstrated. He could be made to compromise, but he had to be bludgeoned. He had little use for the historic trappings of military *esprit*. It remained a mystery to him that the Marines insisted on retaining black belt buckles rather than joining the other services with brass. A junior officer once remarked sarcastically that "McNamara cared a great deal about mankind, but not very much about men." Imprecise as it was, the remark said much about the dominant military view of him.

His lack of sympathy for tradition and his distaste for political finesse were traits that appeared repeatedly in his management of the Pentagon, with enormous consequences. Backed by two Presidents, he chipped away ruthlessly at an encrustation of unneeded and obsolescent bases, a task on which the efforts of his predecessors had been, at best, tentative. There would have been more—it was the Presidents who got cold feet, not he. The war aside, his reforms had saved the nation a great deal of money.

On the other hand, this same refusal to compromise with tradition, and sometimes to accept reality when it defied him, contributed to some of his greatest miscalculations. He failed to comprehend at several points the art of the possible.

For how could the TFX be judged other than as a failure of great magnitude? The TFX became more than an airplane that turned sour. McNamara took a radical design, the movable wing, and added to it the concept of commonality. The plane was to become an essential multiservice weapon in forces finely adjusted to the requirements of graduated response. Commonality failed, in part because of technical barriers, in part surely because of the persistent ill will of the services. There were opportunities to turn it around, to admit defeat, and he never took them. For seven years and longer, the TFX evolved into a grisly comedy piece widely regarded as a monument to his bullheadedness.

Perhaps the central question in the TFX affair was one which had little to do with the plane itself. It was the question whether the Kennedy Administration, with an eye for economic conditions and political circumstance, resolved that General Dynamics should have the huge contract over Boeing, all other things being equal. The choice of contractors was at least as controversial as commonality.

This was a point McNamara never would address beyond the record. The record said the decision was based on the merits. "I will not get into that," he replied firmly when pressed on the political issue. Neither would he defend the TFX itself in retrospect, though he still held commonality to be the wave of the future. In the final analysis, he told an interviewer, the TFX represented "only money" when viewed in the total span of survival issues. It was an answer of small comfort, however, to those who had sacrificed other favorite airplanes, guns, and ships to cost effectiveness.

Senator McClellan of Arkansas made a secondary career for eight years of proving McNamara wrong on the TFX. It and other hardware issues colored McNamara's entire relationship with Congress. In that context the TFX was hardly "only money." The plane appeared with time to become more a product of McNamara the man than a product of his system. There lay its greater cost. For it did provide fuel for his critics. It cast doubt on management techniques of which it was not a result. Cost effectiveness could be more easily ridiculed when the dispenser of the gospel was also the patron of the TFX. An airplane became a symbol of vulnerability in an area where this Secretary of Defense was not supposed to be vulnerable. Capitol Hill thus alternately was overwhelmed by his knowledge and domination of his domain and furious with his reluctance to compromise or admit error.

In the broadest assessment of the McNamara tenure the TFX possibly could be described as an issue involving "only money," and that undoubtedly was the sense in which he used the phrase.

Surely all else fades beside the two themes that dominated his years in the Pentagon: the war in Vietnam and the McNamara strategic design.

McNamara's treatment of grand strategy and the war must be judged in part by the atmosphere in which he encountered them. He had arrived in Washington fairly vibrating with a sense of things to be done, adapting naturally to an Administration prepared to accept every challenge in every area of the globe. Its humanitarian motives were impeccable. With exuberant confidence it proposed to assert America at every level, from economic aid through counterinsurgency through, if it came to that, a nuclear exchange. McNamara would provide the military means.

In time Vietnam became a fundamental trial for an important part of the whole strategy. It did not matter that in another time, another place, other political circumstances, the execution and the results might be different. To the extent that Vietnam did test the strategy, the strategy and its architects and executors were found wanting.

Once the killing stops and the domestic passions are spent, the next generation of historians will be years sorting out the truths of Vietnam. Some of the questions may be unanswerable. Did the national interest dictate intervention on the Eisenhower or Kennedy levels at a time of intense heat in the Cold War? On the Johnson scale, even after the heat subsided elsewhere? Had the world changed enough in just a few years so that the uncertain world-wide consequences of withdrawal had become acceptable to the most powerful nation in history by 1965?

A few were sure of the basic answers quite early. George Ball in late 1964 submitted a long memorandum to demonstrate that U.S. interests did not require intervention. As events unfolded, Ball, who underscored the critical American interest in Europe, became something of a curiosity within the Administration.

At the end as at the beginning, McNamara accepted the underlying premise of U.S. policy in Southeast Asia. Vietnam was an aspect of global rivalry, with freedom from externally imposed

Communist rule as the local objective. It was a place for the application of the latest theories of limited war, uniting political, economic, and military components. But as it worked out, the undertaking in Vietnam unquestionably was a failure as it applied uniquely to Robert McNamara.

The Secretary of Defense understood in 1963 that the United States was demanding a great deal of the unstable Vietnamese society. With its demands for reform, Washington would not permit Ngo Dinh Diem to be an effective dictator, even if he were capable. Neither was Vietnam ready for instant democracy. The reform demanded in Saigon was in large part an American domestic requirement, no less real for that reason.

Nevertheless, when the time came for the commitment of American power or abandonment of the undertaking, McNamara was an advocate of intervention. A former White House official has described McNamara's view accurately: "Bob believed in American power. If there was no government in South Vietnam, we would create one. If there was no army worthy of the name, we would build one. We all thought that with the commitment to bombing of the north and the commitment of men to the war on the ground, it would soon be over."

McNamara himself expressed the same thought in a different way. Once the Communists understand that they "can't win in the south," he said, "we presume that they will move to a settlement."

His adopted doctrine of graduated response, which he had shaped in great measure to his own specifications, was on trial. He lacked complete freedom of execution, however. The historians also must wrestle with what might have happened politically, at home and in Asia, if the Administration had adopted his proposals for national mobilization and funding of the conflict in 1965.

This point becomes important in any retrospective look at the 1960s in Vietnam. McNamara had overestimated the efficacy of U.S. power, and he had grossly underestimated the will of the enemy. All the military criticisms of him were incorporated in the remark of a senior commander: "He gave us enough to deny success to the enemy. He did not give us enough to make the enemy stop trying." But the lessons of limited war were in fact unrefined, with Korea as the imperfect model. The potential effect of American public opinion was an uncertain quantity. McNamara would have tried to mobilize it. President Johnson, hopefully applying the more optimistic prognosis, chose to finesse it.

When the doctrine as applied failed to mold political, economic, and military elements into the anticipated results, it was American public opinion that called time.

Apart from his confidence in American power at the beginning, a second aspect of the Secretary of Defense became critical to his conduct of the war. While he agreed with the American purpose and advised the use of force, he had no stomach for the fighting as the bloodshed increased. "He recognized and pursued the requirement for military power," a respected senior general observed. "It was a great practical and intellectual challenge. Still, he was reluctant to use it as it had to be used. I had to tell him, 'Mr. Secretary, it is sometimes necessary to use force for the greater good of the nation.'"

The Robert McNamara who went to war in 1965 thus appeared in retrospect to be more reluctant than he was popularly supposed to be, but just as dedicated to success as his rhetoric suggested. For critical months of the war, this distinction remained unrecognized even within the executive circle. "I certainly never detected any hesitation on his part about the pursuit of the war," remarked a diplomat who was deeply involved with Vietnam until well past the massive intervention of 1965.

The torments were there nevertheless. All the contradictions began to stand out before McNamara with horrifying clarity as he became more and more disturbed in 1966 and depressed in 1967. The single most disturbing aspect was the bombing of North Vietnam, of course. His testimony of August, 1967, was directed specifically against the bombing, but what amounted to his final advice to the President revealed a more general disillusionment.

In November, when he urged the President to reverse the military course in Vietnam, his turn was complete. If it was not, as he viewed it, an admission of failure and of faulty advice to Lyndon Johnson, it was at least an admission that limited war, as he had practiced it, would have to be fought differently in the future—if indeed the United States ever again would fight such wars. The early evidence was that America, torn over Vietnam, was turning inward.

"I cannot escape the feeling," a former White House official said, "that Bob lost all faith in the hand he was dealing."

If this was the case, it did not apply to the broader McNamara strategy. The application of graduated force, as practiced in Southeast Asia, was an important facet of the strategy, but it was only one of several. McNamara still had unswerving faith in the concept of rationally balanced conventional and nuclear forces, of making the punishment fit the crime, of a range of choice between holocaust and capitulation. Vietnam might represent mistakes in execution, as his behavior in 1967 acknowledged. But the decisions to intervene were, after all, political decisions more broadly reached. He believed it was the political judgment —his own and that of others—that had failed.

As his retrospective perceptions sharpened, he came to several conclusions about the mistakes of Vietnam. Now he could see that the United States must never again commit forces to support a government lacking a sound domestic political base and the unqualified support of its friendly neighbors. What was uncertain, however, until the American public will recycled, was how even these criteria might be applied in the future. The Nixon Administration's later foreign policy implied far more stringent tests of the national interest before intervention.

Beyond Vietnam, the McNamara strategy took a buffeting on the other side of the conventional-nuclear formula in that dismal fall of 1967. Since early in the seven years in the Pentagon, McNamara had come to believe that nuclear superiority was a meaningless advantage once competing powers had the forces of mutual destruction. The attempt to preserve it, he felt, could only continue an endless and mindless arms race. The nuclear nations must settle for deterrence through what he called the power of "assured destruction," a nuclear standoff.

Defiantly he held back the advocates of an antiballistic-missile defense system. ABM deployment, he argued, would only add a new dimension to the arms race at excruciating cost. Then at the end of each lap in the race, the ABM defense would be overcome by less costly offensive missiles.

It was one of the bitterest of many bitter moments when the President, beleaguered in Congress, ordered him to yield on the ABM. The rationale he chose—a marginal justification for defense against China—was crafted to give deployment a minimum justification. The strategist Bernard Brodie has described it, quite accurately, as preposterous. Chinese capability to attack the United States was much more remote than American ability to counteract any moves Peking might make. McNamara, had he spoken his objective conclusions, would have agreed with Brodie.

When he revealed the ABM decision during the September, 1967, speech in San Francisco, most of the tightly reasoned language was in fact an argument to forestall massive ABM deployment against the Soviet Union. It was Soviet, not Chinese, developments that had triggered the pressures on the President. Significant, also, was his treatment of the Chinese rationale when some of his public papers were edited into book form the following year. The rationale and the decision were cut out of the San Francisco speech to become an appendix in the book, banished, as it were, to remove a blot from true McNamara reasoning.

For the rest of it, the San Francisco speech included a rare admission of error. The then current superiority of U.S. offensive weapons, he said, was "both greater than we had originally planned and more than we require." What he called the action-reaction phenomenon already had accelerated the arms race.

Superiority, he said, "does not effectively translate into politi-

cal control or diplomatic leverage." Strategic nuclear forces, however vital to security, played an "intrinsically limited role." But
McNamara knew the Soviet Union was rushing ahead with its
weapons, and something that might be called nuclear parity was
not far ahead. Indeed, strategic parity, in the power of mutual
destruction, had arrived, and he welcomed it.

His treatment of this issue left a heavy residue of resentment
in some quarters, including Congress. The more militant members
had demanded the reassurance of superiority. McNamara continued to provide reassuring figures long after his own analysis
told him they were meaningless in terms of security. In effect, his
analysis for Congress lagged considerably behind his own understanding. His ability to dissemble, under the cloak of higher
truth, ran unchecked for some time on this issue. Not until the
San Francisco speech did he finally complete the semantic transition.

To some, he was guilty of oversimplifying incredibly complex
questions, once he had felt his own way through the maze. But no
one, certainly, would have accused him of underselling his ideas.
It was a point with special application to Europe.

For six years he relentlessly forced the McNamara strategy on
the West Europeans. Suspicious, doubtful, contradictory, NATO
members wanted to hear nuclear reassurance, not doubt. At first,
as the French strategist Raymond Aron wrote, "The McNamara
doctrine left Europeans more troubled than convinced."

He drove ahead with his lectures to NATO, sacrificing personal
popularity and spending considerable political capital in the
process. However subtle his theories, his personal weapon was
the club, not the rapier. Watching the McNamara performance,
diplomats of several nations have speculated as to the kind of
Secretary of State he might have made if Kennedy had survived.

Even within the American diplomatic corps, assessments varied.
"He would have been a disaster," a former senior official declared
with certainty. Another had the opposite view: "He would have

been a great one if the diplomats had remained close enough to handle the political niceties." His personal technique had been heavy-handed, as when he pulled the Skybolt away from Britain and forced West Germany to the wall on purchase of military equipment to offset the dollar drain through U.S. forces in Europe.

"Bob could see in a minute what was motivating a man, apart from what he was saying," an eyewitness to many such encounters recalled. "Then he tended to tune out if the real background substance was something he was barred from dealing with. He wouldn't play the game."

But when the diplomatic wreckage was swept aside, McNamara had stamped an indelible imprint on NATO. The Alliance never accepted fully his prescription for conventional forces, never paid much more than lip service to his appeals for a strong logistics and mobilization base. But he had forced the organization of even the limited conventional forces into greater combat capability despite NATO reluctance.

More important was formal acceptance of the doctrine of flexible response in 1967, though it lacked the impact it would have had earlier. Flexible response was easier to accept as confrontation faded; Europe finally acknowledged the futility of fighting a doctrine for which the United States, in the end, would determine execution anyway. The old tensions, within the Alliance, in East-West relations, by then were abating. In the new atmosphere the Europeans could worry less about strategic details as long as Americans remained on the continent as hostages and their nuclear weapons remained with them.

All of these considerations entered into the NATO decision in 1967. Nonetheless, it also was true that what McNamara described as this "essential first step" reflected a fundamental change, which in fact had evolved slowly, in attitudes on nuclear weapons. If NATO was not ready to provide the men and guns he wanted, neither did it still look upon nuclear response with the desperate certainty it once displayed. McNamara's Nuclear Planning Group had been an important tool in the process, one of his classes in the frustrations of managing superweapons.

"It's taken seven years to get that across to NATO," he told an interviewer later. "But the Europeans are coming along with us now. I think history will record that we did at last get people to recognize the realities of strategic nuclear warfare."

There were even tentative signs, after he left, that the lessons had taken hold elsewhere. In another of the grand ironies, they arose from events in those bleak days when he was simultaneously trying to prevent ABM deployment and turn down the war in Vietnam.

He had convinced President Johnson to propose negotiations on strategic weapons to the Soviet Union as a counter to ABM sentiment. From there, the chain of events ran directly to the strategic arms limitation talks (SALT) of 1970. The Soviet Union still raced ahead with weapons development, and there could be no certainty of its good faith in the negotiations. But Robert McNamara rightly could watch the SALT negotiations from his office in the World Bank with a paternal interest. He had taken the initial step. From that perspective, the nuclear threshold was visibly higher than it had been a decade earlier.

When it was all over, this was the work that stood out most clearly. One did not need to accept all of his strategy. His crowning accomplishment could be simply put: he had caused the world, more than just the narrow circle of American strategists, to look at nuclear weapons with thought, rather than instinct or emotion. It was his own judgment as well. "I am not going to walk away from the war," he said once. "But I believe that twenty years from now this is what history will remember best from this period"—not Vietnam, or a budget that had climbed to $80 billion, almost twice what he had inherited from Eisenhower.

No one could guarantee, of course, that his process would produce answers different from or superior to those dictated by instinct or emotion. But it was a far less risky process, if conducted in keeping with a somewhat awkward McNamara dictum: "We must do our best simultaneously to preserve the constructive aspects of our relationship with Moscow and guard against counting on improvements before they occur." More simply: negotiate, but guard the balance.

This was the criterion—guarding the balance—on which some of his critical decisions on hardware were most controversial. His unrelenting assault on many exotic new weapons, the nuclear aircraft, the B-70 bomber, the advanced strategic bomber, saved billions of dollars. These actions would have looked better, of course, if it had not been for the fiasco of his own TFX. The more important question was whether he had canceled or denied too much, whether, as some critics claimed, he had so slowed the pace as to leave the nation dangerously exposed for the long run.

In retrospect, it was hard to see how this could be so. After he left, there was no sudden, convulsive rush into sparkling new weapons he had spurned, except that the new strategic bomber was restored to favor. The nation still had plenty of time to recover if it had lagged. In the meantime McNamara had showed the courage to organize the march, to shape the strategic balance so that the world, if it would, could come to terms with weapons of mass destruction.

The ingredients of strategy obviously would have to be revised in part. For with the end of the decade, the mood of America and the pressures that influenced the mood had changed. McNamara had built forces for "two and a half wars"—one in Europe, one in Asia, a minor undertaking elsewhere. He had done so at a time of multiple confrontation. When the other confrontations faded, Vietnam continued. For the Nixon Administration, the national mood became a mandate to scale down conventional forces to capability for "one and a half wars."

McNamara, as it turned out, had reached beyond political possibility in his projection of conventional forces in the conventional-nuclear equation. For as they were used, the conventional

forces did not produce quickly enough the anticipated results in
Vietnam. Vietnam, in turn, was large in the background as the
Nixon Administration began reducing conventional forces in its
own plans for the future. America's allies simply never accepted
fully the McNamara prescription for the weight of the arms they
ought to bear.

Even the ABM and the strategic missiles became instruments
subtly different from those with which McNamara argued and
engineered his strategic balance. They still stirred domestic fires
in 1970, but they also had become negotiating cards in the SALT
talks, which were potentially the greatest monument to the McNamara Monarchy.

McNamara knew well where he wanted his achievements to
lead. As he developed his strategy, and as he lived with Vietnam,
he also developed his view of the world as he hoped it would rationally develop. It emerged most clearly in several paragraphs
here taken—out of sequence—from his own book and from the
Montreal speech:

Some of the basic components of power remain obviously unchanged. Great military might remains indispensable. Because science
has produced the new weapons of colossal destruction, the United
States must maintain its nuclear arsenal: not only must it be maintained, but it must be so large as to deter any nation from forcing its
use. Because there are those who still would test our will and under-
mine us slowly with subversion and limited war, we must arm with
conventional forces in common defense with our allies. These are the
old realities, shaped to the world of today. But there are new realities
as well, and we have been too slow to recognize them. For the fact
remains that a negative and narrow notion of defense still clouds our
vision and distorts national policy. . . .

Security is development, and without development there can be
no security. A developing nation that does not, in fact, develop,
simply cannot remain secure for the intractable reason that its own
citizenry cannot shed its human nature.

The United States intends to be compassionate and generous in
this effort, but it is not an effort it can carry exclusively by itself.

Thus it must look to those nations which have reached the point of self-sustaining prosperity to increase their contribution to the development and thus to the security of the modernizing world.

Mutual interest, mutual trust, and mutual effort—these are the goals. Can we achieve these goals with the Soviet Union and with Red China? Can they achieve them with one another? The answer to these questions lies in the answer to an even more fundamental question: Who is man? Is he a rational animal? If he is, then the goals can ultimately be achieved; if he is not, then there is little point in making the effort.

All the evidence of history suggests that man is indeed a rational animal, but with a nearly infinite capacity for folly. His history seems largely a halting but persistent effort to raise his reason above his animality. He draws blueprints for Utopia, but never quite gets it built. In the end he plugs away obstinately with the only building material really ever at hand: his own part-comic, part-tragic, part-cussed, part-glorious nature. I, for one, would not count a global free society out. Coercion, after all, merely captures man. Freedom captivates him.

The appearance of this orderly and moving outline, in the Montreal speech of May, 1966, was a surprise to many. It was the first dramatic public departure from the popular image of the Secretary of Defense. For some it became with hindsight the first public symbol of his frustration with the war. Others followed, in his attacks on racial discrimination, his sympathy for uncertain youth, his assertion of man over technology.

These passions undoubtedly were in part indirect reflections of his concern over Vietnam. But they were more than that. They were the manifestations of the McNamara other than the war minister, the McNamara of Berkeley and Cambridge and Ann Arbor rather than the McNamara of Ford and the Army and the Pentagon.

The frustrations continued to grow, in any case. In 1967 they caused him to violate, with his testimony against bombing of North Vietnam, the spirit if not the text of his often stated concept of loyalty to his chief. Years before, he had said frequently that decisions, once made, were not to be agonized over. He had created a balanced war machine with full acceptance of the need. He had sounded the call to put it to use. But when his system failed him, the nature of the man made the consequences especially painful.

Even his critics could not argue against his right to campaign for a reversal of course in 1967. Policy currents shifted slowly, however, and his influence was waning. McNamara's personal transition pointed him upstream, against the still prevailing currents in Washington. His proposals to scale down the war fell on reluctant ears.

There was a kind of desperate courage in him, however, as his disillusionment deepened. Once U.S. military gradualism in Vietnam had failed to produce the programmed results in an acceptable time, the Administration in its frustration appeared to be moving toward even greater escalation. To him this was intolerable. His efforts to prevent it finally made him an anachronism, out of step, out of favor, a tragic figure. Yet when he proposed an end to bombing, an end to reinforcements on the ground, and a transfer of the war to the South Vietnamese Army, it was, in a sense, a return to the first principles of seven years before. In the final great irony, his recommendations of 1967 ultimately became the policy decisions of 1968 and 1969.

The seven years demonstrated once again the unspeakable burden the nation places on those who will undertake the impossible tasks. Most who do so can live stoically with the reversals, and thereby earn the right to bask in the successes. But failure exacted a special toll from McNamara. "It is much more satisfying," he remarked to friends after he moved to the World Bank, "to be working for the development of nations than to be working with the means of destruction."

This was the other McNamara, a man of emotion who sought to exclude it from his official life. "I've got to think precisely," he told an interviewer. "The cost of being wrong is very, very high."

The emotions had erupted nevertheless, as when his voice

broke in relating to a Congressional committee the impact of the
TFX hearings on his son. (McNamara denied that he had wept.
"I'm saving my tears for the guy who reported that," he snapped.)
There was little of the computer in the McNamara who sustained
Jacqueline Kennedy during her grief, who tongue-lashed a re-
porter who had questioned U.S. strength in Europe, who wept at
the launching of the carrier *John F. Kennedy,* and again at the
departure ceremonies in his honor.

This may have been the key to Robert McNamara as Secretary
of Defense, this conflict between the supremely rational technocrat and the humanist who quoted philosophers and poets. Most
of the military and the Congress saw only the veneer, the cold
perfectionist, incapable of admitting error. His certainty of his
case was almost always total and uncompromising, sometimes
becoming even more fixed when his evidence weakened. In the
end, the humanist betrayed the minister of war.

Exhausted as he was, he left in one respect as he arrived, larger
than life. He was a creature of towering accomplishment and substantial failure; totally self-assured, until the final months in
office, warm in personal relations; sometimes deceiving, sometimes brutally frank; at home equally with his statistics and his
volumes of Shelley and Kipling and especially Yeats; demanding
leader, considerate friend.

Those who worked most closely with him became totally
devoted. "I believe he is one of the great public servants of our
time," said Cyrus Vance, whose own record was impressive. "If
I could pick the President of the United States tomorrow, I would
choose Robert McNamara," Joseph Califano declared without
embarrassment. Even Senator Fulbright, giving him a final merciless grilling on the Tonkin Gulf incidents, could express "regret
to see you leave the government at this very perilous time in our
history." To Barry Goldwater, he was a "loser," a unilateral dis-
armer. To most in the military, he was a brilliant man with
policies the value of which was doubtful, at best.

He would defend or appraise the decisions, but he would not

assess himself for others. "I cannot judge my own performance," he told a questioner.

As he left, he came as close as he would to self-appraisal. "One brings to a post such as this certain ideals and concepts," he said. "In the process of putting them into effect, a great amount of energy is expended.

"Another person could bring in new ideas and new energies to move things farther along. I think the proper order of service here would be four or five years. I stayed longer because of Vietnam. In a way experience is a substitute for innovation."

On February 2, 1968, on national television he quoted T. S. Eliot in a quite revealing way:

> We shall not cease from exploration
> And the end of all our exploring
> Will be to arrive where we started
> And know the place for the first time.

Then he added, "That applies to Vietnam. I am learning more and more about Vietnam every day."

What a splendid time it would have been without Vietnam.

Index

299

About the Author

Henry L. Trewhitt was born on a farm near Cleveland, Tennessee, in 1927. After Navy service and graduation, in 1949, from the University of New Mexico, he reported successively for the Santa Fe *New Mexican*, the Chattanooga *Times*, the Baltimore *Sun*, and *Newsweek*. He studied for a year at Harvard University under a Nieman Fellowship in 1953–54. For the *Sun*, he spent four years covering Europe—NATO, the European Common Market, and the Berlin crisis—then reported on the Department of Defense and Vietnam. As diplomatic correspondent for *Newsweek*, he has traveled in Europe, Asia, Africa, and Latin America. He now lives in Washington.

71 72 73 10 9 8 7 6 5 4 3 2 1